SC/ST STUDENTS' ACCESS TO EDUCATION
Challenges and Opportunities

SC/ST Students' Access to Education

Challenges and Opportunities

MAHENDRA KUMAR SETH

ABHIJEET PUBLICATIONS
DELHI 110 094

ABHIJEET PUBLICATIONS
2/46 Tukhmeerpur Extension
Delhi 110 094
Phone: 22181492, 55698474
e-mail: abhijeet_singh@vsnl.net
abhijeet_singh@indiatimes.com
abhijeetpublication@gmail.com

SC/ST STUDENTS' ACCESS TO EDUCATION: CHALLENGES AND OPPORTUNITIES

First Published 2006

ISBN 81-88683-94-9

PRINTED IN INDIA

Published by J.K. Singh for Abhijeet Publications, Delhi 110094, Lasertypeset by Rajesh Data Services, New Delhi and Printed at Himanshu Printers, Delhi.

Preface

The expansion in the field of education in the post-independence period has been phenomenal. The Education system has provided great access to all sections of the society, including children belonging to Scheduled Castes and Scheduled Tribes. However, owing to a number of constraints, and socio-economic factors, the benefits of expansion of educational facilities have not fully reached the Scheduled Castes and Scheduled Tribes to bring them at par with other Communities. To appreciate the special efforts made in this direction and to know the size of the remaining task, it is necessary that data on progress of education and information needs of these communities be complied and made available to public at large. The absence of such data sometimes leads to lack of appreciation of true dimensions of the problem and the efforts being made in this direction. The present study is an attempt to present Information needs of Scheduled Castes and Scheduled Tribes: students, scholars and faculties in the higher educational system of Orissa and provides picture of various facets of the educational development of the community.

I would take this opportunity to place different suggestions from the findings of my study to Department of Higher Education, Government of Orissa, SC/ST Welfare Department and authorities of different Higher Academic Institutions in the state. I would also like to convey my sincere thanks to the State Governments and other academic institutions that made available the data required for this thesis. It is hoped that the thesis will serve its intended of a reference document and also serve a useful purpose of creating awareness about the educational development of Scheduled Castes/Scheduled Tribes by giving them right to Information through networking.

"This book is an authentic veritable mine of information on diverse aspects of education and information scenario of the country. This will certainly prove an asset and reference tool to scholars, authors, students, officials, journalists, academicians and all concerned."

Mahendra Kumar Seth

Acknowledgements

I express my deep sense of gratitude to my supervisor Dr. Baman Parida, Professor, Department of Library & Information Science, at Utkal University, Vani Vihar, Bhubaneswar in converting my thoughts into action in this thesis, pales into insignificance considering his able guidance and supportive suggestions wherever and whenever wanted. His constructive criticism in course of my professional interactions with him has always accelerated my inveterate interest in the present study. Working with him has been a great pleasure and source of inspiration.

My grateful thanks are due to Dr. D.B. Ramesh, Head, Lib. and Documentation Division, Regional Research Laboratory, Bhubaneswar who have provided all administrative and professional support in this endeavor and meticulous editing of this work, while the same in no less quantum is due to Prof. Manoranjan Mahapatra, Dr. Pitamber Padhi, Dr. Gayatry Mohapatra and Dr. Puspanjali Jena, faculties of the Department of Library and Information Science, Utkal University, Bhubaneswar, for whom I got inspiration and kind support to start this work, and valuable suggestions to finish this book in time.

Mahendra Kumar Seth

Contents

1

Introduction

For the development of human society and the nation there is a need of multifocal effects of government as well as individuals at different levels from local, regional, national and international in the area of education. Education as an instrument of social change focuses mainly on individual behaviour. It shapes economic development of a nation. The quality of planning and programmes framed for better ends depends upon the quality of existing human resources in the respective areas which are generated in the academic institutes having adequate information sources and services. According to UNESCO (1998) report, "Learning: the Treasure Within " popularly referred to as the Dollor's Report, visualize four functions for the Universities—"to prepare students for research and teaching, to provide highly specialised training courses oriented to the needs of societies, to be open to all in order to faster lifelong education in its widest sense and to strive for international cooperation". The report emphasizes that education for all, throughout life, has to be founded on four pillars of learning—to know, to do, to live together and to be. Clearly education goes beyond generating knowledge and applying it for the development of the society. Its objective has to be all round human development. To this, Bacon said, "knowledge is power", it means, the accumulation of facts about material and men in data, which properly organized became information. The rigorous training of gathering information and processing for some purposeful end product leads to human knowledge. Power on the other hand is much more then the ability to enforce certain intentions in the face of resistance stated Tayler (1986). It is remarkable to note what Swami Vivekananda said about education, "Education is not the amount of information that is put into your brain and runs right there, undigested, all your life. We must have life building, man making, character making and assimilation of ideas. If you have assimilated five ideas and made them your life and character, you have more education than anyone who has got by heart a whole library or information center".

In the developing world, the educational progress of the past two three decades has been achieved by introducing new method, plans and projects in their countries time to time. As per the World Education Forum—EFA 2000 (Education Forum Assessment, 2003): The number of children not enrolled in school decreased from an estimated 127 million in 1990 to 113 million in 1998. The net enrolment ratio in primary education worldwide increased from 80 to 84 percent. At the end of the 1990s developing countries as a whole had achieved a net enrolment of 80 percent. The overall adult literacy rate has increased to 85 percent for men and 74 percent for women, though the levels of illiteracy still remain unacceptably high. Nearly two-thirds of the world's illiterates continue to be women although in percentage terms the situation has improved in South Asia from 32 percent in 1990 to 40 percent in 2000. About three-quarters of the world's illiterate live in E-9 Countries: India (which accommodates a third), China, Pakistan, Bangladesh, Nigeria, Indonesia, Brazil, Egypt and Mexico. According to a recent report of Census 2001, India is home to 17% of the World's total population accommodated in an area, which is 2.4% of the world's total area. As against 2820 languages in the entire world, as many as 325 languages are effectively used in India alone. Local dialects change in India almost after every 8-10 kms. The country has witnessed phenomenal educational development—both in quantitative and qualitative terms, since independence. However, the national goals of universal elementary education and total eradication of illiteracy have still remained elusive due to mostly weaker section (disadvantaged) and traditional feelings of girls in the society, where as they constitute majority of the total population of the country. Therefore, Govt. of India is giving various educational provisions and facilities to improve them. It was only after independence that greater thrust was made towards the educational development of the weaker sections.

Ever since independence, education for all has been one of the major concerns of the Indian Government. Even though the education scenario in India in the past few decades has been characterised by massive quantitative expansion at all levels, it is still faced with a staggering backlog of high illiteracy rate of over 34.62 per cent in 2001. "Notwithstanding the enormous expansion of adult, non-formal and elementary education in India, the problem of illiteracy has been lingering on. It is both colossal and complex given the size of the country, its huge population, wide regional and gender disparities, economic and other cultural factors such as poverty, communalism, criticism, etc. Concerted efforts have, therefore, to be made to wipe off illiteracy in the shortest possible time if the country has to take rapid strides in its socio-economic development and right to information." If "Education and Information for All" to be achieved, breakthroughs must take place in these countries. Even though they share a number of challenges because of their physical size, large populations, and vast rural and remote areas, yet, developments in science, technology, information, communications and education etc. complied with the inherent economic potential of these countries present dramatic opportunities to meet these challenges. "Education is a cornerstone of economic growth and social development and a principal means of improving the welfare of individual", according to World Bank (1990) To this, Theodore W. Schultz said, "education contributes to economic and social development. It contributes to economic development through increased national income and individual earning."

The Government is committed to achieving these national goals and has been steadily increasing the budgetary allocation for education. The country has also made significant strides in higher and technical education. India

Table 1.1: Population, Area, Density, Literacy and Public Expenditure in India and Some Neighbouring Countries

Particulars	*Population (millions) (2000)*	*Area (sq. kms)*	*Density*	*Percentage to world*		*Percentage of adult education illiterate (2000)*	*Public on expend. as %age of GNP (1996)*
World	6055.0*	135604354	45	100	100	20.6	NA
Afghanistan	21.2#	652090	33	0.48	0.35	63.7	NA
Bangladesh	129.2	143998	897	0.11	2.13	59.2	2.2
China	1277.6	9596961	133	7.08	21.10	15.0	2.3
India	1027$	3287590	312	2.42	16.96	44.2	3.2
Indonesia	212.1	1904569	111	1.40	3.50	13.0	1.4
Japan	126.9	377801	336	0.28	2.10	NA	3.6
Myanmar	46.4	676578	69	0.50	0.77	15.3	1.2
Nepal	22.5#	140797	160	0.10	0.37	58.6	3.2@
Pakistan	156.5	796095	197	0.59	2.58	56.7	2.7@
Sri Lanka	18.8#	65610	286	0.05	0.31	8.4	3.4
Thailand	62.0#	513115	121	0.38	1.02	4.4	4.8

Source: Statistical Yearbook, 1999 UNESCO* Estimated population for 2000, # Reference year 1999, $ Reference year 2001, & Reference Year 1994, @ Reference Year 1997.

Note: The area figures of India exclude area under illegal occupation of Pakistan and China.

spent 4.02% of its GDP on education during 2001-2002 but about 44% of its adult population still remains to be made literate. Table below compares the population, area, density, literacy rates and level of public expenditure on education in India and some of its neighboring countries. Afghanistan with 63.75% adult illiterates is at the top, closely followed by Bangladesh, Nepal and Pakistan. Population, area, density, literacy and public expenditure of Asian Countries are given below in Table No. 1.1.

Recent news article on Indian's population and literacy development was published in "The Hindu Sunday" July 11, 2004, New Delhi, stated that "India's population has reached 102.8 crores with 53.2 crore males and 49.6 crore females at an annual growth rate of 1.94. On the eve of Population Day, the Registrar-General of India, J.K. Banthia, declared that India's population was all set to exceed China's by 2035 when it would touch 146 crores. India turned 100 crores in May 2000. The 2001 census shows Uttar Pradesh to be the most populous State with a population of 166 million, followed by Maharashtra (97 million), Bihar (83 million) and West Bengal (80 million). Lakshadweep has the lowest population of 61,000. The Scheduled Caste population has touched 16.6 crores (16.2 per cent) and the Scheduled Tribes 8.4 crores (8.2 per cent). The child sex ratio (0-6) slipped from 945 females per 1000 males in 1991 to 927 in 2001. The average literacy rate for above seven populations stood at 64.8 against 52.2 in 1991. The census said 75.2 per cent of the male populations against 53.6 per cent of females are literate.

Education Scenario in India

Education is the most crucial investment in human development. Education strongly influences improvement in health, hygiene, demographic profile, productivity and practically all that is connected with the quality of life. The social and economic development of nations is fundamentally an education process in which people learn to create new institutions, utilize new technologies, cope with their environment, and alter their patterns of behaviour. Education in a broad sense improves the capabilities of individuals and the capacity of institutions, and becomes a catalyst for the closely interrelated economic, social, cultural, and demographic changes that become defined as national development. Precisely how these changes occur is not fully known, and this problem often frustrates attempts at national policy making and planning. However, the evidence is substantial that schooling and other forms of education can, in a supporting environment, make major contributions to the complex processes of technology transfer, economic productivity, individual earnings, reduction of poverty, development of healthy families, creation and sharing of values, learning the responsibilities of citizenship, and enhancement of the quality of life. Yet researchers and scholars also find that education can have negative effects. When formal education is unevenly distributed and information is not properly communicated to the needed people in time, it may perpetuate and legitimize social and wealth divisions in society. There may be inequality in the society. The informal sector has also experienced rapid growth in developing countries and has consequently attracted increasing attention to this. In India, the economy is stimulating interest among academics, researchers, social development activists, and policy planners. It is generally believed that the rapid growth in different sector has been influenced by information. Increasingly, the public and private sectors are developing as a resilient economic base.

The origin of the Indian education comes from thousands of years ago. When great scholars used to teach through the scriptures. A variety of subjects such as philosophy, religion, medicine, literature, drama and arts, astrology, mathematics and sociology were taught and masterpieces on these subjects have been written. Under the Buddhist influence, education was available to virtually everyone who wanted it and some world famous institutions arose out of the monasteries, such as, Nalanda, Vikramshila and Takshashila (now in Pakistan). Nalanda is especially noteworthy, flourishing from 5th to 13th century AD. It had at one time about ten thousand resident students and teachers on its roll, which included Chinese, Sri Lankan,

Korean and other international scholars. During the 11th century, the Muslims established elementary and secondary schools, "Madrassahs" or colleges and even universities at cities like Delhi, Lucknow and Allahabad, using Arabic mostly as the medium of instruction. During the mediaeval period, there was excellent interaction between Indian and Islamic traditions in all fields of knowledge, like theology, religion, philosophy, fine arts, painting, architecture, mathematics, medicine and astronomy etc.

The modern Indian education system dates back to pre-Independence days when for the first time a separate Department was created in 1910 to look after education. However, soon after India achieved its Independence on 15th August. 1947, a full-fledged Ministry of Education was established on 29th August 1947. The nomenclature and responsibilities of the Education Department has undergone changes from time to time since Independence. At present the Ministry has three Departments namely: Department of Secondary Education and Higher Education, Department of Elementary Education and Literacy and Department of Women and Child Development.

Government of India has been providing various programmes for the educational development of the people since independence: Article 45 of our constitution, which enjoins the govt. to provide free and compulsory education up to the secondary level (children unto 14 year) within ten years, but the census count of 1961 placed only 28% of the total population of India as literate and 60% of the same age group could not have primary education. However, the Government of India doesn't stop, on its contrary it provide, planned expenditure on education since the First Five Year Plan, as per the MHRD 2002/2003 report the total public expenditure on education during last five years (in percentage of GDP) are: 3.85% (1998/99), 4.25% (1999/00), 4.30% (2000/01), 4.02% (2001/02) and 3.98% (2002/03) published on 10th December, in The New Indian Express (2003). There are special provision for total literate in India like: Operation Blackboard, District Primary Education Programme, Education Guarantee Scheme, "Education for All" (1993), and "Sarva Shiksha Abhiyan" (2002). Sarva

Shiksha Abhiyan has been launched in partnership with the states. The programme is an effort towards recognition of the need for improving the performance of the school system through a community owned approach and ensuring quality elementary education in a mission mode to all children in the age group of 6-14 years by 2010. Despite dismal performance in the field of education, it is worth recording that during 1991-2001, literacy rates improved remarkably from 52.21 percent in 1991 to 65.38 percent in 2001, the female literacy rate also increased significantly from 39.29 % to 54.16%. At the turn of the twenty first century India has the dubious distinction of being one of the least literate countries in the world. About 50 percent of the total illiterate people in the world live in India, every third illiterate in the world is an Indian.

However, it is really gratifying to record that at the time as 2001 Census the absolute number of illiterates recorded a decline for the first time in the history of Indian Censuses. The absolute number of illiterates declined from 328 million in 1991 to 296 million in 2001, Census of India (2001). Literacy in India has made remarkable strides since Independence. This has been further confirmed by the recently declared provisional results of the Census 2001. The literacy rate has increased from 18.33% in 1951 to 65.38% in 2001. This is despite the fact that during the major part of the last five decades there has been exponential growth of the population at nearly 2% per annum. Some of the important highlights of Census 2001 are given below:

- The literacy rate in the country has increased to 65.38%, which reflects an overall increase of 13.17%, the fastest decadal growth ever. This is the highest rate since independence.
- The male literacy rate has increased to 75.85%, which shows an increase of 11.72%. On the other hand, the female literacy of 54.16% has increased at a much faster rate of 14.87%.
- The male-female literacy gap has reduced from 24.84% in 1991 to 21.70% in 2001. Mizoram has the smallest gap (4.56%) followed by Kerala (7.45%) and Meghalaya (8.27%).

- All States and Union Territories without exception have shown increase in literacy rates during 1991-2001.
- In all the States and Union Territories the male literacy is now over 60%.
- For the first time since independence there has been a decline in the absolute number of illiterates during the decade. In the previous decades, there has been a continuous increase in the number of illiterates, despite the increase in the literacy rates, but now for the first time the total number of illiterates has come down by 31.96 million.
- The number of literate persons has increased to 562.01 million in 2001 thus adding an additional 203.61 million literates in the country.
- Rajasthan has recorded the highest increase in the literacy rate among the States/Uts of India. Literacy rate of Rajasthan in 7+ population in 1991 was 38.55% which has increased to 61.3% in 2001.
- The state also recorded very good increase in the female literacy. It was 20.44% in 1991 which has increased to 44.34% in 2001.
- The female literacy rate of Chhattisgarh in 7+ population in 1991 was 27.52% which has increased to 52.40% in 2001. Thus the rise in female literacy rate in Chhattisgarh has been to the extent of 24.88% which is the highest among all the States/UTs of the country.
- Madhya Pradesh also recorded a good increase in female literacy rate. In 1991 the literacy rate of females was 29.35% which has increased to 50.28% in 2001.

Similarly, there has been a considerable increase in the spread of educational institutions during the period 1997-98 and 2001-2002. This is evident from Table 1.2. During this period the number of Primary Schools increased by 3 times, while the Upper Primary Schools and Hr. Secondary Schools increased by 16 and 18 times respectively. The number of Colleges for general education and professional education increased by about 24 and 12 times respectively

Table 1.2

Growth of Recognised Educational Institutions from 1997-98 to 2001-02

Years	*Primary*	*Upper Primary*	*High/Hr. Sec/Inter/ Pre. Jr. Colleges*	*Colleges for General Education*	*olleges for rof. rof. Education Engg./Tech./ ed. Etc. du.colleges)*	*Universities/ Deemed Univ../Instt. of National Importance*
1997-98	619222	185961	107140	7199	2075	229
1998-99*	626737	190166	112438	7494	2113	237
1999-00*	641695	198004	116820	7782	2124	244
2000-01*	638738	206269	126047	7929	2223	254
2001-02*	664041	219626	133492	8737	2409	272

Sources: Educational Statistics, 1997/98-2001/02, Min. of Edun. Govt. of India

Table 1.3

Percentage of Primary Schools Under Different Management

Year	*Govt.*	*Local Body (LB)*	*Govt.+LB*	*Private Aided*	*Private Unaided*
1973-74	50.88	42.47	93.34	5.01	1.64
1978-79	38.96	55.03	93.99	4.42	1.59
1986-87	41.37	51.71	93.08	4.34	2.57
1993-94	44.63	47.47	92.10	3.78	4.12
1996-97	47.78	43.88	91.66	3.34	5.00
2001-02*	47.45	43.47	90.92	3.07	6.01

Sources: Report of the Ministry of Education, Govt. of India, 1973/74-2001/02.

while the number of Universities increased by 10 times during the period.

In 1973-74 Government primary schools were 51% of the total primary schools in India. In 1978-79, 1986-87 and 1993-94 a large percentage of primary schools were under local bodies but the trend again shifted in 1996-97 and 2001-02 in which the percentage of Govt. primary schools was higher than local bodies. Government and local bodies put together continued to own more than 90% of primary schools. The contribution of private agencies, as indicated in the table, has been small though increasing over the years and was highest in the year 2001-02 (9.08%). The percentage of primary aided schools has been slowly decreasing over the years while the percentage of unaided schools has been increasing.

At the same time, Government continued to manage a majority of upper primary schools, the percentage of such schools managed by Govt. ranging 40% to 51% from 1973-74 to 2001-02. Government and Local Body schools put together accounted for 75.12% to 79.45% of schools; the private sector (aided and unaided) had a percentage share of 21% to 25% over the years.

Table 1.4

Percentage of Upper Primary Schools Under Different Managements

Year	*Govt.*	*Local Body (LB)*	*Govt. + LB*	*Private Aided*	*Private Unaided*
1973-74	50.71	26.86	77.57	17.75	4.67
1978-79	40.31	38.13	78.44	16.90	4.66
1986-87	42.79	32.33	75.12	16.30	8.58
1993-94	45.94	33.51	79.45	9.53	11.02
1996-97	46.41	29.13	75.54	10.25	14.20
2001-02*	47.36	29.05	76.41	7.81	15.77

Sources: Ministry of Education, Govt. of India.

Growth of Enrolment: According to the Department of

education, Govt. of India, the growth of sex-wise school enrolment in different stages of school education from 1950-51 to 2001-2002. The total enrolment at the primary, upper primary, Secondary and Sr. Secondary stages increased by 6, 14 and 20 times respectively since 1950-51. The girls' enrolment increased by 9, 37 and 60 times respectively during the same period in the above institutions. State wise/sex wise details of enrolment by stages and by classes for the year 2001-2002, are given in Tables 5 & 6 respectively. The participation of girls at all stages of education has been increasing steadily through the years as may be seen from educational report govt. of India. Since 1950-51 girl's participation has increased many fold in Primary, Middle, Sec./Hr. Sec. stages and Hr. Education levels from 28.1% to 44.1%, from 16.1% to 41.8%, from 13.30% to 39.5%, and from 10.0% to 39.9% respectively. However, the girl's participation is still below fifty per cent at all stages of education.

The total Scheduled Castes enrolment at the primary (I-V), upper primary (VI-VIII) and secondary/senior secondary (IX-XII) stages of school education from 1997-98 to 2001-2002, increased by 1.9, 3.4 and 3.7 times respectively. The Scheduled Caste girl's enrolment increased by 2.5, 4.9 and 6.6 times respectively during the same period in the above stages of school education. The total Scheduled Tribes enrolment at the primary (I-V), upper primary (VI-VIII) and secondary/senior secondary (IX-XII) stages of school education from the same years increased by 2.5, 4.5 and 5.2 times respectively. The ST girl's enrolment increased by 3.3, 6.4 and 7.5 times respectively during the same period in the above stages of school education (see Table).

Pupil Teacher Ratio (PTR): On the basis of the school enrolment and the number of teachers, the PTR for the years after independence is indicated in table. At the time of independence there was a widespread dearth of educational institutions in the country and the utilization of institutions was also not optimum. During the year 1950-51 the Pupil-Teacher Ratio in primary schools was 1:24, in middle schools it was 1:20 and in High and Higher Secondary schools, the PTR was 1:21. In 2001-2002 this ratio has now increased

Table 1.5

Total Enrolment of Scheduled Caste & Scheduled Tribes Students in Schools During 1997-2002 (in 000')

Year	*Primary (I-V)*			*Middle (VI-VIII)*			*High/Hr. Secondary (IX-XII)*		
SC	*Boys*	*Girls*	*Total*	*Boys*	*Girls*	*Total*	*Boys*	*Girls*	*Total*
1997-98	11898	8659	20557	3786	2283	6069	2026	1048	3074
1998-99	11123	8377	19500	3748	2388	6136	2068	1149	3217
1999-00	11810	8625	20435	3881	2420	6301	2385	1399	3784
2000-01	12059	9136	21195	4066	2628	6694	2418	1394	3812
2001-02	12251	9253	21504	4551	2945	7496	2693	1622	4314
ST	Boys	Girls	Total	Boys	Girls	Total	Boys	Girls	Total
1997-98	5667	4000	9667	1541	943	2484	778	396	1174
1998-99	5312	3989	9301	1589	967	2556	856	452	1308
1999-00	6139	4511	10650	1804	1101	2905	918	504	1422
2000-01	6330	4665	10995	1879	1205	3084	955	535	1490
2001-02	6691	5040	11731	2054	1306	3360	1079	622	1701

Sources: Ministry of Education, Govt of India, 1997-2002.

Table 1.6

Dropout Rate Among SC/STs at School Education During 1980-1999

CATEGORY	*Classes I-V*	*Classes I-V*	*Classes I-V*	*Classes I-VIII*	*Classes I-VIII*	*Classes I-VIII*	*Classes I-X*	*Classes I-X*	*Classes I-X*
	80/81	89/90	98/99	80/81	89/90	98/99	80/81	89/90	98/99
General	58.70	48.08	39.74	72.70	63.40	56.82	82.46	71.34	67.44
SC	60.16	49.03	44.27	76.84	72.09	63.58	86.91	80.58	76.63
ST	75.66	63.81	57.36	86.71	80.10	72.80	91.18	86.00	82.96

Sources: Educational Development of SC/STs (1995) and 10th Five Year Plan(2002-2007), Vol. II, Planning Commission (2002, p. 421-454).

to 1:43 in primary schools; 1:34 in upper primary schools and 1:34 in High and Higher Secondary Schools. Though the number of educational institutions has considerably increased after independence, the higher PTR indicates that the utilization of the educational facilities has also increased. The increased enrolment at various levels also underscores the need for opening of a greater number of educational institutions for improving the quality of education (see Table).

Table 1.7

Pupil Teacher Ratio (PTR)

Year	*Primary*	*Upper Primary*	*High/ Hr. Secondary*
1950-51	24	20	21
1960-61	36	31	25
1970-71	39	32	25
1980-81	38	33	27
1990-91	43	37	31
1995-96	43	37	32
1996-97	43	37	32
1997-98	42	37	32
1998-99	42	37	31
1999-00	43	38	32
2000-01	43	38	32
2001-02	43	34	34

Sources: Ministry of Education, Govt of India, 1950-2002.

The Public Expenditure on Education (1951-52 to 2001-2002). The expenditure on the education sector was slightly less than 1% of the GDP in 1951-52. The percentage expenditure to GDP shows an irregular rise and fall. It rose to 2.33% in 1972-73 but in 1973-74 declined to 2.15%. It increased to 3.07% in 1979-80 and decreased to 2.83% in 1981-82. Continuing to rise and fall slightly, it has reached a level of 4.02% in 2001-2002. Similarly, the percentage of expenditure on education and training to total expenditure of all sectors during the last five decades indicates that it has increased from 7.92% in 1951-52 to 13.17% in 2001-2002 i.e. by 5.25 percentage points during the last five decades. This translates to an annual average growth of 0.11% during the period 1951-52 to 2001-2002.

1. Issues Related to School Education

The National Policy on Education (1986) has committed to achieve the goal of universal elementary education by 1995. Further, India as a signatory to the World Declaration on Basic Education made in Jomtein more than eight years ago, agreed to achieve the target by the year 2000. Yet, the goal has remained elusive, despite the fact that there is a primary school within 1.5 kilometres for children in 95% of the villages. Different studies have revealed that universalisation of basic education cannot be achieved without addressing the issue of cultural and socio-economic barriers. Interestingly, the results of a survey conducted by the National Sample Survey Organisation in 1992 revealed that school-related factors are responsible for at least 22-25 per cent of non-participation of children in primary schooling. The issue of bringing all children to school cannot be tackled with the single point proposition of opening more schools. The problem has deeper roots in the socio-cultural and economic conditions of the people. Moreover, the problem of quantitative coverage cannot be solved in isolation without paying adequate attention to improving school quality.

The above statistics indicate that the rate of growth of schooling beyond the lower primary stage is low. The ratio of upper primary to lower primary schools in most part of the country is still around 1:4, as against the official commitment of making it 1:2. The ratio of secondary to primary schools is around 1:6. This is far from the norms achieved in the developed world or even with the situation in many developing countries. In India, the Gross Enrolment Ratio (GER) for the secondary stage is only 48%, while the figure for China is as high as 66%; in the developed regions of the world, secondary education has been fully universalised. While improved provision of primary education facilities in the country has to be tackled on a priority basis, it may not prove to be effective if steps are not simultaneously taken to meet the demand for further education. Taking Kerala as an example, it is apparent that children are not likely to stop their education at the end of five years or even at the end of 7-8 years, given that, 75-80 per cent of children complete secondary schooling in Kerala. This apparent stagnation in the growth of post-primary education will also directly impinge on the quality of human resources and in turn, affect the process of economic development.

Low efficiency and effectiveness of the public schooling system, coupled with inadequate financial resource allocation has tended to push more and more people to seek even primary education through privately managed institutions. May one rationalise this trend as positive, as it helps to reduce dependence of those who can afford to pay on the government institutions? However, there is no reason to believe that people are voluntarily moving away from the public system, which is free, towards private education. It is important to note that this trend is likely to lead to further increase in inequity. In fact, one can observe that in urban areas this divided system of school education has contributed to a vertical division in the society on the basis of economic status of the parents. Can the state silently watch this phenomenon of education becoming an instrument of division and perpetuation of inequality in the society? Is it desirable to throw open the education system to the vagaries of the market when a large majority of the population are still deprived of even the basic levels of education?

Recent statistics show that even though GER for girls has risen to more than 90 per cent at the primary stage, it has remained practically static around 50 per cent at the upper primary stage for the last several years. In fact, even at the primary stage, the male-female disparity remains not fully bridged. School education has to address this issue by designing special strategies to overcome the barriers and bridge the gap between boys and girls on a priority basis. It is a well-known fact that millions of children in the country are forced to enter the labour market instead of pursuing education in the schools. Even among those who begin attending the school, a large number as indicated by high dropout rates and low transition rates, enter the workforce at a very early stage of life. It is in this context that the school curriculum that remains academic in nature has come under repeated criticism for not being able to add any value to the lives of such children and rather making education a drudgery and burden. Notwithstanding deliberations by several committees and commissions, we have yet to establish a meaningful structure of schooling, which can benefit both streams of students—those who terminate at elementary or secondary stage and those who continue their education to the tertiary level.

School education cannot be impervious to the fast changes taking place in the economic sector through liberalisation and globalisation of the market. Demands on the school, particularly with regard to those who enter the production sector straight from the school are two-fold. On the one hand, school education, particularly at the secondary stage has to keep pace with the needs of a competitive market, dependent on continuously improved knowledge and skill levels. On the other hand, school education has to recognise that the liberalised market framework directly affects the microeconomics of the poorer sections of the population, often corroding their fragile occupational base. The school education system has to become pro-active in preparing the curriculum and processes not only as a matter of social concern, but also to meet the basic needs of those entering the emerging economic framework.

Information Technology (IT) presents an excellent opportunity for making a quantum jump in the provision of school education in a need-based manner. Unfortunately, very little attention has been given in the country for exploring the tremendous potential of IT in school education, both for its quantitative expansion and for improving its quality. It is, therefore, urgent that immediate attention is given in school education to imparting basic IT skills to all learners. Learning from the past efforts, it is important that adequate provisions are made for development of software and capacity-building for teachers in order that it does not remain only as an additionally to the existing subject areas, but becomes an integral part of the learning experience of all children.

Examination statistics show that about 60 per cent of children routinely fail in the public examination conducted at the end of the secondary school; and of those who succeed and join higher secondary, only 40 per cent succeed in the higher secondary examination. Curriculum reforms, examination reforms and large scale efforts for introducing progressive pedagogy and so on, are being made in almost all the states. However, given the large size of the school education system, these system level reforms seem to be making very little impact on the functioning of the school. Direct actions for changing the functioning of people and institutions operating at the grassroots level have not received adequate attention. The situation demands a total reversal of perspective so that school occupies the centre stage and improvement in the quality of the school becomes the major agenda of all reform processes.

Non-suitability of a standardised model of full-time formal schooling to create a universal mass education system in the country was emphatically pointed out by Mahatma Gandhi much before we embarked on the task, fifty years ago. It is now fully realised that a monolithic approach to delivery of school education cannot meet the legitimate demands of the people for provision of educational facilities of a reasonably acceptable quality. Yet, it has been difficult to break the monopolistic hold of full-time formal schooling on the education system. Interestingly, society has begun adjusting its expectations to the limitations of formal schooling, instead of more actively pursuing the task of designing alternatives.

Suggestions

Elaboration of issues and problems of school education confronting the country should not be construed to imply that we are saddled with an impossible situation. Rather, it points to the need for acting with a sense of purpose and determination. What are the priority areas in which well-planned action holds promise for taking the school education system in a progressive direction? Some of these are indicated below.

Liberalising the curriculum framework: An important area that needs immediate attention is the introduction of a flexible and dynamic curriculum framework that meets the varying needs and aspirations of the diverse profiles of children entering school education. This is essential, if school education is to be made more joyful and relevant to the lives of the people. Actions have to be initiated, therefore, to avoid increased standardisation of the curriculum and allow for more decentralisation. This, again requires curriculum development to be a participatory endeavour of the direct stakeholders replacing the high bureaucratisation that characterises the current scene.

Breaking the monopoly of the full time formal school: Creating an institutional framework of delivery and organising the inputs in meaningful learning units are relevant only to the extent that they facilitate easy and effective transaction of learning processes. But, when the format of organisation begins determining and delimiting the nature and scope of education, alternative means have to be sought, in order to effectively pursue the basic purposes of organised education. In the current state of development of school education in India, this seems to be a matter for priority action.

It is not that no effort has been made in this direction, in India. Yet, one can easily see that a monolithic set- up of age-grade organisation in hierarchical learning units has become the predominant means. The monopoly of this dominant mode is so powerful as to seriously jeopardise the emergence of a pluralistic framework through apparently innocuous instruments such as equivalence, comparable learning inputs, comparable length of learning, common public examinations and so on.

Harnessing advances in information technology to the advantage of school education: In India, use of technology has invariably been identified with prosperity and affluence. With the relatively under-endowed state of the public education system, technology is seen as an alien element, which has no place in the school education programme. This perspective has failed to fully grasp the potential of technology to overcome some of the very barriers arising out of inadequate resources. It is important to take positive steps for building a more meaningful interface between modern developments in the field of information technology and school education programmes.

It is paradoxical that whereas the national leadership harbors aspirations of making the country a global leader in the IT sector, there has been no plan at all to make even basic computer literacy a part of the larger school system. It should be worthwhile that a national taskforce examines all the issues involved and comes out with a pro-active and futuristic framework for creating a sustainable interface between IT and school education.

It is essential that the task of quality improvement in school functioning is addressed in a more holistic manner by viewing teacher capacity-building and managerial skill development in an inter-related framework. Without bringing substantial improvement in the managerial efficiency of the schools, no amount of investment in pedagogy training will make an impact.

Therefore, there is a need to abandon the traditional concepts and practices of training the school teachers and managers through centralised arrangements involving the use of generic packages of training inputs. These have to be replaced by more localised and sustainable support mechanisms and delivery modes that are capable of providing contextualised learning inputs directly at the workplace.

If efficiency and quality improvement are our concerns, there appears to be no alternative, but to go for more local initiatives within a participatory framework and move towards the creation of more easily manageable organisational arrangements.

In spite of the hyperbole created with regard to decentralisation under the banner of recent Constitutional Amendments on Panchayat Raj Institutions, no perceptible change has come in most of the states with regard to the educational management scenario.

The benefits of ushering a decentralised system of management are enormous. The most important one is that smaller systems built through participatory processes are in a better position to remain sensitive to the local needs and aspirations; they allow for creative alternatives to emerge; and they are more likely to bring in a sense of ownership as well as accountability (Govinda–1998).

2. *Higher Education Scene in India*

Higher Education System in Indian Universities and specialized institutes are the centers for higher learning in India. The studies and disciplines cover a wide range of subjects from poetry to computer engineering to space research. Most of the universities and higher centers of learning and research are autonomous in function. A good number of universities have a federal structure composed of affiliated colleges on one tier and the university departments on the other. The affiliated colleges teach, in general, undergraduate courses, whereas the university departments conduct postgraduate teaching and advanced research. The university decides the criteria of admission into colleges and coordinates the first-degree examination in the undergraduate programmes and award of degree. Some other types of universities teach both undergraduate and postgraduate courses in general disciplines as well as in technical and professional courses. There are no affiliated colleges attached to them. There is a third category of universities and institutions where technical and professional courses are taught at undergraduate and postgraduate levels. Names like Indian Institute of Technology, Birla Institute of Technology, All India Institute of Medical Sciences, Indian Forest Research Institute, Indian Veterinary Research Institute can be quoted. Some institutes only offer postgraduate and research courses such as Indian Agricultural Research Institute and Post Graduate Institute of Medical Research.

There are three principle levels of qualifications within the higher education system in the country. These are: Bachelor/Undergraduate level, Master's/Post-graduate level and Doctoral/Pre-doctoral level. Diploma courses are also available at the undergraduate and postgraduate level. At the undergraduate level, it varies between one to three years in length; postgraduate diplomas are normally awarded after one year's study. Bachelor's degree in arts, commerce and sciences is three years of education (after 12 years of school education). In some places there are honors and special courses available. These are not necessarily longer in duration but indicate greater depth of study. Bachelor degree in professional field of study in agriculture, dentistry, engineering, pharmacy, technology and veterinary medicine generally take four years, while architecture and medicine, it takes five and five and a half years respectively. There are other bachelor degrees in education, journalism and librarianship that are second degrees. Bachelor's degree in law can either be taken as an integrated degree lasting five years or three-year course as a second degree. Master's degree is normally of two-year duration. It could be coursework based without thesis or research alone. Admission to postgraduate programmes in engineering and technology is done on the basis of Graduate Aptitude Test in Engineering or Combined Medical Test respectively. A pre-doctoral programme—Master of Philosophy (M.Phil.) is taken after completion of the Master's Degree. This can either be completely research based or can include course work as well. Ph.D. is awarded two year after the M.Phil. or three years after the Master's degree. Students are expected to write a substantial thesis based on original research, generally takes longer. There are three types of institutions engaged in importing higher education on different courses viz., Unitary Universities, Affiliating Universities and Deemed Universities and also Government of India has passed a bill to set up private Self Financing Universities, not requiring any financial support from the government, according to Website (http://www.ntu.edu.sg/sci/is/resgrps-14.htm#Anc_ISP7) education India.

The Ministry of Human Resource Development, Govt. of India, estimates that at the beginning of the year 1999-2000, the total number of students enrolled in the universities and colleges was 74.18 lakh-12.25 lakh in university departments and 61.93 lakh in the affiliated colleges. Eighty per cent of the total enrollment was concentrated in the three faculties of Arts (40 per cent), Sciences (20 per cent) and Commerce (20 per cent) while the remaining 20 per cent was absorbed by the professional faculties. Enrollment at the degree level was 65.20 lakh (87.9 per cent), at the PG level 7.25 lakh (9.8 per cent) and the remaining at research and diploma/certificate levels. The strength of the faculty went to 3.42 lakh this year. Out of the 76,587 teachers in the university department, 17, 385 are professors, 27,188 are readers/associate professors, 30,558 are lecturers and the rest are tutors/Demonstrators. In the affiliated colleges the number of senior teachers are 71,588, the number of lecturers 1,89,309 and the rest are tutors/demonstrators. The enrollment of women students in the year 1999-2000 was 25.74 lakh at the graduate and post-graduate levels. This accounts for 34 per cent of the total enrollment. The enrollment of women students was the highest in Kerala (53.8 per cent) and lowest in Bihar (19 per cent). Eighty-Seven per cent of the total women enrolled were in the non-professional faculties of Arts, Commerce and Science and 13 per cent professional faculties. MHRD Annual Report (1999-2000). UGC Annual Report 2001-2003 has given the folloing strength of total higher educational institution and faculties (see Tables 1.7, 1.8).

Table 1.8

Type of Institutions in Higher Education

S.No.	*Institutions*	*2001/02*	*2002/03*
1.	Central University	18	18
2.	State University	178	183
3.	Deemed University	52	81
4.	Institutions Under State Legislature Act	5	5
5.	Institutions of National Importance	12	13
6.	Colleges	13,150	13,343

Sources: UGC Annual Report 2002-2003.

Table 1.9
Faculty Strength

S. No.	Category	Affiliated College %	University Dept./ Colleges %	University and Colleges %
1.	Lecturers	43.68	4.91	48.59
2.	Sr. Lecturers	12.42	2.55	14.97
3.	Readers/ Equivalent	18.67	5.25	23.92
4.	Professors/ Equivalent	NA	3.49	3.49
5.	Principals/Prof. Equivalent	5.17	NA	5.17
6.	Others (Tutors/Demonstrators)	83.37	16.63	100.00

Sources: UGC Annual Report 2002-2003.

The National Policy on Education, 1986, with modifications undertaken in 1992, proposed that in the near future, the main emphasis would be on the consolidation of, and expansion of facilities in, existing institutions. Autonomous colleges would be helped to develop in large numbers until the affiliating system is replaced by a freer and more creative association of universities with colleges. Autonomy and freedom would be accompanied by accountability. Besides, courses and programmes would be redesigned to meet the demands of specialization better and state level planning and coordination of higher education would be done through councils of higher education and the UGC and these councils would develop co-coordinative methods to keep a watch on these standards. The teaching methodology would be technologically advanced and the teacher's performance would be systematically assessed. A suitable mechanism would be set up by the UGC for coordinating research in universities, particularly thrust areas of science and technology.

Despite all the efforts by the UGC and the Government over a period of time, on observes that there has been a decline in the standards especially because of increase in innumerable colleges. In addition, Science education in colleges and universities too is undergoing a decline owing to non-availability of modern laboratory equipment and lack of connectivity of syllabi with dynamics of job market. Another is the lack of accountability, both of teachers and students. There is also a concern regarding the most dissipate character of the graduates that the universities are turning out every year and the high level of unemployment that prevails among them. Nevertheless, a university degree or diploma continues to be a requirement for most jobs and consequently, the college and university continues to be a crowded the students aiming to get a degree or a diploma. It is very important to improve the quality of higher education as well as streamline the system itself. According to Arvind Panagaria a professor of economics (Maryland) advocates three mutually reinforcing reforms—private entry, greater autonomy, increased tuition fees—to alleviate the quantitative and qualitative crisis in University education in India, published in *The Economics Times* (2002), 23rd October.

Thus, India has the third largest scientific and technical manpower in the world. There are also more than 36 million educated unemployed. Consequently, it is felt that there is an excess supply for graduates and the university system can do with a reduction in size. The reality is that in India, per thousand of population, the number of graduates, engineers, doctors, etc. is one of the lowest in the world and also their average quality is suspect. This is a result of both poor quality of instructions and the migration of the cream to greener pastures abroad (Brain Drain). The engineering graduates remaining behind in the country do not go in for research and development, but join management schools and civil services in large numbers. The challenges before the country are innumerable. There has been a phenomenal proliferation of University and Higher Education in the country since Independence. The higher education system has been a twelve-fold increase in the number of universities and twenty-two-fold increase in the number of college since independence. There are now 185 universities, 42 deemed to be universities and five institutions established through State and Central legislation, and nearly 11,100 colleges in the country in addition to the unrecognized institutions in the higher education sector.

Total 1.10
Total Number of Recognized Educational Institutions in India (1998-99) Sate/UT-wise

Sl. No.	States/UTs	Primary Junior Basic Schools	Middle/ Senior Basic Schools	High Sch./ Hr. Sec Intermediate/Pre-degree/ Jr College	Colleges for General Educational	Professional Education	Universities Deemed Uni. and Instt. of National Importance
1.	Andhra Pradesh	51836	8713	11225	923	189	20
2.	Arunachal Pradesh	1277	326	171	7	1	1
3.	Assam	33236	8019	4590	265	33	6
4.	Bihar	53697	13761	4910	742	74	17
5.	Goa	1042	98	436	21	10	1
6.	Gujarat	14789	20044	6011	339	109	11
7.	Haryana	10269	1788	3785	169	45	5
8.	Himachal Pradesh	7732	1189	1525	57	6	3
9.	Jammu & Kashmir	10483	3104	1351	38	12	3
10.	Karnataka	23690	24142	10073	838	346	15
11.	Kerala	6755	2966	3109	186	42	9
12.	Madhya Pradesh	86858	21108	8341	413	70	17
13.	Maharashtra	41804	22196	14471	838	538	26
14.	Manipur	2570	630	582	50	3	2
15.	Meghalaya	4679	946	493	33	1	1
16.	Mizoram	1244	741	378	27	2	0
17.	Nagaland	1469	470	295	29	1	1
18.	Orissa	42104	12096	6813	524	49	8
19.	Punjab	12633	2527	3325	193	64	5
20.	Rajasthan	35077	14807	5633	267	76	10
21.	Sikkim	501	131	108	2	1	1
22.	Tamil Nadu	30844	5538	7357	365	174	21
23.	Tripura	2065	414	589	16	4	1
24.	Uttar Pradesh	94476	20675	8339	676	174	28
25.	West Bengal	52123	2864	6652	389	66	14
26.	A&N Islands	188	51	82	2	1	0
27.	Chandigarh	48	34	107	12	7	2
28.	D&N Haveli	144	54	15	0	0	0

29 Daman & Diu	53	22	25	1	1	0
30. Delhi	2676	601	1459	64	24	11
31. Lakshadweep	19	4	13	0	0	0
32. Pondicherry	356	107	175	8	7	1
INDIA	626737	190166	112438	7494	2130	240

Source: Annual Report 199-2000, Ministry of HRD, Government of India

Main Agencies in Higher Education

The Government of India established University Grants Commission (UGC) by an Act of Parliament in 1956. It discharges the Constitutional mandate of coordination, determination, and maintenance of standards of teaching, examination and research in the field of University and Higher Education. UGC serves as a vital link between the Union and State Governments and the institutions of higher learning. It monitors developments in the field of collegiate and university education; disburses grants to the universities and colleges; advises Central and State Governments on the measures necessary for the improvement of university education; and frames regulations such as those on the minimum standards of instruction. University Grants Commission (UGC) is responsible for coordination, determination and maintenance of standards, release of grants.

Central Government is responsible for major policy relating to higher education in the country. It provides grants to the UGC and establishes central universities in the country. The Central Government is also responsible for declaration of Educational Institutions as 'Deemed to be University' on the recommendation of the UGC. Some of the State Governments are also responsible for establishment of State Universities and colleges, and provide plan grants for their development and non-plan grants for their maintenance. The coordination and cooperation between the Union and the States is brought about in the field of education through the Central Advisory Board of Education (CABE). Special Constitutional responsibility of the Central Government on the: Education as mentioned in the 'Concurrent list' subject to Entry 66 in the Union List of the Constitution. This gives exclusive Legislative Power to the Central Govt. for co-ordination and determination of standards in Institutions of higher education or research and scientific and technical institutions.

National Policy on Education (NPE), 1986, a scheme to provide career orientation to education at the first-degree level was launched in 1994-95. Under the scheme, a university/college could introduce one to three vocational courses in 35 identified subjects. In 1986 (NPE), a scheme of autonomous colleges was promoted to develop and propose new courses of study to the university for approval. They are fully responsible for conduct of examination. It has been proposed that the programme of autonomous colleges would be fully central Govt. for 5 years and fund would be made available for the purpose to the UGC. However the assistance expenditure would be met by the existing system of usual resources. Currently, more than 138 colleges have been functioning as autonomous colleges in eight states in the country. NPE–(updated 1992) states that the new policy will lay special emphasis on the removal of disparities and to equalize educational opportunity by attending to the specific needs of those who have been denied equality so far (Para 1 NPE 1992). The objectives specified in the NPE are in the best interests of a democratic society and for the first time "equality" is prioritized over other gender, race, religion, region or cast together with an improvement of quality.

National Assessment and Accreditation Council (NAAC): To improve the quality of higher education several schemes like Faculty Development Programme, University Leadership Programme, National Eligibility Test, Academic Staff College, Autonomous College and National Assessment and Accreditation Council have been launched by UGC. National Assessment and Accreditation Council (NAAC) has been set up as autonomous affiliate of the University Grants Commission (UGC) under the provisions of the UGC Act., to evaluate the qualitative merit of the higher education. These schemes have been in operation for quite some time now. But the success is not remarkable. This is due to half-hearted and ritualistic implementation. Though higher education is not coming under fundamental right is considered to be essential for the cultural, social and economic development of the nation, it is necessary to improve the infrastructure in our academic institutions, create facilities, adopt a more flexible academic structure, introduce major academic reforms, gather market information and adopt other measures that will make Indian education attractive to others.

Indira Gandhi National Open University (IGNOU): Established in 1985 for introduction and promotion of Open University and distance education system. Major objectives include widening of access to higher education. It offered 43 programmes during 1998. Total number of students registered for various programmes was 1,63,000. Students' Supports Services in 1998 consist of 19 Regional Centres and 346 Study Centres. IGNOU programmes telecast on Doordarshan Network six days a week. Its jurisdiction is through out the country. It can set up Study Centres outside the country. This was allowed vide amendment of the IGNOU Act in 1997. Distance Education Council (DEC) under IGNOU has the responsibility for coordination and maintenance of standards in open and distance education system in the country.

Technical Education is a crucial component of human resource development with great potential for adding value to products and services and contributing to the national economy. Five Year Plans have laid great emphasis on the development of technical education. During the past five decades, there has been a phenomenal expansion of technical education sector in the country. Apart from the Government Sector, private and voluntary organizations were involved in setting up of Technical and Management Institutes in the expansion of the system. From 43 Diploma level Polytechnics with an intake of 3,400 students at the time o independence, the number has grown to 1,128 Polytechnics with the intake of 1.90 lakh students in 1997. Similarly, the number of Degree level institutions and the corresponding intake figure rose from 38 and 2,940 in 1947 to 552 and 1.36 lakh in 1997. Today, 185 institutions conduct Post

Graduate courses in Engineering and Technology with an annual intake capacity of 16,800. Facilities for doctoral studies in Engineering, Technology and Applied Sciences have also been created in a number of technical institutions. For more information on this area - log on to the website of Department of Education Government of India: http://www.education.nic.in/htmlweb/unhighedu.htm

Issues and Problems to Higher Education

Higher education in India since its inception in 1947 has been following the same road. The road has therefore reached dead-end from several perspectives. As the nature of occupations has been constantly changing with rapid developments in science and technology but curricula have practically remained unchanged, therefore, students no longer have confidence in higher education institutions for preparing them for entering the world of work. For a long time the principal employer of the educated youth in the country was the State. State as an employer generally did not look beyond academic certifications such as graduate, post-graduate, and occasionally at the level at which the degrees were obtained. It is only in the recent past requirement such as National Eligibility Test coupled with the level of pass at the post-graduate level were introduced as essential criteria for appointment of lecturers in colleges and universities.

The hard reality is that majority of employment opportunities now are in the private sector and this sector is very choosy, to say the least. The private sector employs only those who possess skills and competencies required by it. Its requirements are continually changing because this sector has to keep pace with its global competitors. Education now has to be tailor-made to the requirements of the private sector. Also, foreign institutions are making inroads in the higher education sector by providing alternative learning opportunities leading to award of degrees of their universities. They claim that their certification will be preferred by multinationals to the degrees awarded by our universities.

To add to the complexity of issues of higher education

in India, its demand and asymptotic saturation of state investment in higher education have been exploited by the private sector in a big way in setting up institutions with the hidden agenda of making money. In the period since 1990 the number of universities has nearly doubled; there has been manifolds increase in the student numbers. Many states passed acts for setting up of Private Universities. Private universities emerged like mushrooms under the provisions of Private University Acts, and institutions including those, which were newly created, obtained deemed to be university status. At the same time, the traditional structure of higher education in the state funded institutions has continued to remain around teacher-student contact, and finds that it is no longer adequate in meeting its demand and relevance. There are not enough lecturers, library books or rooms, and there is not enough time. New organizational structures are therefore required to support new learning processes.

In such a scenario, an obvious conclusion is that the road of higher education seems to have reached at a crossroads. The need of the hour is to give a fresh look to the higher education and introduce such changes as will restore confidence in the ability of the state universities and colleges for providing, cost effectively, education relevant to the present context of the world of work. If 'traditional' working practices are no longer efficient in the modern context of higher education, then we must determine effective ways of successfully achieving change. We have no choice but to do things differently. New organizational structures are required to support new learning processes. The key to meeting this challenge has been quality assurance that too cost effectively. Customer satisfaction is the key for upgrading quality, as without full customer satisfaction it is not possible to increase market share. The customers of education are students. Decline in interest in general education courses has hit the universities and colleges. It is perhaps due to dissatisfaction with the present education system, students seeking tertiary education. clamor for joining professional courses of study than courses in general education. The widespread impression is that unlike professional education courses, the general education courses have failed to keep pace with changes that are taking place in the world of work. The courses offered by the general education colleges are determined by traditional mindset and have continued to remain inflexible. Also, the general perception is that contents of courses that are being offered at present may not be helpful to them in acquiring skills and abilities required by their future employers.

Student satisfaction may have to be used as an effective instrument for raising the quality of programmes of study. This will require acceptance of the sovereignty of learners by the higher education system. New courses and course combinations may have to be offered for meeting varying learning needs of students. The other driving force for raising quality will be the commitment of teachers to their students and to the pursuit of excellence. The main task of teachers will be bringing out the inner potential of their students and chiseling of their mental faculties. Yet, another perspective that brings out the need for bringing in change in the content and process of education is the recognition that unlike in the industrial age when production of goods was the accepted means for generating wealth, in the information age it is the knowledge-based work that generates wealth. Instead of large capital investment of funds that was required for starting an industry for production of goods at a competitive cost, a knowledge-based enterprise requires human capital of knowledge workers only. Already the information age is transforming the way we work.

Like the brains of the other species that have evolved on Earth, the human brain can also store information. But the human brain has the privileged faculties of thinking, imagination and creativity. The computer can store a vast amount of information but it cannot think. It can process information as per the direction given to it by its user. The directions are the outcome of thinking by the human brain. Lord Rutherford, the great pioneer of nuclear physics once said, when he was told that America was going ahead in nuclear physics because they had a lot of money, "Americans have money. .We do not have it, and so we have got to think." There is no substitute for hard and serious thinking;

and with sustained and serious effort we should be able to go long way even with our meager resource and capital. It will, therefore, be an anachronism to continue to use the human brain for memorizing information when it should be used for solving problems, creative thinking—the skill attributes of knowledge workers. Therefore, any system of education unless it is learner centred, is flexible, is around developing thinking skills and is able to help learners in acquiring the ability of learning how to learn will gradually lose its relevance. We should not be surprised that now the good students rarely select the conventional courses offered by the colleges as their first choice for higher studies. Therefore, there is now an urgent need to reorient teaching learning in the universities to meet the requirements of the youth for living and contributing effectively in the 21st century.

The dimensions of the Information Revolution and its limitless possibilities are widely accepted and generally understood, even by lay people. Nevertheless, to make the most of it, we must also acknowledge that there are challenges before the education system particularly the higher education system, and we must make important choices. We can extend opportunity to all or leave many behind. We can accelerate the most powerful engine of growth and prosperity the world has ever known, or allows the engine to stall. History has taught us that choices cannot be deferred; action or inaction makes them. There is no such thing as virtual opportunity. We cannot point and click our way to a better future. The tools of information and communication technologies that are available today offer themselves for introducing the paradigm shift that the higher education system needs for making it relevant to the needs of the 21st century. Before too long, each student has to be enabled to stretch a hand across a keyboard and reach every book ever written. Also, information that is being generated, nearly in real time, is being made available online with the Internet. For the first time in our history, it is now possible, in principle, for a student in India to have access to the same world of knowledge at the same instant as a student in the most affluent country of the world has.

We know from hard experience that unequal education hardens into unequal prospects. We know the Information Age may perhaps accelerate this trend. The fastest growing career presently is in computer related fields, offering far more than average pay scales of other professions. History teaches us that even as new technologies create growth and new opportunity, they can heighten economic inequalities and sharpen social divisions. As we move into the Information Age, we have it within our power to avoid these developments. We can reap the growth that comes from revolutionary technologies and use them to eliminate, not to widen, the disparities that exist. But until every student has a computer in the classroom and a teacher well trained to help, until every student has the skills to tap the enormous resources of the Internet, until every high-tech company can find skilled workers to fill its high-wage jobs, India will miss the full promise of the Information Age. We cannot allow this age of opportunity to be missed. Everyday, we wake up and know that we have a challenge; now we must decide how to meet it. Every student deserves the chance to participate in the information revolution.

Suggestions

I would like to say that the nation looks towards its universities for initiating the deep and fundamental changes that we require. The faculty members should consider themselves agents of social change who can influence and mould the minds of the young. Universities should consciously reach the weaker sections/disadvantaged/SC/ST in the society and encourage them to pursue higher education so that they became bright and confident citizens of the future. Therefore, time has come for redesigning curricular concerns in higher education. The challenge is to introduce innovative interdisciplinary programmes of study appropriate to the concerns of the 21st century. If teachers continue to work in isolation and curriculum concerns are tackled by each institution individually without drawing benefit of each others experience it may become a race in which goal post is receding at a pace faster than the speed of approach. The end result will be that reaching the target may forever remain illusive. The key issues that I have tried to bring out are multidimensional and are overlapping. Suggestions for reengineering higher education for excellence can be as follows:

1. Information technology literacy to be made a compulsory component of all courses whether offered as campus programmes or as distance education programmes
2. Access to the state of the art learning resources through CD-ROM and the Internet be made available to all students.
3. Networking of teachers for collaborative development of teaching-learning resources.
4. Institution to recognize sovereignty of learners and teaching learning be made learner-centred programmes be made modular and choice be given to students to select modules for earning the required number of credits for the course of study
5. Transfer of credits be allowed for enabling students to study part of a course at another institution.
6. Theoretical component of courses to be taught by the teachers of the institution and courses for skills development be taught by practicing professionals, and the skill component be kept updated with the developments in technologies
7. Internship arrangement for each student with potential employers for obtaining practical experience.
8. Marketing of higher education or self-financing can be possible in some cases.
9. Changing the old methods/system/structure of the education plan.
10. Educational quality should be improved by introducing more technical and professional education.

Education and SC & ST Communities

Importance and relevance of formal education continues to occupy major space in the process of social development and change. This is more so in the case of developing country like India that has been traditionally and historically based on the principle of inequality and hierarchy through religion and the caste system. Education was the monopoly of few upper castes (especially Brahmins) whereas majority masses were denied access to education. However, at that time the objectives of education were limited to rites and rituals and three R's—Reading, Writing and Arithmetic. The nature, objectives and contents of education have undergone change only after the advent of British. Although the Britishers' goal of introducing modern education was limited to their vested interests, it was secular in nature and open to all. The industrial revolution brought modern values of life, such as equality and humanity to India supported by modern system of education. During British period, access to education was opened for all and therefore it could reach the castes other than Brahmins. For the first time in the history of India's education, these castes could access formal education. Further, the role of Christian missionaries has been very crucial in introducing modern values of equality and human dignity through education. Consequently, generations of intellectuals and social reformers came up under modern, western influence of education that served the cause of downtrodden. Thus, British rule, Christian Missionaries, industrial revolution and process of modernization and the contributions of social reformers could prove responsible for spreading education among the masses. The freedom struggle could be taken as ultimate outcome of these processes.

The term Scheduled Castes (SCs) is of recent origin based on legal and constitutional connotations (Article 341), broadly covering the castes (or outcastes) that have been treated as untouchables until independence measuring to 16.33 per cent (Census 1991) of total India's population. However, they have been also known by different names like Exterior Castes, Outcastes, Depressed Classes, Harijans, Ex-untouchables and Dalits in current situation. In addition to the scheduled castes, there are 8.8 per cent Scheduled Tribes (STs) (Census 1991, Article 342[1]). Besides, there also exist other backward classes (not untouchables) who are constitutionally recognized for the purpose of providing special facilities for their upliftment forming 52 per cent of total population of India. These communities are spread all over the country mainly based in rural parts. Previously, these castes had no right to education, to property, to occupation of their choice and suffered from various disabilities. It was the British officials with modern values, who for the first time, employed the ex-untouchables as domestic servants. This was further supported by their entry into modern and secular occupations like servants, construction workers, messengers and military service. Thus, the traditional social suppression of these communities, although to a little extent, was evading due to these factors. During British period we find some evidences of educational enrolment among the Scheduled Castes then slowly to Scheduled Tribes. Growth rate of SC/ST population in all census reports (1951-2001) starting from our independence shows a slow trends in decadal growth as per the below mentioned table.

Table 1.11

Trends in Decadal Growth of Scheduled Caste and Scheduled Tribe Population in India (1951-2001 Census)

Census Year	*SC*	*Proportion of SC*	*Decadal Growth Rate*	*ST*	*Proportion of SC*	*Decadal Growth Rate*
1951	51.3	14.4	–	19.1	5.4	–
1961	64.4	14.7	25.5	30.1	6.9	57.6
1971	80.0	14.6	24.2	38.0	6.9	26.2
1981	104.8	15.7	30.9	51.6	7.8	35.8
1991	138.2	16.5	31.9	67.8	8.1	31.2
2001	166.6	16.2	20.6	84.3	8.2	24.5

Population in Million

Thus, SC/ST constitute 24.54% of the total population of India, where SC's are 16.46% and ST's constitute 8.08 percent of the total population. Most of these people live on the peripheries of villages in rural India. Except 2 or 3 percent cream layer most of the SC/ST are illiterate. They were considered untouchables before independence. Though unsociability is a crime under the constitution, it is silently practiced. On the other hand Scheduled Tribes live largely on the hills and in the dales of India. They are cut away from the mainstream of life. They are the most backward people with traditional customs and superstitions. They live hand to mouth with scarce facilities. Most of these people though they have languages of their own, don't have literature and scripts to there languages. Their communication system is still oral. Therefore, Government of India has made some Constitutional provisions relating to the educational development to these communities.

Socio-Economic Profile of SC/ST

Education should be a gift of wings—its rich potential in harmony with the divine order of nature: "Wholeness unites truth, beauty and goodness in one majestic symphony of education" (Marjorie Sykes). To this Jyotiba Phule, who opened the portals of education to the dispossessed and weaker sections of the community once said—"Without education, wisdom was lost, without wisdom, development was lost; without development, wealth was lost, without wealth the Shudras were ruined". Thus, in the knowledge society of the 21st century, education will be increasingly valued as an end in itself and not as a means to an end, Presentation, (2002). Now in order to underscore the importance of education to the SC/ST, let us begin with by presenting their broad socio-economic profile surveyed by Ministry of HRD (1999) and Census of India (1991). Here we have used terms Scheduled Castes (SCs) and Scheduled Tribes (STs).

As Table 1 shows, in 1991, population of SCs and that of STs were 13.82 and 6.76 crores, respectively, constituting 16.48 and 8.08 percent, respectively. So far other indicators are concerned, it is observed that total literacy among the SC and ST male population was 37.41 and 29.60 percent respectively; while the average literacy for the country as a whole was 62.21 percent. Again the literacy rates, among SC and ST male population were 49.91 and 40.65 percent, respectively compared to 64.13 percent for the population as a whole. In terms of female literacy rate, the comparative figures were 39.29, 23.76, and 39.29 percent, respectively. This shows that in the area of literacy SC and ST population lags much behind the national average. The reason is mainly due to rapid urbanisation and privatisation in the country.

Table 1.12
Socio-Economic Profile of SCs, STs & Total Population (All India)

Sr. No.	*Indicator*	*SCs*	*STs*	*Total Population*
1	Population (Crore)	13.82	06.76	83.86
	(Percent)	(16.48)	(08.08)	(100.00)
2	Literacy (%), Total	37.41	29.60	52.21
	Male	49.91	40.65	64.13
	Female	39.29	23.76	39.29
3	Urbanisation (%)	18.72	07.39	25.73
4	Agricultural Labourers	48.00	-	
5	Cultivators	28.17	-	
6	Average Status of Cultivators	Marginal	-	
7	Percentage of People below Poverty Line	50.00	-	
8	Bonded Labourers	66.00	-	
9	Employment (%), Primary Sector	77.11	90.03	67.53
	Secondary Sector	09.83	03.85	11.97
	Tertiary Sector	13.06	06.12	20.50

Note: Information at Sr. Nos. 1,2,3 and 9 pertain to the year 1991 and from 4 to 8 pertain to 1987-88.
Source: (i) *Sarvekshana*, Vol. XII, No. 4, April-June 1999 and (ii) Population Census, 1991.

The various privileges for them in the country is a slogan for political leaders only, in practice the reservation for the SCs/STs is predominately in the government sectors either for Job or education. Whatever small opportunities for the SCs/STs in the government sector have been on constant decline because of changing Industrial policies, socio-economic compulsions and part of privatization move over the years by the successive governments that has seriously hindered the growth of the SCs/STs. Urbanisation is one of the most significant indicators of geographical and economic mobility and therefore over-all economic progress. It is disappointing to observe that in 1991 the rate of urbanization was only 18.72 percent for SCs and as low as 7.39 percent for STs compared to 25.73 percent for the national average. It is further observed that 48 percent of SC population comprised agricultural laborers, while cultivators were barely 28 percent. It is needless to say that generally SC cultivators are 'marginal'. What is worse, 66 percent of the bonded labours in the country belong to SCs. Below mentioned table shows the growth trends of urban population of SC/ST's comunities India as per our different census reports.

Table 1.13

Growth Trends of Urban Population of SCs/STs in India (1961-2001 Census)

Census Year	*Proportion of SCs*	*Proportion of STs*	*Proportion of Non SC/ STs*
1961	10.7	2.6	20.7
1971	11.9	3.4	22.9
1981	16.0	6.2	27.1
1991	18.7	7.4	29.2
2001	20.2	8.3	31.6

If we glance at the employment profiles of the SCs and STs vis-à-vis the population as a whole, it could be observed that 77 percent of the SCs and 90 percent of the STs have been employed in the primary sector as against 67.53 percent for the country as a whole. Further, only 9.83 percent of SCs and 3.85 percent of the STs worked in the secondary sector compared to 11.97 percent for the national average. Lastly, 13.06 and 6.12 percent of the SCs and STs worked in the tertiary sector compared to 20.50 percent for the populations as a whole. Representation of SC/ST in central government Services are given in the following table.

Table 1.14

Representation of SC/ST in Central Government Services

Group	Total	SC	Percent	ST	Percent
A (Executive Level)	60067	6155	10.21	1840	3.06
B (Gazetted Level)	94111	11649	12.38	2840	3.02
C (Non-Gazetted Level)	1959477	314995	16.08	122903	6.27
D (including sweepers)	818748	176368	21.54	54931	6.71
Sweepers	1551137	61149	39.42	12812	8.26
Total (excluding sweepers)	2932403	509149	17.36	182524	6.22
Total (including sweeper)	3087540	570296	18.47	195326	6.33

Source: Department of Personnel & Training. Quoted in National Commission for SC and ST, 5th Report 1998-99, p. 130.

In literacy level its growth rate is very poor in comparison to general community, as per the recent census report 2001, literacy rate at national level is 65.38% whereas in case of Scheduled Castes, it is 54.69 with gap of 10.69% and Scheduled Tribes is 47.10% with a gap of 18.28%. The literacy rate male is 75.26 comparatively, the SCs is 66.64 and STs is 59.17 and the gap being 9% & 16%, whereas general female literacy is 53.69% compared to SC/ST gap 12% and 19% respectively.

Table 1.15

Literacy Rate: General, SC, ST, Gap

Literacy Rate	Male	Female	Persons	Gap in Male/ Female	Gap in Person Gen/ SC/ST
General	75.26	53.67	65.38	21.59	
SC	66.64	41.90	54.69	24.74	10.69
ST	59.17	34.76	47.10	24.41	18.28

Sources: Census Report, 2001.

Table 1.16

Five States/Uts in Terms of Lowest Literacy Rate & Female Literacy Rate of SC/ST Population in India (Census-2001)

States/UTs	*Literacy Rate SCs*	*States/UTs*	*Literacy Rate STs*
Karnataka	52.9	Jammu & Kashmir	37.4
Rajasthan	52.2	Orissa	37.3
Uttar Pradesh	46.3	Andhra Pradesh	37.1
Jharkhand	37.6	Uttar Pradesh	35.1
Bihar	28.5	Bihar	28.2
	Female Literacy Rate		*Female Literacy Rate*
Orissa	40.3	Andhra Pradesh	26.1
Rajasthan	33.9	Jammu & Kashmir	25.5
Uttar Pradesh	30.5	Orissa	23.5
Jharkhand	22.6	Uttar Pradesh	20.7
Bihar	15.6	Bihar	15.6

Table 1.17

All-India Literacy Rate of SC/ST and Others During 1961-2001

Years	*SC*	*ST*	*Rest of Population*
1961	10.27(3.29%)	8.54(3.16%)	24.00
1971	14.67(6.44%)	11.29(4.85%)	29.45
1981	21.38(10.93%)	16.35(8.04%)	36.23
1991	37.41(23.76%)	29.60(18.19%)	52.21
2001	54.34(41.40%)	46.34(34.42%)	64.38
% INCREASE IN 1991-2001	16.93(17.68)	17.24(16.33)	13.17

Note: Figures in brackets show percentages of Female Literacy.

Source: Census of India, 2001, New Delhi.

The above literacy percentages showed that a percentage of rest of the population is higher than SC/ST in all the census of India. The percentages level of literacy has been increasing in all the census records. ST literacy are increasing faster than SC, it is perhaps due to more government initiative towards them. The recent

The 2001 census shows that nearly 47 per cent of the Scheduled Tribes (STs) were literate in the age group 7 and above, compared to 65 per cent in the total population. Even the literacy rate among Scheduled Castes (SC) was much higher (55 per cent) than the STs. Among the Scheduled Tribes again, the literacy rate among the tribes of Central India was one of the lowest in the country. The recent data on poverty also show that the Scheduled Tribes have the highest level of poverty. Nearly half the rural population belonging to scheduled tribes is found living below the poverty line compared to one-fourth in general population (excluding Scheduled Castes). Poverty is also much higher among STs compared with SCs particularly in rural areas.

The development process has displaced sizable number of tribal people from their natural habitat and from the sources of their livelihood in recent times. This has further kept them below poverty line. In tribal areas there is a lack of infrastructure particularly related to the supply of drinking water, electricity and educational and health services. The tribal territory is rich in mineral, forest and water resources, but the poorest of the poor live here. The area has also an abundance of rare flora-fauna and is rich in bio-diversity. Despite this, tribes have to migrate in search of their livelihood, have low access to heath care and education and have higher morbidity and mortality. Thus, it is required that the development processes are speeded up in the tribal areas ensuring that the fruits of development must reach the tribal communities.

Again, the all India scheduled caste and scheduled tribe education was surveyed during 1999, April and June and found the levels of middle, secondary and higher secondary education among the male as well as female population in both rural and urban areas among the SC/ST population are much lower compared to non-SC/ST population. The percent distribution of Persons of Age 15 years and above by general education for different social groups in India given below—

Thus, relatively low school attendance rates accompanied

Table 1.18: Percent Distribution of Persons (15+) by Level of General Education-1999

Social Group	*Not Literate*	*Literate unto Primary*	*Middle*	*Secondary*	*Higher secondary*	*Graduate & above*	*Not recorded*	*All*
				Rural Males				
ST	58.80	24.50	9.60	4.30	2.10	7.00	-	100.00
SC	54.20	25.00	11.60	5.50	2.60	1.10	1.00	100.00
Other	34.90	28.90	17.30	10.50	5.00	3.40	-	100.00
All	41.10	27.60	15.40	8.90	4.20	2.60	-	100.00
				Rural Females				
ST	84.30	10.10	3.50	1.40	4.00	2.00	-	100.00
SC	82.40	11.60	3.90	1.60	4.00	1.00	-	100.00
Other	65.50	19.00	8.70	4.40	1.50	7.00	-	100.00
All	70.80	16.60	7.30	3.60	1.20	5.00	-	100.00
				Urban Males				
ST	25.00	27.60	17.10	14.30	7.60	8.00	2.00	100.00
SC	31.90	29.00	17.80	10.40	6.00	4.80	1.00	100.00
Other	13.70	22.40	18.60	18.60	11.80	14.80	1.00	100.00
All	16.20	23.30	18.40	17.50	11.00	13.40	1.00	100.00
				Urban Females				
ST	50.50	19.10	13.30	7.90	5.30	3.50	3.00	100.00
SC	62.00	17.80	10.10	5.50	3.20	1.20	-	100.00
Other	32.20	22.20	14.90	13.90	7.80	8.90	1.00	100.00
All	36.30	21.60	14.30	12.70	7.20	7.80	1.00	100.00

Source: Sarvekshana, Vol. XII, No. 4, April-June 1999. Govt. of India, New Delhi.

by high drop-out rates among the SC/ST children create an unequal opportunity structure and sow the seeds of low ability of the their children to benefit from the available opportunities in the various spheres of the society which ultimately result in socio-economic discrimination. Accordingly, efforts have been made to ensure greater access to the disadvantaged groups by making provisions in the constitutions and special facilities for them, like—freeships, scholarships, hostel facilities and reservation etc.. On 4th May 1999 the state cabinet (of Orissa) decided to have 49 percent reservation for SC/ST/ OBC in all the disciplines of education i.e. medical, engineering, management, pharmacy etc. (16% for SC, 12% for ST and 21% for OBC) and in some educational institutions admission qualifications are also relaxed for them. This provisions coupled with the expansion of the system and helped in reducing disparities to some extent among SC/ST and non-SC/ST. For the educational upliftment of Scheduled Castes and Scheduled Tribes, funds are earmarked under Special Component Plan for them and are utilized through different schemes of both the Departments i.e. Department of Elementary Education & Literacy and Department of Secondary & Higher Education. Due to these affirmative actions done by the governments (Centre and State), their percentage of literacy is slowly increasing. This can be seen from the different census records.

Table 1.19: Totai Enrollment of Scheduled Castes and Scheduled Tribes in Higher Education

Year	*Non-Scheduled*	*Scheduled Castes*	*Scheduled Tribes*	*Totul*
1978-79	2,337.221 (91.35)	180,058 (7.03)	41,081 (1.6)	2,558,360 (100)
1988-89	3,448,087 (90.90)	279,720 (7.29)	69,169 (1.8)	3,836,976 (100)
1995-96	5,532,998 (89.24)	496,872 (8.01)	170,239 (2.74)	6,200,109 (100)
1996-97	5,898,407 (89.49)	512,291 (7.77)	180,142 (2.73)	6,590,840 (100)

Sources: 1) Twenty-Eighth Report of the Commissioner for SC/ST, 1986-87, Government of India, New Delhi, 1987. 2) Select Educational Statistics: 1988-89, Ministry of Human Resource Development, Government of India, New Delhi, 1989. 3) Annual reports – 1996-97 and 1997-98, Ministry of Human Resource Development, Government of India, New Delhi, 1997 & 1998.

Table 1.20

SC/ST Students in Elite Technical/Engineering Institutions (1994-95)

UG=undergraduate; PG= graduate

	IIT Delhi		*IIT Kanpur*		*IIT Kharagpur*		*IIT Chennai*		*IIT Mumbai*	
	UG	*PG*	*UG*	*PG*	*UG*	*PG*	*UG*	*PG*	*UG*	*PG*
Total seats	2457	483	375	53	527	450	348	261	408	422
No.of seats reserved										
SC	355	72	53	19	28	67	57	40	61	17
ST	176	36	26	10	3	33	29	20	31	9
No.Cand. Selected										
SC	132	21	19	14	28	54	28	48	32	0
ST	20	3	3	0	3	7	3	13	4	0
Shortfall percentage								Excess		
SC	62.82	71	64.2	21.4	0	19.5	51	20%	48.6	100
ST	88.64	92	88.5	100	0	78.8	90	35	87.1	100

Sources: Report on the Reservation for Employment of SC/ST in IITs Including Reservation for SC/Scheduled Tribes in Admissions therein. Standing Committee on Welfare of SC/ST-Fifth Report (1998-99), Lok Sabha Secretariat, New Delhi, pages 21, 23, 25, 27, 29.

As a result of all these multiple but inter-related factors 50 percent of the total SC population was below poverty line. In view of this, it would be interesting to see the extent of land ownership by SC/ST households. This is because in rural areas ownership of access to land is the single crucial factor that enables one to share the benefits of agricultural development and also serves as a symbol of social prestige. This may be attributed to the nature and features of the tribal economy and should not mislead one to conclude that agriculture as an economic activity is more favorable with the STs compared to the SCs, let alone the non-SC/ST population, quoted by Louis (2003).

Special Facilities for Educational Advancement

There are Constitutional provisions relating to the educational development to the citizens of India, may be provide under two categories: provisions which are applicable to all the citizens including the Scheduled Castes and Scheduled Tribe, such as Article 45, and Articles which have been specially provided to protect the interest of the SC and ST like Article 15(4) and 46. Articles 15(4) and 46 of the Constitution of India provides special safeguards for the educational development of SC/ST and enable the state to make special provisions for their educational advancement. The directives enshrined in the constitution have been reflected in various Five Year Plans, which have sought to raise the level of education among the SC/ST. Gradually the scope of programmes for educational development in the various FIVE-YEAR PLAN periods broadened. The National Policy on Education (NPE) 1986 as updated in 1992 lays special emphasis on removal of disparities and equalisation of educational opportunities attending to the specific needs of those who have been denied equality, particularly scheduled castes, scheduled tribes and educationally backward minorities. Some of the important programmes of the Department of Education are:

- Norms of opening of primary school has been relaxed to have a primary school within one-kilometer walking distance from habitations having a population of 200 persons.

- Abolition of tuition fee in all states in government schools at least up to Upper Primary level. Most of the states have abolished tuition fee for SC/ST students up to senior secondary level and also provide incentives like textbooks, uniforms, school bags, etc., to these students;
- The major programmes of the Department of Education like Universalisation of Elementary Education, Operation Blackboard, Non-Formal Education, District Primary Education Programme, etc., accord priority to areas of concentration of scheduled castes and scheduled tribes. Lok Jumbish and Shiksha Karmi projects which are community based non-formal education projects have a specific focus on SC/ST inhabited areas;
- Reservation of seats for SCs and STs in Central government institutions of higher education including IITs, Regional Engineering Colleges, Central Universities, Kendriya Vidyalayas and Navodya Vidyalayas, etc. Reservation in universities and colleges and technical institutions apart from relaxation in the minimum qualifying cut off stages for admission.
- In order to improve the academic skills and linguistic proficiency of students in various subjects and raising their level of comprehension, remedial and special coaching is provided for SC and ST students- like, appearing NET, joining IITs and for entry in services;
- Scholarships are provided to SC/ST students under the scheme of National Scholarship at the secondary stage for talented children from rural areas. Other scholarship like—Junior Research Fellowship, scholarships, Research Associate ship/Fellowships are also awarded by UGC exclusively to SC/ST students;
- University Grants Commission provides relaxation of five percent from 55 percent to 50 percent at the Master's level for appointment as Lecturer for SC/ST candidates. The Commission has also reduced minimum percentage of marks required for appearing in the NET examination to 50 percent at Master's level for SCs/STs.

- NCERT prepared/developed/published textbooks in tribal dialects and teaching/learning material in tribal dialects. The Central Institute of Indian Languages (CIIL), Mysore, has worked on 75 tribal and border languages.
- Establishment of SC/ST Cells in Universities, introduced by UGC during 1983 to ensure effective implementation, monitoring and evaluates the reservation policy in the universities.
- In our 9th Plan for the empowerment of weaker sections of the society there are extension programme. The purpose is widening adult education, population education, continuing education etc

Affirmative Actions: Issues and Problems

The issue of equality and justice gained high relevance in contemporary societies. However, the goal of equality cannot be achieved without special planning and programmes; especially for those communities that have been traditionally-historically deprived on various grounds of race, ethnicity, caste or gender. Social deprivation is universal but methods of combating it are different in different societies. Most of the democratic countries have adopted the special measures to do away with deprivation and introduced policies and programmes to achieve equality in social and economic spheres. The social and economic development is directly linked to higher education and the employment. However, growth of higher education in India has taken place more in response to political pressures and demands from the upper sections of the society than to cater to the development need of the nation as a whole (Aikara, 1994). India has completed 57 years of experimentation with the policy of Affirmative Action and it is time to review its gains and drawbacks. The conclusion, which emerges from various studies, reports etc. that the impact of the policy is that the situational constraints highlighted by the various studies should be removed through an integrated programme for the dispersal of the benefits. The benefits of the protective discrimination should not be allowed to become concentrated; rather they should be dispersed to cover their total population to prevent the creation of a sub-elite among the Scheduled Castes and Tribes (Ahmad, 1978).

The issues and problems emerged during last five decades pertaining to the Affirmative Actions are manifold: the political; social, economic and educational. Studies have revealed that the policy has certainly contributed to the educational progress of the Scheduled Castes but the progress is steady and minimal at higher level of education. It is because of the drawbacks within the system itself. Moreover, the socio-economic background that has direct links with educational access, retention and performance got thoroughly ignored. Consequently, a few urban-based families/castes within the Scheduled Castes have benefited. This led to regional and caste-to-caste imbalances. With reference to implementation of the provisions, it has been very poor due to bureaucratic attitude of upper castes, lack of will power and politicization of the issue; on one hand, and on the other, these communities in general, lack awareness. The people in general carry prejudice against the Scheduled Castes and Scheduled Tribes due to inherent feelings of superiority resulting into anti-reservation protests and litigations. It is also argued by some sections of people that the caste criteria should be replaced by economic criteria with certain time limit for such provisions. And very importantly, there has been an argument that the reservation policy lowers down the quality and standards. However, a small section of educated Scheduled Castes elites has emerged that is always being targeted against fall victim to new forms of discrimination and crisis.

There has been a constant nagging voice of protest, despair and disapproval from some of the sections of privileged India against the policy of reservation. "The dark and ugly demon of reservation has been looming over the future of our sons and we see no hope of its end—it is now here to stay to shake our existence." This line pithy sums up the frustration of privileged Indians and they often vent it in the forms of protest rallies or letters to the editors with headlines like: 'When will reservation end?' or 'revoke reservation'. It used to haunt the anxious parents and their sons/daughters over the academic future and job prospectus. The reservation for the SCs/STs is predominately in the government sectors either for Job or education. Whatever small opportunities for the SCs/STs in the government sector have been on constant decline because of changing Industrial policies, socio-economic compulsions and part of privatization move over the years by the successive governments that has seriously hindered the growth of the SCs/STs. The recent government in finding another avenues to resolve this problem has thought to exercise an option of reservation for SCs/STs in private sectors. I think, in the wake of this new problem and remedial solution in offer has taken unfortunate turn, therefore, it has absolutely become necessary to look at the problem of reservations through different angle taking some of the past and contemporary social factors into consideration.

As the National Policy on Education-1986 says: "priority will be accorded to opening primary schools, there educational development and welfare in the tribal areas". The backwardness of ST's is total when compared with other communities. Some of the states in which large number of tribal people living are North Eastern States—Arunachal Pradesh, Tripura, Nagaland, Assam and Madhya Pradesh, Bihar, Orissa, Maharashtra, Gujarat, Rajasthan and West Bengal. The Tribal communities are characterized by a high percentage of illiteracy. They need on priority, education and mobile libraries with audio-visual materials. They need more and more Bare-Foot Librarians to take information to their doorstep on matters of health, education, agriculture, environment, etc. Community libraries should be established in tribal areas under special plans to bring socio-cultural changes among them. The National Policy on Education-1986 laid stress on the education of SC/ST and suggested various measures for improving their position. The following common points are evaluated from different academic survey and kept for careful solutions.

1. Scheduled Castes and Scheduled Tribes students are not aware about various schemes/facilities for them lack of proper information/guidance. There should be academic support centers, library orientation and

users education program for them.

2. Due to their backwardness and unfavorable social status, the SCs/STs are not in a position to use the village libraries.
3. There are no book deposit centers and mobile libraries in their inhabitations.
4. The SCs/STs largely depend on their manual work for their livelihood. Therefore the SC/ST children also drop out from their school education due to pressure of family.
5. They need information on labor, agriculture, health, housing, forestry, education etc.
6. The SC/ST were oppressed and suppressed for many centuries. They need social justice. For that the SC/ST should have access to education and information.
7. The areas where the SCs/STs live should liberally be provided with Book Deposit Centers, Book Clubs and Mobile Libraries.

Impact of Educational Incentives

In general, incentives for the education of weaker sections (SCs/STs) have benefited a large number of students in educational institutions without which they can't get admission in the schools and remain deprived. Now, it helped them to develop self-confidence, awakened awareness in them of their rights and they are in good numbers in government services. Moneylenders, local landlords and government officials used to exploit the illiterate and ignorant weaker sections in all the time but due to spread of education they are aware of their rights as well as of the evils social practices. Percentages of their enrolment in all classes are increasing and witnessed during the NCERT survey and census report 2001. According to our educational statistics the growth rate of female literacy is at faster as compared to male during last couple of years. But, there are drawbacks/limitations at the developmental process—in the level of policymaking, implementing and proper management of it. As per different research and survey since independent it has reveals that education to the scheduled caste and scheduled tribe has been slow to reach them in several reasons:

- Traditionally, they are living in remote villages or hill areas which has been away from our general mainstream and had no proper formal education in their societies until recently and they were unaware of the advantages of education.
- Economically these backward people want their child to assist them from childhood in various household works and they are not aware about education and incentives.
- The educational curriculum is not according to their societal/cultural environment, which make them boring, and difficulties to cope. Due to some efforts and incentives they are enrolling but majority of them living out without success.

There are also other limitations on the developmental way like:

1. The unnecessary paper works and multiplicity of department's etc. delay in the welfare activities.
2. Lack of proper awareness about government incentives due to disseminations of timely information.
3. Due to Paucity of funds some of the welfare activities have not been properly implemented. It is more in backward states like Orissa, Jharkhand, and Bihar etc.
4. The various incentives like grants of scholarship, books, dress materials, mid day meal etc. for them in the educational institutions creates undue delay in its implementation.
5. There is need of proper supervisions to check the incentives and its record in time without political pressure and local vested interests.
6. The budget for the incentive should be prepared at the District Level after negotiation with the Head/ Principal of the school/college and student should disburse this through a bank or post office without much formalities.

7. Sometimes, incentives given to them are not properly utilized or wrongly recorded, it should be verified and should be given at the beginning of the session.
8. In order to have an effective control over the progress, strategies and measures, periodical meeting of the heads of the institutions with guardian of the students should be done to evaluate the benefits/schemes.
9. There should be a standard of education in the country, so the quality of education must be the same as urban area to remote location.

Conclusion

Thus, to my conclusion the existing educational system in India is profoundly shaped by its past. A highly unequal society evolved during centuries of colonialism and exploitation, and was stamped with extreme forms of segregation and discrimination during the decades of apartheid. Racial differentiation and discrimination within higher education created a divided and fragmented system in which: Resources were inequitably and inefficiently allocated, Governance structures were undemocratic, Access was highly skewed on racial lines, There was a lack of coordination, common goals or systematic planning, There was an inability to respond to the economic and social needs of the majority of the SC/ST population. Now, time has come to fight for education and knowledge for the betterment of the community, but without awareness or proper information this can't be satisfied. Right to Information Act is the right path, if its purposed can be understood in the country for its betterment. Therefore, library and information centers in their environment can also play a crucial role on it. Before going to it, we can discuss all about various aspects of information and knowledge.

There is a saying "If you have knowledge, let others light their candles by it." This is the philosophical underpinning of the freedom of information movement. Freedom of information and in particular, the right of access to information held by public bodies, has attracted a substantial amount of attention recently. In the past several years, many countries have taken steps to enact legislation giving effect to this right. By doing so, these countries join others around the world which have a long tradition to right to information, such as Sweden, the United States, Finland, the Netherlands, Australia and Canada. At this time the importance of freedom of information as a cornerstone right is more than an accepted notion; it is an obvious fact of life, which has been articulated as a fundamental right in numerous international conventions such as the Universal Declaration of Human rights and the International Covenant on Civil and Political Rights. However, the right to access to information has not been realized by the majority of India's people. Rather than protecting citizens right to information, India and other developing countries have created a "poverty of information" through sanctioning an official culture of secrecy.

Freedom of information should be analyzed on several different levels. For certain segments of society, for example, the middle and upper classes, access to information often times simply makes life a bit more secure or stable. However, for those who are poor and struggling for literacy, right to information becomes crucial for them. Without access to information, the most vulnerable become even more disenfranchised. In the past, right to information has often been an academic exercise in transparency couched in esoteric terms detached from the realities of grassroots organizations and movements. However, we know from the struggles of these groups that the right to information, if guaranteed and implemented in the right spirit, can empower communities to take charge of their lives by participating in decision-making and by challenging corrupt and arbitrary actions at all levels. This empowerment is particularly significant in developing countries, such as India, which is a nation afflicted with low literacy rates, high birth and infant mortality rates, social and economic tensions, class, caste and communal conflicts, gender discrimination and a relatively poor record of civil rights.

Climbing down from the ivory towers of academia results in a greater understanding of the significance of right to information. A walk around any slum or disadvantaged community reveals a multitude of concrete examples where the people right to information is not simply an academic exercise, but rather a matter of survival, security, or sustenance of life. Education underpins a person's ability to access important information. When there is no freedom of information regarding educational opportunities, the entire project of obtaining information is jeopardized. For example, while attendance at a college or university often guarantees a continuance of the status quo for those in the middle and upper classes, for a scheduled caste or scheduled tribe person from a lower class, admission to university often means an escape from poverty.

2

The State of the Art Review

2.0 Introduction

Any library and information centers are meant for the users, so all its activities and operations are centered towards users satisfaction. Therefore, it is the role of librarians to keep a very close contact with the users knowing their reading interests, behavior, and information privation attitudes towards the library. Thus it is very much essential to study the previous research on users, which has been a subject of frequent discussion. The first survey was made by Bernal (1948) to have real impact of user's in library information science field, which was carried out in 1948 and it is valid till today's research. Bernal's result indicated that pure and applied research had different needs and that work activity was a factor that could affect use of libraries and other sources of information. Other investigators have also correlated with the finding of Bernal. Another information scientist Menzel (1964) who has reported that the end of 1963 seems to have been something of a take off point for empirical research on the information needs and user of scientists and technologists. Thus this is a continuous process in the field of LIS.

There are different studies on LIS and has been a subject of frequent discussion It must be stressed here that most of these studies have been concerned with user demands rather than user needs and accordingly is lost without limitation. This is certainly a defect as there is a great deal of difference between a demand and a need. Demands made on libraries reflect not only the basic needs of users but also the nature and sometimes the deficiencies of the system that is being used to satisfy these needs. The possible reason for the earlier studies being restricted to the study of demand or use is perhaps because it is difficult in practice to separate the two and that it is easier in practice to study demand and reduce needs.

2.1 Methodologies Used in Earlier Studies

User studies' is a term which covers a very wide range of potential research, from the study of users' choices of books from a university library, through reactions to on-line search outputs, to the in-depth analysis of the underlying needs that result in information-seeking. It should be equally clear that this implies the use of not one model of the research process or one method of research but multiple models and methods. However, in the past the dominant method has been that of 'scientific method' (often mis-interpreted) with the large-scale social survey as the predominant method of data collection. It is not suggested here that the 'scientific method' is necessarily inappropriate in the study of information users. The process of problem definition, classification of phenomena, hypothesis formulation, data collection, hypothesis testing and so forth, and the interaction of theory and method, is probably relevant to any kind of study. The point at issue, however, is whether quantitative methods have been employed in user studies inappropriately.

Quantitative social survey methods are powerful data collection devices, so much so that they are often misused to collect a great deal of data without the researcher having a theoretical (or even descriptive) framework into which to fit the data. In effect, collecting data becomes a substitute for thinking about the problem. This is to criticise the unthinking application of methods, rather than the methods themselves. As a result, it might fairly be said that the practitioners of information work have been disappointed by user-studies research, largely because they fail to find within it recommendations for service provision. Equally, information researchers have generally failed to make an impact within any social scientific discipline because their work lacks integration with theories within those disciplines. It is suggested below that the answer to the first of these problems may lie in turning to a different model of research, where its application or utilization is considered to be part of the process. An answer to the second problem is more difficult to propose because it is bound up with the problems of socialisation into research within a field of practice without a research tradition: 'qualitative research' is proposed as a way of confronting directly the issue of the lack of theory in user studies. Wood (1969) has taken a bird's eye view of the methodologies used by earlier investigators on information needs of library users. He has discovered and enumerated the following five methods for the assessment of the information needs of library users. — Questionnaire; Interview; Diary method (systematic self observation by the user); Observation (by the person studying the user); and analysis of existing data.

The Citation Analysis Method and analysis of circulation and other statistics maintained by the library may be taken to cover by the final category in Wood's List. Each method of investigation has its own merits and demerits. Moreover, because of the variant nature of the information needs of the various types of users, no one method can be applicable in all the studies with the same accuracy of results.

Questionnaire and Interview Method, although not devoid of limitations, are the two well established and to a certain extent reliable methods. Among the direct studies questionnaire is found to be favorite method of study, with interview running second and observation a poor third.

Interview is a face-to-face interpersonal role situation in which, the there interviewer asks respondents questions designed to obtain answers pertinent to the research hypothesis. The questions, their wording and sequence define the extent to which the interview is structured. The structured interview involves the use of a set of predetermined questions and of highly standardized techniques of recording. Against this, the unstructured interview appears to be the central technique of collecting information research studies. Interview of users, most of the time, reveals data on user and non-user attitudes and perceptions about library use. The response received there from gives the greatest amount of probing and answer seeking. Another method of survey of users is telephone interview. It is characterized as a semi personal method of collecting information. This method as gained general acceptance during the last few years as a substitute for personal interviewing. It is convenient and produces a significant cost saving and higher response.

Questionnaire method is normally regarded as an impersonal survey method. In this process, a clearly and specifically defined group of users are asked to answer a number of identical questions. These individuals are administered with a questionnaire either by local distribution or through mail with a request to fill out on their own. This method seems to be the most suitable and convenient due to its lower cost, greater autonomy and accessibility. A questionnaire is the most common accepted device used in measuring library use and users' attitudes towards library resources. This technique gives detail information about users habit, perception on the functioning of the library and opinion on improving the standard of existing library services.

Observation is regarded as the basic, most primitive and widely accepted modern method of scientific research. Scientific research begins with observation and ends in observation. It includes the most casual, uncontrolled experience and practical experimentation. User study in the library environments can be undertaken in observing the phenomena primarily associated with the library use. By observation, information concerning to different behavior patterns of the users can be collected in the library without putting any obvious burden on the part of the users. Most of the user studies conducted through observation method in the libraries are confined to the use of card catalogues, circulation of library materials, type of reference queries they put and the extent of their independent approach to library resources.

The Diary Method involves the analysis of the user-records of information related activities. Otherwise being the most reliable source of information on the subject, its usefulness is undermined by the difficulties in getting access to it. Herner (1967) records the experiences of two investigators.

The limitations of the individual technique of study and the multidisciplinary trend in the development of subjects has made it imperative on the part of the investigator to use more than one technique so as to patch up the limitations of one technique with the help of another one. Earlier investigators perhaps realized this fact too, but not many studies with combination of techniques are found to be on record. Usually two and in some cases three techniques have been used for similar studies.

2.2 Research Trends in Users Studies

USA and European countries have witnessed the beginning of systematic trend in research in the field if library science during 19th centuries. The USA witnessed systematic research activities under an institution when Graduate Library School at the University of Chicago opened Ph.D. programme in 1928. In U.K. only in 1963 formal research programme (Ph.D.) was started with the initiative of PG school of Librarianship and Information Science at the University of Sheffeld. Library Science education in India though started as early as in 1911, it was only after the World War II that it was gradually recognized as a full-fledged discipline and separate departments were set up in universities offering courses leading to bachelor and master degrees. There were only 5 universities in India offering Diploma course before 1947. In 1948 S.R. Ranganathan started Ph.D. programme at the University of Delhi. Dr. D.B. Krishna Rao was the first Ph.D. awardee in Library Science (1957), though in 1950 Calcutta University awarded a Ph.D. degree in Science to M.N. Basu for his work on preservation of museum articles and library materials. However, all such works were carried out in departments other than LIS and under the guidance of scholars belonging to other fields. Besides some library personnel and LIS teachers have done research work leading to Ph.D. in LIS at universities abroad or Ph.D. on subjects other than LIS. Thus, there are four categories of research work conducted by Indian Library personnel, including library workers and LIS teachers, relating to LIS or inter disciplinary topics involving LIS. Since, then the pace of research in LIS in India was quite slow till 1970, but during the next decades, it accelerated considerably. Today, there have been several studies in LIS field and the numbers of publications are estimated to be more than 2000 with several review articles.

Researchers in the library and information science, as the time marches, have laid much emphasis on user studies, particularly in the field of LIS research. As a result, the research literature in the field of library and information science, particularly during the last decade, witnessed a spectacular growth in all its ramifications. During the 1930s, when early research on user studies was under taken, the scope then was mostly limited to inside the library. But taking into consideration the variety of users in multidisciplinary field, such studies were undertaken concerning to the problems of the users beyond the library premises. The same phenomenon can be exemplified through an illustration in which, two such studies i.e. one concerning to inside the library or other outside the library of the university o Colorado were undertaken. The study concerning outside the library i.e. student union is a better represented study of library use compared to the study made within the library premises.

Library being the center of information for both science and social science research, researchers have stressed the need for developing an effective communication setting so as to make a sound system for free flow of information. To practice the same, communication, as scientific method of dissemination, was adopted to providing a comprehensive description of all facts of the subjects concerned. APA project of scientific information exchange in psychology, for instance, applied several method and techniques to bring out a comprehensive picture of the free flow of information in psychology and of the characteristics of all major media used to acquire and disseminate information in the concerned field. This study was more concerned with the participants who were seeking specific information through their attendance, their success in obtaining it, and the nature of information they sought.

Another well-known trend is the recognition of the social role of scientific communication as reflected in the studies of invisible college. Since the information generators are also among the principal users, they stem continuously fed back on itself. With the adoption of system approach to the study of scientific communications, inter-relations and interdependence of various methods of communication system too have received increased attention.

Satish (1994) in his work "attitude towards information...", mentions one definite trend that is being however discerned towards comprehensive description of all facts of scientific communication in particular disciplines. There major trend in the communication research which he maintains including growing awareness of social characters and social organization of scientific communications as reflected in the studies made by Donohew Lewisn (1978) on invisible college defining the role of scientific meeting and enhancing its effectiveness as a means of information exchange.

Early models of user studies are more related to the document seeking and library use. Researchers used to confine their work on the practical aspects of library usage by the users. The center of their attention was more of the library than that of the user. All the early models of user studies were primarily concerned with document seeking or library use that with the characteristics of behavior, which might usefully discriminate among information users and provide guidance to service planning. On the other hand, Wilson (1981) also recognizes the necessity of identifying the ends served by the information seeking behavior within the wider contact of users' totality of experiences or users life-world centered upon the individual as an information user. He feels much of the user studies in the past have suffered from a concentration as the means by which people discover information, analyzed in terms of how the users ought to have been seeking information.

However, during the later period, there was a shift in the focus. The behavior of the users and the coverage received utmost attention in most of the studies. Information user, as an organizational user, influences the whole spectrum of information environment and was taken as a model of study. "Information requirement of social scientists (INFROSS)" a study taken at Bath University Line et al, during 1971 can be accepted as a remarkable example in the field of user studies. This study, in fact, gave a new direction to the problem associated with the user study especially in social sciences have identified the deep understanding of the behavioral pattern of the social science users.

Another study conducted at the Bath University in 1973 on 'Design of Information systems for social science project' a milestone in analysis of the requests made to the National Children's Bureau Questions and Answers Service, is a user evaluation of an information service in Social Welfare conducted by Satish (1994) This study, in fact, had shown that while 65% of the enquirers were for information in a great variety of particular subjects, less than 35% of users, on the other hand, asked for references, various research findings and statistics.

A three phases research project on information needs and information services in local authority social science department (INISS) undertaken in 1975 to experiment the multifaceted problems of the users aptly concludes that, specialization of information services according to the scheduled work roles where common needs can be discerned is desirable and information services should be integrated in the organizations communication pattern stated by Wilson and Stretfield, (1979).

The foregoing studies have, therefore, established the fact that more comprehensive description of all facts of scientific communication in a given discipline becomes the perquisite for every information system. The scholars in present trend should, therefore, agree that user studies should primarily be concerned with the document seeking approach of the library users rather than their behavior.

2.3 Need Based Users Studies in General

Several studies have been conducted on need based user studies in general; some of the studies are given bellow alphabetically.

Agrawal and Lal Manohar (1997) discussed the scope of user education and the value, methodology and assessment of user education programmes, describing international and Indian developments in user education and proposing the formation of a national policy on user education and a national agency to administer its programmes. Alvin and others (1970) of MIT group have described about the communications stars that serve as "gatekeepers" and facilitate the flow of information from outside and transmit it to their colleagues. Brooke (1980) in looking at the scientific communication system commented on the importance of informal channels of communication.

Auster, E. and Choo, Chun Weiv (1991) proposes a conceptual framework for studying the information-seeking behavior of executives when they scan the business environment and literature. The framework could be especially useful in designing research to investigate some basic questions about executive scanning behavior. The questions address issues such as what information do executives require, which sources are used by them to obtain the information, and how is environmental information used in decision making. Auster (1982) studied the area of organizational behavior and the areas of information seeking are separate fields that have produced literatures relevant to librarians. Neither of these two fields, however, is concerned with librarians as their primary focus. Nor does the literature of librarianship generally take into account the findings from these disciplines. Presents a brief review of both areas and comments on their relevance for librarians.

Bates (1997) develops an analytical framework to support the analysis of conversation in information seeking contexts. It brings together linguistic and social linguistic issues, which serve as viewpoints for exploring how information-seeking conversations differ from casual conversations and conversations in restricted conversational domains (e.g. teacher-student, and physician-patient). A sample of 9 conversations from 2 information-seeking contexts (i.e. school library media centre, and public library) is used to test the utility of the framework and explore possible characteristics of information seeking conversations. The findings support the utility of the framework for various purposes including: training of information specialists, feedback on their performance, design of human computer dialogues, eliciting of decision making processes during information seeking, and support for natural language processing.

Brown (1991) in his study brought together various aspects of information-seeking behavior, projected over an organisational and behavior framework, into a general survey of the literature. Three dimensions of information-seeking behavior were determined: the conditions, the context, and the process including the interaction among these dimensions. Selected barriers to information-seeking behavior are reviewed. Burdick, (1996) describes an exploratory study of the impact of gender on information seeking. The study took place during the fall trimester of 1994 at the laboratory school of a large university in the USA. The sample consisted of 47 females and 56 males enrolled in 4 English classes (one an honors class) in 10th, 11th, and 12th grades. Addresses the importance of investigating gender issues; presents a conceptual framework; reviews research questions methodology, and study site; presents a brief summary of findings; and outlines implications.

Chatman (1991) reported a study on which gratification theory (essentially, that certain populations live in an environment in which the emphasis is on immediate gratification and satisfaction of needs) was applied to an information-seeking behavior of a lower-working class population. Respondents were janitorial workers at a southern US university. Results show that, although members of this population expressed a number of areas in which they needed information (e.g., employment, everyday coping advice, etc.), they were not active seekers of information outside of their most familiar social milieu. Findings indicate that a possible explanation for this was the perception that outside sources were not capable of responding to their concern. Thus, there was little motivation in exploring the relevance of these sources. Moreover, items of most interest to them were those things that were accessible, had a firm footing in everyday reality, and responded to some immediate, practical concern.

Chen (1982) had given results of a study, supported by the Office of Libraries and Learning Technologies, US Department of Education, of the information needs and information seeking patterns of New England residents. 400 residents in each of the 6 New England States were interviewed over the telephone by researchers at Simmons College, Boston. The detailed questionnaire covered information searching both in work and in personal life during the previous month and the results is reported statistically in Tables, charts and graphs. Ellis (1993) describes an approach to the design of an information retrieval system for academic social scientists and attempts to determine their information-seeking patterns conducted by the Department of Information studies at the University of Sheffield by means of informal, semi-structure, in-depth interviews. 6 characteristics appeared in the patterns and at the same time to provide a framework for a flexible model to underpin recommendations for information system design and evaluation. These are: starting, chaining, browsing, differentiating, monitoring and extracting. Herner and Herner (1967) conducted a survey on the information requirements of the social scientists by the Bath University library group in England describes the different sources of information according to their use. Also the use of informal channels for locating relevant references and keeping up with the current research is described. It was observed during the survey that older and more experienced researchers tended to use fewer libraries than others do.

Itoga (1992) presents an interdisciplinary study of research into the social aspects of information communication by bridging the existing gap between cognitive and phenomenological views of information needs and uses.

Limberg (1995) aimed at to understand the interaction between information seeking and learning outcome in education. The hypothesis of the study is that what students learning about the subject content of an assignment are affected by the way this student searches and uses information for the assignment. Studies will be carried out on upper secondary and college level. Lonnquist (1990) reports a NORDINFO study designed to study the information-seeking behavior and information needs of scholars in the humanities from a holistic perspective. 64 people from Denmark, Finland, Iceland, Norway and Sweden were interviewed and result show that scholars in the humanities do not have a homogeneous information-seeking behavior or homogeneous information needs. Compared to other information channels research libraries, as expected, turned out to be of greatest importance for scholars seeking information and printed materials for their research. The study also showed that what subject search for a scholar means, in most cases, is looking up individual names of persons, (author of a book or article, or searching for information about a person). Scholars used bibliographies only to a small extent and their bibliographical awareness was rather low.

Maheswarappa and Trivedi (1986) made a study on the information needs of Indian Food Scientists a case study at CFTRI; Mysore studied the information requirements of food scientists through questionnaires and also evaluated the services provided to them. Results of this study are aimed at planners and designers of information systems to help them in designing effective information systems to help them in designing effective information services in the field of food science and technology. Nicholas (1997) studied the potential impact of the introduction of the Internet into the workplace. It is proposed to do this through a case study of one of the first groups to feel this impact: journalists and information professionals working in the print media. Of particular interest will be the empowerment of end-users, the changes in work practice that the Internet may bring about, and the effect these changes will have on information professionals as intermediaries in the information-seeking process.

Ocholla (1996) analyzes information-seeking behavior by university academics at Moi University, Kenya. A pilot study was conducted and data collected through questionnaires and interviews among 27 academics randomly sampled from: health sciences, information sciences, environmental studies and education faculties. Reports the results which covered: departments and faculties where academics belong, rank and position in the academics, information resources frequently used by academics, gaining knowledge of the existence of information sources, generation of professional ideas, reasons for looking for, where the academics get the information resources they use, and dissemination of information. Make recommendations to support information provision capacity in a university. Oliver and Oliver (1997) tests the hypothesis that information-seeking activities based on contextual and social purposes would lead to higher levels of knowledge acquisition and learning than those achieved through activities where the purpose and context was absent. Results provide tacit support for hypothesis. When students participated in information-seeking activities and tasks, the context and purpose of the activity influenced the amount of knowledge gained and retained.

Osiobe (1988) reports a study undertaken at Port Harcourt University Library, Nigeria, which investigated student's information seeking behavior. Results of the study show that browsing is the prevalent source of reference to the literature among undergraduates followed by faculty staff and the library card catalogue in 2nd position and the subject librarian in 3rd place. Abstracts and indexes are poorly used and ranked 6th in the study. Prentice summarises the interview findings of the 5 papers in this special section. Each individual has his special information needs and each works in a field in which current information is both essential and often hard to locate. Co-workers are the most often consulted information sources, and libraries were rarely if ever used for on the job needs-perhaps there is little or no role for the library in this sphere for many workers. Library staff, too, consults co-workers when planning the libraries reference activities. Potential users know what they need. Librarians need to know the extent to which they can fill those needs.

Sasikala (1994) reports results of a study of the information and library use behavior of 436 managers in 3 groups (senior, middle, and junior) from 20 industrial organizations in Andhra Pradesh. These show that: managers seldom visit libraries; that they try to satisfy their information needs from other sources as well as from libraries; managers need data type information firstly and descriptive information on specific topics secondly; managers collect information to keep abreast of current knowledge, to solve immediate practical problems, and additional information relating to the job. There are some differences in search and use behavior among the 3 groups. Savolainen (1995) offers a framework for the study of everyday life information seeking in the context of way of and mastery of life. Way of life is defined as the 'order of things', manifesting itself, for example, in the relationship between work and leisure time and models of consumption, and nature of hobbies. Mastery of life is interpreted as 'keeping things in order'; 4 ideal types of mastery of life with their implications for ELIS are outlined, namely optimistic-cognitive, pessimistic-cognitive, defensive-affective and pessimistic-affective mastery of life. 2 major dimensions of Ellis are reviewed: seeking orienting information and seeking practical information. The research framework was tested in an empirical study based on interviews with 11 teachers and 11 industrial workers. Discusses the main features of seeking orienting and practical information and gives suggestions for refinement of the research framework.

Selden (1992) describes the research patterns of social science researchers and humanist scholars and assesses the state of business studies. Discusses Kuhlthau's model of information searching and presents a behavioural model for information system design based on information seeking activities. Examines the conditions for research and researchers' use of libraries. Discusses the research career and the information-seeking career covering information socialization of the junior researcher, steps in the research career and information outcomes of the research career.

Contrasts the structure of science and engineering information with that of business researchers and humanities scholars. Stam (1989) studies the information-gathering activities of art historians have been studied from 3 different perspectives: in terms of the books they use; through their own accounts of their working processes; and by informal, systematic observation, written up as 'user studies', by art librarians. While observation implies objectivity, a distance between observers and observed, in practice art librarians are very much involved with the art historian in the work of art history and in the development of its methodologies.

Wiberle and Jones (1989) describes how humanists in a small, interdisciplinary group seek information, confirming findings of previous research, although with significant variations. They ignore on-line databases and seldom consult reference librarians, but they do rely on archivists and special collection librarians. Their use of formal bibliography is limited to 1 or 2 sources and occurs only when exploring new topics, their preference being to find information by going to the person or location that can supply it.

2.4 Need Based Users Studies in Information Field

Different need based user studies have been conducted so far in general. But the most relevant information studies pertaining to the above areas are of very importance to the libraries for the all-round development of it. Some of the studies are reviewed and given as the following lines. An in-depth review of literature on the subject clearly shows that a considerable number of user studies have been conducted concerning to the use of initial libraries by the various scientists and the general public alike. The outcome of few such studies which a set examples for the future scholars and the LIS professionals, testing the gravity of the individual library environment, provided a sufficient scope for the library concerned to revamp the whole system and to rebuild the library collection so as to make it more purposive, need based and meaningful for those it is intended.

Weedman (1992) conducted a study on University of Delhi Library in 1965 was the first of this kind in India, which gave a detailed account of the library development in regards to its services. No definite standard for use in developing a university library programme exists. Among other things, the quality aspects of the library development rather than users approach seem to have been predetermined in his recommendation.

Krishan Kumar (1987) conducted a study on the use of Sapru House Library servicing social science teachers an scholars provides sufficient clue concerning the average number days and hours the library is put to use, along with the priority of information sources being explored, thereby giving a scope for the library administrator to reorient the library system suitable to the requirements of social scientists.

Dhanyi (1986) conducted a survey of 100 readers at Rajasthan University Library in 1974 which revealed that readers demonstrated their interest more in using the library at college level with an optimal approach to library catalogue and handling reference books. They study stressed the need for user education for the new entrants of the college library.

The other such studies that deserve mention include the study made by Kaul (1999).) On the quantum of library use and pressure demand from various categories of users; the study of Karki (1982) on 'Analysis of industrial information service in india' was conducted by Sridhar (1989) on users of library and information science periodicals are some of the notable works in the field. The seminar on user studies and user education held in Osmania University on 1985 also stressed the need for conducting user studies in Indian university libraries. The libraries have to conduct user studies so that they can prepare an acquisition policy that can help in acquiring appropriate information best suited to their clientele.

Reddy and Karsiddappa (1997) conducted a survey on information seeking behavior on 160 medical scientists on the use of formal and informal channels of communication which showed that journals are preferred for formal source on information for preparing course/teaching materials. Books are used more for providing consultation and offering therapeutic/diagnostic services. The time spent in borrowing/reading literature for various purposes has also been studied.

Prasad and Tripathy (1998) conducted a study with physical and social scientists to find out their information seeking behaviors. They also enumerated the various sources of information used by the scientists. The primary journals were used by both groups of scientists, but there was a difference in the usage of abstracting and indexing periodicals. Wilson, dividing the research field of information needs and uses in system studies and user studies, subsumes the studies conducted until the beginning of the seventies under the general heading of library surveys in his review of research in information needs and uses. Also, attitudes of students towards libraries and their staff and the extent to which students borrow books have been explored in the surveys. These studies report that students seldom buy books, they have difficulties in using libraries and they often use the neighboring public library and that seminars on library use have little effect. Wilson (1994) has made the new review of information behavior research. In his Vol. 1: Studies of Information Seeking in context ISIC III, The Third International Conference on Research in Information Needs, seeking and use in different contexts

The third collection of papers presented at the International Conference on Information Seeking in Context held in Göteborg in August 2000, represents a huge variety of research conducted in this area as well as a rich range of approaches and aspects and wide geographic distribution of researchers. A part of this wealth of studies is included in the first volume of the *New Review of Information Behaviour Research* published annually by Taylor Graham (2002). The editors have grouped the papers in this volume into three categories: on theoretical perspectives (5 papers), on contexts of information seeking (7 papers) and on information searching issues (3 papers). Some papers in all three groups may attract a wide audience as fascinating readings. The exploration of information habits from small world perspectives by Elfreda Chatman; the metaphorical approaches to information use by Reijo Savolainen; the differences between novices' and experts' information behaviour by Charles Cole and Carol Kulthau; the impact of information technology on the success of the management of British 'pubs' by Alistair Mutch, or sharing information among Web users by Sanda Erdelez and Kevin Rioux are intriguing and attractive by the very serious and humanistic scientific attitude to recognisable everyday areas.

On the other hand, the works that would scare off an occasional reader by specific language or statistical data are no less interesting for their new insights and approaches. There is an impressive attempt by Brittain (1982) to build a general theory of information seeking on the basis of general principles of psychology. The rigorous "quantitative investigation of the ideas developed through qualitative research", by the group of UK and USA researchers allows to identify interesting relations of uncertainty to other variables experienced in information seeking stated by Wilson and others (1991). The study done by Kuhlthau (1993) reveals the direct relation between task complexity and use of information sources. Together with the study of steelworkers' behaviour conducted by Christie, Bruce (1981) and information behaviour of software designers by Morten Hertzum it once more proves the importance of people as information sources.

Some of the authors apply specific paradigmatic approaches or methods to information behaviour studies. Lonnquist.(1990) introduces the results of phenomenon graphic studies and their potential. Trivison, Chamis, Saracevic, Kantor, and Kantor (1987) uses long-term ethnographic observation for better understanding of relevance judgments, with a group of researchers applies a cognitive work analysis framework to explore collective information seeking. A rare treat to the eyes of the reviewer from Central Europe is the presence of the only by Appleton (1994) paper on information needs in Estonian industry. As a general conclusion we would say all these have a good support to many research projects, providing new perspectives and supplying unexpected research results from a related field.

Studies in information needs and seeking are a central part of research in information studies. Studies have been conducted from the 1940s and the perspective was first the view of information systems. This research tradition has been called the system-oriented paradigm. In those studies the aim has been to obtain knowledge to support organizational development and administrative decision-making. The approach has been criticized because of insufficient theories, concepts and research methods and because it hasn't taken into consideration the needs of the information-seeking persons. In analysis of data quantitative methods usually has been used by Dervin & Nilan (1986), Gould & Handler (1989).); Julien & Duggan (2000) and Wilson (1994).

At the end of 1970's and in the beginning of 1980's researchers began to realize that questions in information needs, seeking and use couldn't been seen only from the systems point of view. The user of the information and his/her needs came into focus and research in cognitive science was applied in the studies. The new view was called the new paradigm or the cognitive views of Dervin, Nilan and Wilson. Today the cognitive view has been criticized for not taking into consideration peoples social and cultural contexts in studies of information needs and seeking brhaviour stated by Case (2002); Mick Colin (1980), Vakkari (1998). To obtain better knowledge about human information behaviour there is a need for a more holistic view, which takes contextual aspects in to account in the research in information behaviour.

It has been pointed out that information seeking and use should be studied as a whole stated by Savolainen (1993, 1995) and Wilson (1981). Use of information has been studied in information as studies in scientific communication, for example citation analysis. There has been an effort to explore the question of use by studies in use and relevance of different information channels and sources. Savolainen mentioned in Brenda Dervin's Sense-making theory, and Robert S. Taylor's Information use environments etc. as examples of the few researchers who have tried to conceptualize questions concerning use of information more deeply. Existing theoretical and methodological problems have influenced that use of information hasn't been successfully studied and it has been suggested that also results of research in other disciplines (e.g. artificial intelligence, cognitive research in learning, memory and thinking) should be taken into consideration when information scientist try to conceptualize processes in information use by Savolainen.

A qualitative study of information seeking and use in the professional workplace context: using the sense making approach was, investigators by Prof Schubert Foo, Mr Mark Hepworth (Department of Information Science, Loughborough University, United Kingdom) and Ms Bonnie Cheuk Wai Yi (Internet Search). This study investigates the information seeking and use process in the workplace. Three professional workgroups are being studied: auditors, engineers and architects. This research project adopts Brenda Dervin's Sense-Making approach, which aims at developing a process model of information seeking and use in the workplace. The model will have implications to improve current practices of information literacy education as well as improving information/knowledge management and systems design in the workplace.

2.5 Need Based User Studies in Educational Field

Many of the studies in information science concerning aspects in university students' information behaviour has described students' use of library services and problems in using those services.

Wilson, dividing the research field of information needs and uses in system studies and user studies, subsumes the studies conducted until the beginning of the seventies under the general heading of library surveys in his review of research in information needs and uses. Also, attitudes of students towards libraries and their staff and the extent to which students buy books has been explored in the surveys. These studies report that students seldom buy books, they have difficulties in using libraries and they often use the neighboring public library and that seminars on library use have little effect by Wilson (1994).

Kalervo Järvelin and T.D. Wilson (2003) have studies

on several kinds of conceptual models for information seeking and retrieval (IS&R). The paper suggests that some models are of a summary type and others more analytic. Such models serve different research purposes. The purpose of this paper is to discuss the functions of conceptual models in scientific research, in IS&R research in particular. What kind of models are there and in what ways may they help the investigators? What kinds of models are needed for various purposes? In particular, we are looking for models that provide guidance in setting research questions, and formulation of hypotheses. As a example, the paper discusses [at length] one analytical model of task-based information seeking and its contribution to the development of the research area.

Studies of undergraduate students relations to libraries has been conducted in the Nordic countries in Danmark, Sweden and Finland. The results show that students are rather frequent library users quoted by Höglund et al. (1995), although there are large differences in how students of different disciplines utilize library services mentioned by Höglund. The students want more study carrels, more course literature and more generous opening hours according to Pors (1995). The students do not frequently use the user education programs of libraries. According to the Finnish and Swedish studies students themselves ask for more education in information seeking and library use. The students also expect a traditional service from the library and look at the library as a depot for literature and do not identify the library as an information center or as a place for studies. The results indicate also that systematic cooperation is needed between teachers and librarians, both regarding education in information seeking and in support of information service to students.

In these studies the perspective is the user and knowledge has been obtained about the role of libraries in the students information needs and seeking. More generally students' information behaviour has been studied by Carol C. Kuhlthau (1993). She has made empirical research about students' information seeking behaviour in libraries and developed a general model of the information seeeking process (ISP). ISP consists of 6 stages: initiation, selection, explication, formulation, collection, and prestation. Students experience the ISP holistically with interplay of taughts, feelings, and actions. Limbergs study concerns the interaction between information use and learning outcome, when high school students work at an assignment implying independent use of information. According to the study, which has been done by using the phenomenographic method, variation in information seeking and use interact closely with variation in ways of experiencing and understanding the content of infôrmation. Questions concerning the relation between teaching methods and students' information behaviour has not been investigated thorougly—although PBL—students' information seeking behaviour and libray use have been compared in a few studies, which are described later in connection with medical students' information behaviour.

In Finland, in addition to the study of students' library use mentioned above, a few master and licentiate theses have been done in the area of students information needs and uses at the departments of information studies in Tampere and Oulu. For example Rissanen (1994) has studied health care students information needs, uses and information literacy in a case study. Teachers, staff, and the collections on the practice department, the library of the college and the public library, textbooks and journals were the most important information channels for the studied students. Their information gathering was restricted by lack of time and money, language problems and poor skills in information seeking. He has explored instruction given to students in seeking and using literature as a part of university education. The findings showed that, teachers do not usually teach the central literature in a domain and teachers regard information skills of students as satisfactory. The subject field strongly influences on teachers' thinking and actions connected to instruction given in seeking and using literature.

In 62nd IFLA General Conference, 1996, Devadason and Pratap (1996) presented a case study paper on "methodology for the Identification of Information Needs of Users" said

Information needs are of various types. Apart from expressed or articulated needs, there are unexpressed needs which the client is aware of, but does not like to express. Another category of needs is the dormant variety, which the client is unaware of. Though identification of information needs is essential for designing information systems in general and for providing effective information services in particular, it has been found to be a difficult task as it is almost an investigative or detective work. In order to identify information needs one should adopt various methods to gather information on the various factors that influence the information needs. No single method or tool will serve entirely. A careful selection and blending of several techniques depending on the client whose need is being studied is necessary. In fact, the "information needs identifier" should study, prepare and equip him/her-self thoroughly to perform the task of identifying information needs. A formal step-by-step procedure that can be adopted to study the information needs of a majority of clients is proposed in this paper. Besides gathering and recording the information needs, a careful analysis is to be made to distil actual needs from the data gathered. It is hoped that the methodology discussed here, would be easy to perceive and be translatable into practice. It is to be noted that the methodology would become clearer and clearer as each step is put into practice enhancing the understanding of the scenario and help in fine-tuning the procedure to suit particular situations. Moreover it has been found that the proposed methodology is not only useful in identifying the information needs, but also has a profound impact on finding ways and means of satisfying such needs. In other words, the information needs identifier (INI) would discover, as a bye-product, several ideas, tools, methods and techniques of satisfying the clients in meeting their needs as well as design new and novel information services and products to meet those needs.

In 64th IFLA General Conference, 1998, Nazan Ozenc Ucak and S. Serap Kurbanoglu, presented a study on Information need and information seeking behavior of scholars at a Turkish university and said Knowledge generated by user studies can help to develop information systems and information services. Information need and information seeking behavior, two of the most important research areas of the user studies, are two complementary concepts, which are affected by many factors. Research results in these areas of user studies indicate that the type of information need and information seeking behavior of scholars are dependent on their field of research, and vary from one discipline to another. Understanding such behavior help us to design services and products, which would transmit the required information most effectively. Such different needs in turn may necessitate offering services (e.g. user education) in academic libraries depending on the academic discipline users come from. In this paper we report the result of our research conducted at Hacettepe University, Ankara, Turkey on the effects of occupational factor in library usage by the scholars in science, engineering, social sciences and humanities. We also compare these findings to those reported in scholarly literature. Based on these findings we make several recommendations to improve the interaction between library staff and the scholarly community

2.6 User Studies on Information Seeking Behavior

The important studies based on the above heading are reviewed as under alphabetically.

Akeroyd, J. (1990) studies 3 different interfaces for on-line public access catalogues were evaluated using transaction logging as a methodology. In two cases exercises were set and run against each interface so that results could be critically evaluated to indicate areas of weakness. In all cases a random transaction log was derived and this was used to diagnose system problems and identify patterns of behavior. Results showed that searches were often difficult to categorise, users employing different approaches to the same end. Users were also prepared to undertake sustained searching until something was retrieved; however they then frequently stopped. Search input problems are also identified and possible areas for further research suggested.

Albrechtsen and Hjorland (1997) presented an interview

with Birger Hjorland, Danish author of a new book on knowledge organization entitled 'Information Seeking and Subject Representation: An Activity-Theoretical Approach to Information Science'. The book presents a new general theory for information science and knowledge organization, based on a theory of information seeking. Gives the author's views on knowledge organization and subject representation. Bystrom and Jarvelin (1995) studies the relationships of broad job types and information seeking characteristics have been analyzed both conceptually and empirically, mostly through questionnaires after task performance rather than during task performance. Analyzes at the task level on the basis of a qualitative investigation of the relationships of task complexity, necessary information types, information channels, and sources. Tasks were categorized in 5 complexity classes and information into problem information, domain information, and problem solving information. Moreover, several classifications of information channels and sources were utilized. The data were collected in a public administration setting through diaries, which were written during task performance, and questionnaires. The findings were structured into work charts for each task and summarized in qualitative process description Tables for each task complexity category. Quantitative indices further summarizing the results were also computed. The findings indicate systematic and logical relationships among task complexity, types of information, information channels, and sources.

Chamis, Saracevic and Trivison, Donna (1986) reported on a project on the cognitive aspects of information seeking and retrieving. Analyses the variations in search results obtained by 9 searches on a series of questions. The objectives of the 1st phase of this project were: to analyse the degree of agreement in search results and search strategy among intermediary searchers searching the same question; and to test the cognitive characteristics of the searchers and correlate these with the effectiveness and efficiency of the search results obtained. Indicates wide variations in the number of citations retrieved by the 9 searches. Analyses the number of unique citations in the set of 9 searches for each question.

Derr (1984) in his study reported that 5 types of information seeking expressions of users has identified by an analysis of a sample of such expressions and of analogous expressions in another social context. The treatment of these expressions in the literature of information retrieval is reviewed. 2 recommendations are offered: information specialists should call questions 'questions', requests 'requests', statements 'statements', commands 'commands', and truncated expressions 'truncated expressions' and both the search interview and the search itself should focus upon user questions. Hjorland (1993) provides a summary of a dissertation which presents a theory of information seeking behavior based on the theory of knowledge, thus uniting the two areas in which this subject is usually studied: user studies and information retrieval. Chapters deal with the following areas: definition of subject retrieval; an overview of the field of subject representation data; subject analysis; theories of subject, interpreted, characterized and criticized from the viewpoints of objective idealism, subjective idealism and realism; methodological problems in information science; analysis of information seeking from a methodological collectivistic methodology; the concept of information needs; and the relationship between the proposed concept of subject and tendencies in philosophy and psychology.

Hyldegaard (1997) aimed to study the potentials, if any, of using a Virtual Reality (VR) user interface for visualizing, retrieving and manipulating information. A VR user interface represents the next generation of user interfaces by allowing for a high degree of transparency and non-command based interaction. Discusses the different factors affecting transparency and considers information retrieval through browsing. Kuhlthau (1991) discusses the users' perspective of information seeking. Presents a model of the information search process derived from a series of 5 studies investigating common experiences of users in information seeking situations. The cognitive aspects of the process of information seeking suggest a gap between the users' natural process of information use and the information system and intermediaries' traditional patterns of information provision.

Kuhlthau (1993) proposes an uncertainty principle for

information seeking. The principle is based on the results of a series of studies conducted into the user's perspective of the information search process. A basic principle of uncertainty is elaborated by six corollaries. Proposes the principle to explain the constructive process of information seeking and use bringing affective considerations to what has usually been regarded as a cognitive process. Liddy and Jorgensen (1993) attempted a study which aimed to empirically investigate book-index usage, behaviors, and the extent to which specific print index features affect a user's search for information; and to examine these features in an electronic environment and to determine the optimum specifications for indexes in electronic texts by gathering evidence from a controlled user study. Provides an overview of the research project, focusing on a subset of the results from the study of hard-copy book indexes. Describes observable behaviours of a sample of users when consulting different variations of a hard copy book index. Suggests a preliminary model at three levels of abstraction repressing users' behaviours when using a book index.

Malmsjo (1997) reviews the factors related to the environment and situation influencing users' information seeking behavior and the various models and equations reported in the literature to describe this activity in a quantitative manner Overall, the aim is to examine the degree to which these models of information seeking behavior can be of use in designing practical information systems.

Marchionini (1989) conducted an exploratory study on elementary school children searching a full-text electronic encyclopedia on CD-ROM. 28 third and fourth graders and 24 sixth graders conducted 2 assigned searches, one open-ended, the other closed, after 2 demonstration sessions. Keystrokes captured by the computer and observer notes were used to examine user information-seeking strategies from a mental model perspective. Older searchers were more successful in finding required information, and took less time than younger searchers. No differences in total number of moves were found. Analysis of search patterns showed that novices used a heuristic, highly interactive search strategy. Searchers used sentence and phrase queries, indicating unique mental models for this search system. Most searchers accepted system defaults and used the AND connective in formulating queries. Transition matrix analyses showed that younger searchers generally favored query-refining moves and older searchers favored examining title and text moves. Suggestions for system designers were made and future research questions were identified.

Reneker (1993) studied the information seeking activities of 31 members of the Stanford University academic community were examined over 2 week periods, the 2,050 information seeking incidents being tape recorded and supplemented by interviews. Qualitative and quantitative analysis was used to examine the information needs in relation to perceived environment, source use, personal characteristics, and satisfaction with the result of information seeking. Results revealed information seeking to be embedded in day-to-day tasks and relationships and triggered both by articulation of need and availability of information. Describes the methodological approach adopted and the use of the ETHNOGRAPH and SPSS/PC Plus software to facilitate data analysis. Saracevic, Kantor,

Chamis, Alice and Trivison, Donna (1988): The objectives of the study were to conduct a series of observations and experiments under as real-life a situation as possible related to: user context of questions in information retrieval; the structure and classification of questions; cognitive traits and decision making of searchers; and different searches of the same question. The study is presented in 3 parts: Part 1 presents the background of the study and describes the models, measures, methods, procedures, and statistical analyses used.

Savolainen (1993) studies based on the sense-making theory, which is based on constructivist assumptions on human information seeking and use. Focuses on the epistemic and practical interests of the theory, discussing them in relation to the interests of the traditional intermediary-centered approach. Sense-making theory is a programmatic research effort suggesting user-centered ideas for the conceptualization of the information seeking and use. Its contribution to LIS researches its critique to the limitations of the traditional intermediary-centered approach. Sitter and Stein (1992) presents a dialogue model that incorporates the illocutionary aspects of information-seeking dialogues. Directives, commissive, and assertive types of dialogue acts (asking, offering, rejecting, answering, and evaluating) are represented by a complex transition network. The model determines all legitimate types and sequences of dialogue acts and regulates the role assignments (when the information seeker and the information provider temporarily exchange their roles). Such an integrated model can serve as a basis for the design of human-computer dialogue systems. The model was worked out in the COGITO (Cognitive Interaction Tools) at the Integrated Publication and Information Systems Institute, Germany.

Spink (1996) reports results of an exploratory study to investigate the ability of novice searchers to recognise stages in a user's information seeking process. The study follows a research project, which investigated the ability of experienced search intermediaries to recognise and assess the stage of a user's information seeking process. 2 aspects were examined in the study: problem definition level; and the work stage that the user was experiencing at the time of the online search. The study aimed to investigate whether the ability of searchers is limited to skilled and experienced intermediaries or is a more fundamental human cognitive activity. Results suggest that novice searchers were able to judge the user's problem definition level more successfully than the users work stage. Implications of the results are discussed in terms of a general process model of information seeking behavior. He further goes on to argue that information science is beginning to explore feedback as a key concept within information seeking and retrieving models. Feedback has been a fundamental element in many cybernetic and social models. Gives an overview of feedback within the cybernetics and social frameworks. Compares these feedback concepts with the interactive feedback concept evolving within the framework of information seeking and retrieving, based on their conceptualization of the feedback loop and notion of information.

Summers, Matheson, and Conry (1983) suggested that on current research on information retrieval, greater attention be given to the study of information habits and needs of users of information. It has also been suggested that the user be viewed more broadly as existing within interacting cognitive, emotional, and social systems. The findings of the study offer support for the notion that information source use by educators is the result of a complex set of interactions among variables and examination of the interaction of personal, professional, and psychological attributes of users provides a useful beginning in understanding the dimensions influencing the use of information sources. Talja, (1995) discusses the theoretical foundations of information seeking research, theories of the nature of information and its users are metatheories which guide the information of concrete research programmes in IS research. The basic ontological and epistemological assumptions of these metatheories are analyzed in this project, and their implications for the development of research strategies are discussed. Trivison, Chamis, Saracevic, Tefko, Kantor and Paul (1987) describes a study made to validate a model of information seeking and retrieving and to observe the effects of a selected set of cognitive variables involved in on-line searching. Professional searchers were observed searching prepared questions in their subjects on DIALOG. The degree of agreement in search strategies was low.

Vakkari and Kuokkanen (1997) describe a study whose aim was to analyse theory growth in information science by using a case from information seeking studies. Scientific growth is identified with the growth of theories. Differentiates 3 contexts of theoretical work: unit theories, theoretical research programmes and metatheories. States that for analysis of theory growth, tools based on the current theory of science are needed. Introduces tools for the analysis of theory growth and theory reconstruction and applies them to analysis of a theory on information seeking. Vakkari, in an independently published article analysed some theoretically most advanced studies of information seeking will to reconstruct the theoretical structure of unit theories presented in the studies. The structure of a unit theory includes a set of concepts and assertions relating those concepts in an account of some information behavior phenomena. With the help of the reconstruction linkages between unit theories are analyzed in order to reveal possible theory relations. Theory relations might refer to the fact that theoretical research programmes exist, i.e. family of interrelated unit theories. Finally on the basis of interrelated unit theories, conclusions are drawn from the nature of growth of theories of information seeking.

Wilson (1981) reviews work on information-seeking behavior and information needs in a number of disciplines, other than information science. The aim is to identify models and methods that may be transferable to information science. Wilson (1995) further explores the information-searching behavior with the framework of a model of information-seeking behavior based on the concept of uncertainty-reduction. A number of models will be tested, and the role of individual psychological factors will be investigated. A sample drawn from the staff of the University will be used, and qualitative data relating to their information behaviour will be gathered using semi-structured interviews, observation of searches, and transaction logs. Psychometric data will be measured using Riding's cognitive style analysis. Data analysis will seek to establish both statistical and qualitative evidence of relationships between different elements of information seeking. While the project is seen essentially as a contribution to the basic understanding of information behavior, a number of practical lessons should arise from it, both for the design of information retrieval systems and for the training of information intermediaries. Information provided by the British Library.

Yoon (1997) studied for his doctoral thesis about the use of certainty in information seeking in an interpersonal context. Certainty is what users know or think they know in relation to their information need whereby they describe their need using what they already know. That is, users employ certainty in order to point to what they do not know and need to find out. The uncertainty has been widely accepted as the information need in many information retrieval and user studies. The certainty, however, has not been explicitly addressed. The purpose of the study is to explore the extent to which the user's communication for information seeking relies on certainty, and what characteristics are in relation to uncertainty.

2.7 Users Studies on SC/ST Communities

The Constitution of India provides certain special Constitutional safeguards for the welfare of Scheduled Castes and Scheduled Tribes and other weaker sections of the population, so that they could take their rightful place in society. But they are occupied very distinct place in the communication system of country, they have no ideas, events, contacts and links with the government provisions and facilities to words them, in terms of their developments that tremendously influence the society. SC/STs are backward and remain in poverty since our independence, which apparently reflects their social position, profession and missionary objectives in making the nation more informative. Since, education is more crucial and viable force for the all rounds development of a nation. it is also the responsible of the government, the different communication media and library professionals to make them more educative and informative.

Disadvantaged communities of the developing countries in particular, very often make the right to seek information imperative without any hindrance so as to develop their community effectively. Hence, in India SC/STs' access to information and need for information appears to be of great significant for research scholars of Library Information Science. It is the distinct obligation of a librarian or information scientist, among other things, to know the user community (specially those are not regular user) better by assessing their information needs and determining their information seeking behaviour. In performing such a difficult tasks, the librarian has to understand the users and to acquaint himself with their myriad information requirements so as to ascertain the impact of the library on the life style of the users who can contribute substantially to social, political and economical environment of the nation.

Studying users and use of resources will ultimately pave the way for the librarian to design an effective information system tailored to the needs of the target audience. Hence, users study is one of the crucial weapons through which the information requirements of the SC/ST can be better addressed and the significant results thereof can be analysed to find out the most suitable methods of service/delivery, which can help to develop an appropriate information system for them in India. Since no such comprehensive study has yet been undertaken concerning to SC/ST as potential users of the libraries, the present study becomes imminent. There are many survey, case studies conducted by different government, NGOs, private organizations, agencies and institutions in the country on their socio-economic condition, education, health, status etc. to see the real problem.

Chakrabarti and Basu (1999) conducted a study on information needs of Tatos (sub-Himalayan tribal community) reveals that everyday information need of any community is incumbent upon its economic conditions and its reactions to these conditions. Socio-economic aspects include various needs of the community people such as areas of their earning, livelihood, availability of communication facilities etc. Information on political conditions relationship with the community deals with electoral process; roads, electricity and entertainment etc. are also the factors for the development of the community.

Dr. Ambedkar Research Institute (1991) Conducting various survey and studies on socio-economic status of SC/ST, research in specific and general areas to undertake ethnographic and anthropological studies on castes and sub-castes, synonyms for inclusion for inclusion/deletion pertaining to reservation policy, undertake evaluation study and sample survey during the course of implementation of SCP/TSP. to assist the research scholars (M. Phil/Ph. D.) who are interested in undertaking studies on problems of SC/ST in different regions of Karnataka, Special studies will also be taken on atrocities & unsociability and measures to be taken on preventing them, evaluation studies to examine the impact of Government welfare measures implemented by both State & Central Government.

Wankhede (2003) presented a paper on affirmative actions and the Scheduled Castes: access to higher education in India and reveals that the issues of equality and justice gained lot of importance and such programmes have been introduced by constitutional commitments in India for these sections of the society, i.e. the Scheduled Castes. This paper addresses the issues pertaining to the Scheduled Castes and their education with reference to Affirmative Actions. Higher education is considered as an important mechanism for their development that is directly linked to better jobs and higher income. However, it is not possible for these communities to access, sustain and perform better in education due to their poor social and stigmatized background without governmental support. That is why they have been provided with various material and non-material facilities including reservation of seats in admissions at all levels of education. However, during last five decades of the experimentation of the policy; studies have revealed that their progress in higher education is unsatisfactory due to the education system itself followed by the unfavourable socio-economic conditions and biased attitudes of the upper castes. However, this does not mean that facilities do not help them improving their plight. Their access to higher education is made easy by these programmes but could be made more effective and result oriented by implementing them properly. Since last decade, the globalization has posed a new threat to the policy supported by privatization.

National Council of Educational Research & Training (NCERT), New Delhi (2001) studied on educational problems of tribal children, aims at mapping the existing provisions for primary education in the tribal areas as well as their utilization by the recipient population. It has been carried out in seven DPEP States viz. Assam, Karnataka, Kerala, Maharashtra, Madhya Pradesh, Orissa and Tamil Nadu. The aspects studied include educational infrastructure and facilities available, status of teachers in tribal areas, status of curriculum and teaching learning materials, use of tribal language, status of school enrolment and school dropout, monitoring, evaluation and community participation.

A national research project on Scheduled Caste and

Scheduled Tribe college students and teachers in Orissa was conducted during 1972-1975, by Prof. Rath (1975), Dept. of Psychology, Utkal University, Bhubaneswar, sponsored by the Indian Council of Social Science Research (ICSSR), New Delhi. The aim of the study was to find out educational problems faced by SC/ST in Orissa, suggested different schemes on socio-economic development to ICSSR.

Thus, there are different studies conducted by Dr. Ambedkar Research Institute, Ministry of Human Research Development, Social Welfare Organisations and SC/ST Welfare Department of India, to find out their socio-economic conditions, socio-educational development and different social needs for planning, designing and overall development of these communities in different period of time. Any such studies are necessarily not only for planning and designing information system for the government for the sake of development but also for their efficient and effective operation and implementation as a whole. This can be also applicable for the librarian to study their information needs for their educational advancement. There are likely to be many surprises to even an experienced librarian about his own clientele, as he would not have heard them all in a systematically planned set up in his day-to-day work. The obvious drawback in relying on experience is a bias towards outspoken and intensive users, which is, at times, either too pleasant or too bitter. These types of user studies on SC/ST students in academic environment of Orissa can also help to improve the relation of the library with users in an objective way, provided it is done with the organisation concerned. Accurate and objective knowledge about users and their information behaviour are the essential ingredients for designing an information system in Orissa for the betterment of the disadvanced community. The effectiveness of educational planning and library information system depends on the extent to which the system characteristics correspond with the user and on how much the potential user is willing and able to make use of it.

2.8 Research Gap and Rationale for the Present Study

All the major works on users studies have been done in this field in the western countries, especially UK, USA and China. Very little work has been done on the information needs of library users in India and especially in the field of higher education; perhaps no comprehensive study has so far been pursued. Typical Indian user studies represent an over emphasis on bibliometric studies in general and citation studies in particular. But the utility of such studies in understanding the users dynamism is limited. Most of the studies conducted earlier have adopted individuals as the unit of analysis taking the similarities and differences among the users in terms of their backgrounds like status, age, experience, education, discipline and specialisation into account. Very few studies have been conducted taking an organisation as the unit of analysis treating organisation as the composite entity with sample individual respondents as the typical representative. As indicated in the above a numbers of 127 total doctoral theses have been awarded by different universities in India. Since, last 6 years on LIS field, out of which only 21 numbers are specifically made on users study based on information needs of student teachers and faculties in general. But on the other hand, there has been a number of theoretical and review type of works carried on by government departments, private agencies and NGO's for educational development of minority communities in Orissa. Yet, no single comprehensive user study has been reported in the state relating to SC/ST in higher education). Therefore, the present study is the outcome of the need to fill up this very gap as a sample from Orissa State.

I come forward to find out the real problem for them for seeking information in various fields for their socio-economic development as well as their education and information needs. Hence, this study is focused on the information needs and seeking behavior of the SC/ST student/researcher/faculties with specific reference to higher education and a need for networking of these educational institutions without any preconceived expectations or hypothesis. The study also suggests a model for need based information system among the Colleges and Universities in Orissa and cooperation at all levels starting from the local to the global level. Cooperation is a pre-requisite for all types of networking for resource sharing. Therefore, the following must be ensured before preparing the plan for linkages between university and college libraries of Orissa.

1. Institutional commitment to accept the given measures.
2. Fund and support resource sharing solution.
3. Attitudinal changes in library staff to undertake additional responsibility in resource sharing environment.
4. Training of library staff to understand and appreciate the changed situation.

If these pre-requisites are made available the university libraries could plan for resource sharing programmes, apprenticeship in libraries for learning new skills and IT training programmes, consultancy in retro-conversion and in developing IT infrastructure. All these put together will be the basis of preparing a perspective plan and evolve a vision for academic libraries in the State. In fact research in library and information science like this is more meaningful if the findings increase the efficiency and effectiveness of information flow to suit the interest of the SC/ST communities in the state and attract them towards the library information sources to minimize their illiteracy.

3

Research Context and Framework

In the concluding section of the previous chapter it is clearly pointed out the various limitations in the on going research project done by different researchers in different period of time and highlighted the various challenges faced in most university and college libraries in India as well as in Orissa. Therefore, suggested a model to face the challenges of actually preparing a perspective plan from scratch i.e., from collection development to networking through IT solutions, and will need a complete blueprint to develop these libraries during the coming centuries. I thing this educational network model can work from the primary level to university level all over the state, due to following reasons: Firstly, the state government has already adopted the new IT policy of 1998 in both—governmental and educational field. Secondly, the Government of Orissa enacted the most demanded Orissa Public Libraries Act in 2001. Thirdly, Orissa has links with different national computer networks like—NICNET, I-NET, INFLIBNET, ERNET, SIET etc. Before going to the chapter dealing with suggested Academic Library Network of Orissa, this chapter deals with the "Research Context and Framework" of the study and also include various objectives of it. Again, discussion on profile of Orissa, it 's educational policy in general and scheduled caste and scheduled tribe community in particular has been discussed prior to the framework.

3.1 Profile of Orissa

The state of Orissa is situated on the eastern coast of India, surrounded by West Bengal in the northeast, Madhya Prodesh in the west, Andra Prodesh in the southeast, and the Bay of Bengal in the east. The state was 13 districts before 1999, and then it became 30 districts. It was one of the last Indian Territory to come under the British rule and therefore was exposed much later to the liberal education introduced by them. Moreover, Orissa is an economically backward state with conservations deep rooted in the society. The population constitutes 3.6% of the Population of the country. The density of population lower than the country's average (324), increased to 236 persons per sq.km in 2001 from 203 in 1991. The sex ratio 972 females per 1000 males, is higher than the country's average. It is also one of the least urbanized states in India with only 15% of the total population living in urban areas while for the country as a whole the corresponding percentage is 27.8%. Probably this is the single largest obstacle to the educational development of the state. Again, scheduled castes and scheduled tribes together constitute nearly 40 percent of state population—the highest percentage compared to other major states in India in 1991. Districts like Malkangiri have SC & ST population to the extent of almost 80 percent. Owing to these historical and socio-economic constraints, Orissa still continues to the closeted among the educationally backward states of the country. It is also one of the low literacy states, ranking 13 among the 16 major states in the country. About 64 % of the total population has been enumerated as literates in the 2001, Census (2001).

Demographic Information of Orissa as Per Census 2001

Total Area Sq.M.	*Rural*	*Urban*	*Total District*	*Total Tahsil*	*Total Block*	*Total Town*	*Total Villages*
155,707	152,912	2,794	30	171	314	138	46,989

Distribution of Population by Religion

Hindus	*Muslims*	*Christians*	*Sikhs*	*Buddhists*	*Jains*	*Others*
94.67	1.83	2.10	0.05	0.03	0.02	1.26

Total Population and Literacy (2001)

	Item (in Lakh)	*Population*	*Literacy*
1.	Urban Population (Total)	54.96	80.95
2.	Male	29.00	88.32
3.	Female	25.95	72.68
4.	Rural population (Total)	312.10	60.44
5.	Male	157.11	73.57
6.	Female	154.98	47.22
7.	Total	367.06	63.61
8.	Male	186.12	75.95
9.	Female	180.94	50.97

Sources: Census Report 2001

Living Condition of the People

Orissa is one of the poorest States of the country. Compared to coastal region, the incidence of poverty is more in northern and southern regions of the State. It is higher among the scheduled tribes as compared to scheduled castes and general castes. Further more, the percentage of rural families living below the poverty line is found to be much higher in the State (66.37 per cent, as per the estimate made by Panchayati Raj Department, Govt. of Orissa in 1997). Besides structural poverty, the State also faces the poverty like conjunctural poverty (due to floods, cyclones, droughts, etc.) and destitute poverty (of persons lacking either money or material to survive). In terms of the development indicators like literacy rate, infant mortality rate, per capita income, etc, the living conditions of the people of the State are considerably lower than the national average. Greater inter-district variations in the living conditions of the people are found within the State. The performances of the welfare activities like EAS, PDS, ICDS and MDM are also found to be very poor.

There are a number of remedial measures to reduce the incidence of poverty among the people in the State. Economic growth is necessary to improve the living conditions of the people. For this, development indicators like literacy rate, per capita income, infant survival rate, per capita foodgrain production, per capita net value added by manufacturers, etc. have to be improved through appropriate and adequate investment in the concerned sectors. Adequate funds should be diverted to the rural area to reduce the higher concentration of rural poverty in the State. Further more, efforts should be made to remove the present loopholes and a problem in the rural developmental programmes and programmes aimed at alleviating poverty through government initiatives. Increase in agricultural production and stability in foodgrain prices are very much necessary for improving the levels of living of the rural poor. Government should take necessary steps to control the climatic crises like flood, drought, cyclone, etc., so that the conjunctural poverty causing mass structural poverty (headcount index) in the State can be reduced. Inter-district variations in the living conditions of the people should be reduced to improve the standard of living of the people. Lastly, necessary steps should be taken to improve the performance of the welfare activities of the government (i.e. EAS, PDS, ICDS and MDM), so that the living conditions of the people can be increased.

Like the infrastructure sector provision for different social infrastructures and services required to be rendered to the people under social sector development by the State is not so discouraging in Orissa. However, the nature of implementation of various services and their delivery across space and people is highly unsatisfactory. In the front of health and education the State has to pay more attention for the development of infrastructure and amenities in the backward tribal and highland districts. Particularly, in the health sector there is a necessity for ensuring the services of doctors and other paramedical staff in the interior and tribal pockets of highland districts. It is found that the infant mortality rate, morbidity rate and death rate of population in Orissa are much higher and the life expectancy rate is much lower than the other major neighbouring States making almost same level of investment on the health sector. Similarly, in education sector the State should not remain complacent by mere setting up of primary schools and constructing school buildings alone. It is observed from the village survey that the primary school education in the interior and tribal villages of the highland districts are in total disarray. Further, there should be policy formulation for giving preference to vocational education for increasing self employment opportunities. The State has much lower level of literacy among the female population particularly, in the tribal districts like, Koraput, Rayagada, Malkangiri, Nabarangpur, Kalahandi, Nuapada, Kandhamal, etc. Apart from health and education, the other welfare schemes and beneficiary oriented anti-poverty programmes should pay more attention on their monitoring aspects and selection of right beneficiaries in order to protect the interest of the poor and weaker sections. There is a need to check the malafide transfer of social security benefits to the actual non-poor category of rural population.

3.2 Education Scenario in Orissa

Education plays a pivotal role in the socio-economic development of a nation. In recognition of this basic proposition Universalisation of Elementary Education (UEE) which implies provision of free and compulsory education to all children up to 14 years of age has become a major thrust of the State's educational policy. UEE which is targeted for achievement by 2000 A.D. has three aspects namely: *(a)* universal access and enrolment, *(b)* universal retention of children up to 14 years of age and *(c)* achieving essential leaves of learning by all children by improving the quality of education. The emphasis so far has mainly been on the access in terms of construction of class rooms and appointment of teachers etc. In order to meet challenges of the task and to ensure total involvement of people, Government of India have launched "District Primary Education Programme" (DPEP), a new strategy in the selected districts of some states including Orissa.

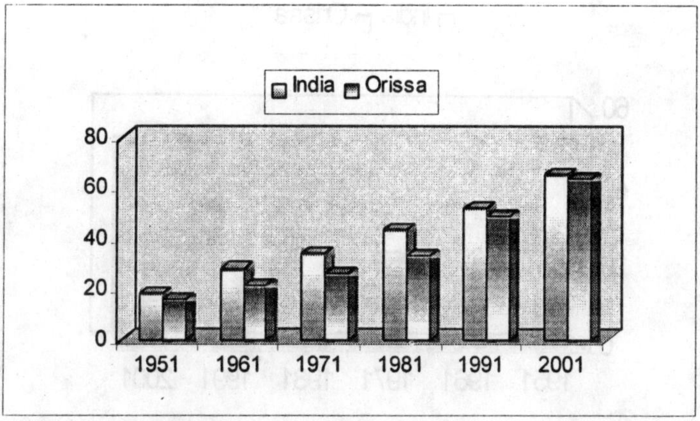

Fig. 3.1(i) By Persons

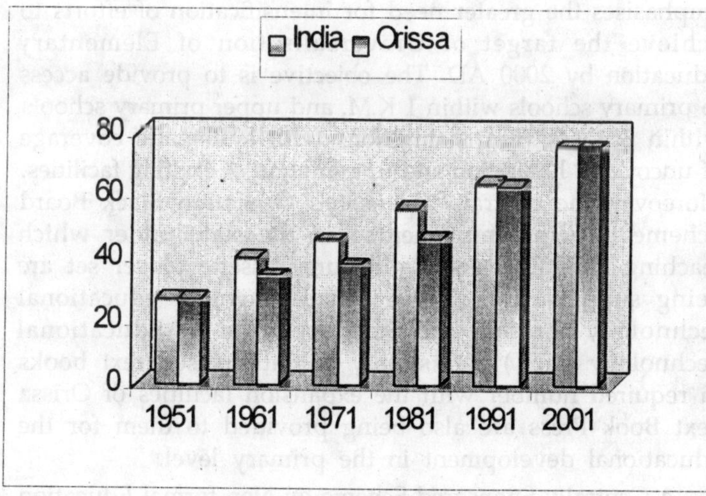

Fig. 3.1(ii) By Male

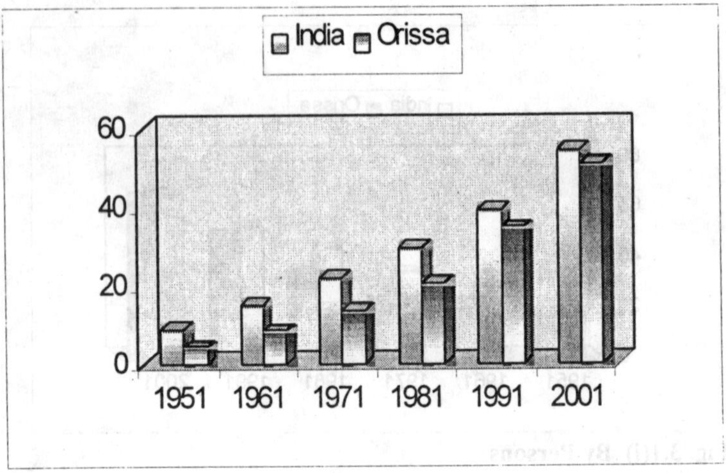

Fig. 3.1(iii) By Female

Primary education is expected to cover children in the age group of 6 to 14. Literacy rate of 49.1 percent in the state as against national average of 52.1% as per 1991 census emphasises the greater need for intensification of efforts to achieve the target of Universalisation of Elementary Education by 2000 AD. The objective is to provide access to primary schools within 1 K.M. and upper primary schools within 3 K.Ms from habitations with systematic coverage of uncovered habitation and upgradation of existing facilities. Moreover, the centrally sponsored Operation Black Board Scheme is being implemented in the state under which teaching aids T.V. sets, Radio-cum-Cassette player set are being supplied to schools. Development of educational technology through the State Institute of Educational Technology (SIET) and supply of nationalised text books in required number with the expansion facilities of Orissa Text Book Press are also being provided to them for the educational development in the primary level.

A Centrally Sponsored Scheme on Non-formal Education is in operation in the state to supplement the formal stream of primary education. The non-formal system aims at covering school drop-outs working children and children under socio-economic stress. The primary objective of this scheme is to impart minimum levels of learning to create awareness in the segment of children (specifically girl children and backward area) for coming over to the main-stream of education. 14,552 NFE centres are functioning in the State with an enrolment of 3,78 lakh students. The enrolment of students had been increased by 14,000 in 1995-96 to over 3,64 lakh enrolled during 1994-95. It is proposed to extend the coverage of these center's in association with N.G.Os. SECONDARY EDUCATION: The Secondary stage of Education comprises Class VIII to Class X the academic control of Board of Secondary Education, Orissa and the Higher Secondary State of Education (+2) is under the academic control of Council of Higher Secondary Education. In Orissa, most of the Higher Secondary classes remain attached to general colleges due to historical reason and infrastructural limitation. Table below presents the number of High Schools, and enrolment of students in the state from the 7th Plan period to 1995-96. The figures reveal a significant upward trend in the Secondary Education. The teacher-pupil ratio during 1995-96 was 1 : 17 as against 1 :18 in the previous year.

Table (a)
Number of Primary Schools and Students in Orissa

	By the End of 7th Plan	*1995-96*	*1996-97*
Primary Schools (in nos.)	49,705	56,656	65552
i. Normal	39,593	42,104	42104
ii. Non-formal	10,112	14,552	23448
Enrolment of student (in '000 No)	3,875	4,265	4531
i. Formal	3.580	3,887	3945
ii. Non-formal	295	378	386

Source: Director, Elementary Education, Orissa, BBSR.

Table (b)

Number of High Schools and Students in Orissa

	By end of 7th Plan	*1995-96*	*1996-97*
No, of High Schools (in No.)	4,487	5,808	5967
No. of Students (in 000 No.)	770	822	866

Source: Director, Elementary Education, Orissa.

Table (C)

Number of General Colleges, Students and Teachers in Orissa

	By end of 7th Plan	*1995-96*	*1996-97*
No. of Colleges	459	893	967
No. of Students in ('000 Nos.)	263	440	474
No. of Teachers	10,949	15,909	16610

Source: Directorate of Higher Education, Orissa.

According to the recent educational statistics all the districts (30) in the state have hundred percent enrolments for boys at the primary level, but this is not true for girls. However, it is evident that Orissa has achieved 98% enrolment at the primary level. The disparity between the enrolment of boys and girls is found to be a little more than 30% for the state. Sundergarh district has the lowest disparity (12.52%) and Kalahandi the highest disparity (50.73%). The dropout rate of all children at the primary level is found to be 58% in all areas, with the dropout rates for boys and girls at 56.52% and 59.83%, respectively. Mayurbhanja (Tribal region) records the highest drop-out rate with respect to all children, while Kalahandi (predominantly tribal) records the highest drop-out rate for girls. In urban Orissa, the average enrolment rate is 102%—109.32% among boys and 94.50% among girls.

At the same time, Orissa has always made concerted efforts to provide quality education to all. Prospects of a brighter future are evidently in the offing in view of certain major initiatives of the Government of Orissa and the

Government of India. These steps provided by Higher Education in Orissa (http://www.education.nic.in/htmlweb/iamr1.htm) are directed towards the reform and renewal of state's education system, include:

- Under the National Programme of Nutritional Support to Primary Education, mid-day meals are supposed to be provided to certain categories of schools. But the basic information regarding number of beneficiaries and number of schools covered under the programme, have not been received for last five years.
- Non-Formal Education (NFE) Programme is to provide education to the children under the age group of 6-14 years, who cannot attend school for entire day. They include working children, school dropouts and children in habitations without schools.
- Expansion of Operation Blackboard Scheme to encompass more primary and upper primary schools.
- Out of 30 districts in the state of Orissa, inclusion of eight and further 14 districts in the state's District Primary Education Programme (DPEP). But the progress of implementation of the programme has been extremely tardy in the State.
- Having a separate component in education plan for KBK districts (KALAHANDI, BOLANGIR & KORAPUT) for more focused and targeted development.
- Administrative mechanism of the state to be geared-up and political will strengthened for development of education in the state.
- Inter and intra-sartorial convergence for planned holistic development of education.
- Empowerment of Panchayti Raj institutions.
- Total Literacy Campaign (TLC) has been started in the state since 1990-91. Out of 30 districts, 28 districts and Rourkela (special project) have been included in the programme.

Now it has been decided to introduce Continuing Education Programme in two districts—Ganjam and Malkangiri on experimental basis. The other districts will be taken up after final approval of the 1st phase districts. Thus, Orissa is expected to steer clear the initial inertia, with unstinting support from the Union Government. Orissa was one of the developing states in India and improving and competing with other states of India, to become a prosperous state in the field of education. The literacy percentage of Orissa is improving highly. The comparative growth rate of literacy of Orissa with Indian is given below since first census of India.

It reveals from the above that the literacy rate in Orissa is always lower than that of the national level thought the period from 1951 to 2001. During this period the male literacy rate in Orissa has also been lower than the national rate except the year 2001. It also good sign for the state that percentages of female literacy was 4.52% during 1951, now it is 50.97%, which indicates that it is increasing rapidly with national female literacy.

Table 3.1

Comparative Literacy Rate of India and Orissa: 1951-2001

[See also Figs. 3.1 (i-iii)]

	Persons		*Male*		*Female*	
Year	*India*	*Orissa*	*India*	*Orissa*	*India*	*Orissa*
1951	18.33	15.80	27.16	27.32	8.86	4.52
1961	28.30	21.66	40.40	34.68	15.35	8.65
1971	34.45	26.18	45.96	38.29	21.97	13.92
1981	43.57	33.62	56.38	46.39	29.76	20.60
1991	52.21	49.09	64.13	63.09	39.29	34.68
2001	65.38	63.61	75.85	75.95	54.16	50.97

Sources: Provisional Literacy Tables, Census of India 2001.

Table 3.2

Literacy Rank Among the Districts of India: 2001

	Name of the Districts	*Persons*	*Male*	*Female*	*Rank Among the District of India*
*	ORISSA	63.61	75.95	50.97	*
1.	Khurda	80.19	88.38	71.06	57
2.	Jagatsinghapur	79.61	88.96	69.94	65
3.	Puri	78.40	88.73	67.80	78
4.	Kendrapara	77.33	87.62	67.29	91
5.	Cuttack	76.13	85.46	66.94	114
6.	Bhadrak	74.64	85.44	63.62	139
7.	Jajapur	72.19	82.69	61.45	174
8.	Jharsuguda	71.47	83.04	59.23	184
9.	Nayagarh	71.02	83.23	58.10	193
10.	Baleswar	70.94	81.75	59.57	195
11.	Dhenkanal	70.11	81.31	58.55	210
12.	Anugul	69.40	82.02	56.01	222
13.	Sambalpur	67.01	78.87	54.79	260
14.	Sundergarh	65.22	75.69	54.25	297
15.	Baragarh	64.13	77.93	50.03	314
16.	Sonapur	64.07	80.30	47.28	315
17.	Ganjam	62.94	78.39	47.70	334
18.	Debagarh	60.78	73.79	47.56	368
19.	Kendujhar	59.75	72.53	46.71	389
20.	Baudha	58.43	76.86	39.78	412
21.	Balangir	54.93	70.36	39.27	460
22.	Kandhamal	52.95	69.98	36.19	478
23.	Mayurbhanj	52.43	66.38	38.28	485
24.	Kalahandi	46.20	62.88	29.56	537
25.	Nuapada	42.29	58.78	26.01	557
26.	Gajapati	41.73	55.14	28.91	560
27.	Koraput	36.20	47.58	24.81	578
28.	Rayagada	35.61	47.35	24.31	581
29.	Nabarangapur	34.26	47.37	21.02	586
30.	Malkangiri	31.26	41.21	21.28	588

Sources: Provisional Population, Census of India: 2001.

Table 3.2, gives the districts of Orissa arranged in descending order of literacy rate of persons along with their corresponding ranks among the districts of the country. Among the districts in India, Aizawl district of Mizoram occupies the top position having 96.64 percent as literates. The second position in terms of literacy has gone in favor of Serchhip, which is also a district of Mizoram having a literacy rate of 96.16 percent. 13 district of the country are having more than 90.00 percent literates out of which eight belong to Kerala state alone and four belong to Mizoram and the remaining one district belongs to Pondicherry, out of 593 districts of the country 294 districts are above the national average of 65.38 percent. The lowest rate of literacy of 30.01 percent has been recorded in the districts of Dantewada in the state of Chhattisgarh, in Orissa the highest literacy rate of 80.19 percent has been recorded in the district of Khurda which occupies 57th position among the districts of the country whereas the lowest literacy rate of 31.26 percent has been observed in the district of Malkangiri which occupies 588th position among the districts of India. Orissa is having 63.61 percent of literacy rate among the states and union territories of the country. The male literacy rate of Orissa is 75.95 percent and ranks 24th while in terms of female literacy rate it occupies 27th position among the states and union territories. The highest literacy rate for both the males (94.20 percent) and females (87.86 percent) has been recorded in Kerala whereas lowest literacy rate in both the sexes has been recorded in Bihar. In Orissa, 13 districts are having above national level literacy rate and among 260 districts of Indian literacy position. Again, all other 17 districts are coming under below national level of literacy rate.

The Table 3.3 reveals that during 1991 census the total percent of literacy in Orissa was 49.09% where as in 2001 it was increased to 63.61, a growth rate of 13%. Among the districts, it has reveals that there is a literacy hike in all the districts of Orissa during the 2002 census. Again, it was found that among all Khurda is the highest literate and Malkangiri is the lowest literate district in the state.

Table 3.3
Comparison of Litaracy Rate of Orissa During 1991 and 2001

	DISTRICT	*1991*			*2001*		
		Persons	*Males*	*Females*	*Persons*	*Males*	*Females*
	Orissa	49.09	63.09	34.68	63.61	75.95	50.97
1.	Bargarh	47.65	63.78	31.21	64.13	77.93	50.03
2.	Jharsuguda	52.73	67.29	37.11	71.47	83.04	59.23
3.	Sambalpur	51.52	65.90	36.43	67.01	78.87	54.79
4.	Debagarh	44.45	59.43	29.26	60.78	73.79	47.56
5.	Sundargarh	52.97	65.41	39.60	65.22	75.69	54.25
6.	Kendujhar	44.73	59.04	30.01	59.75	72.53	46.71
7.	Mayurbhanj	37.88	51.84	23.68	52.43	66.38	38.28
8.	Baleshwar	57.64	71.23	43.40	70.94	81.75	59.57
9.	Bhadrak	60.54	74.62	46.35	74.64	85.44	63.62
10.	Kendrapara	63.61	76.82	50.67	77.33	87.62	67.29
11.	Jagatsinghapur	65.77	78.27	53.05	79.61	88.96	69.94
12.	Cuttack	65.46	77.41	52.44	76.13	85.46	66.19
13.	Jajapur	58.00	70.50	45.29	72.19	82.69	61.45
14.	Dhenkanal	54.91	68.80	40.33	70.11	81.31	58.55
15.	Anugul	51.53	67.66	34.32	69.40	82.02	56.01
16.	Nayagarh	57.20	73.00	40.74	71.02	83.23	58.10
17.	Khordha	67.72	78.74	55.39	80.19	88.38	71.06
18.	Puri	63.30	76.83	49.41	78.40	88.73	67.80
19.	Ganjam	46.72	63.88	29.87	62.94	78.39	47.70
20.	Gajapati	29.37	41.76	17.44	41.73	55.14	28.91
21.	Kandhamal	37.23	54.68	19.82	52.95	69.98	36.19
22.	Baudh	40.98	60.61	21.01	58.43	76.86	39.78
23.	Sonapur	42.62	61.48	23.38	64.07	80.30	47.28
24.	Balangir	38.63	55.64	21.30	54.93	70.36	39.27
25.	Nuapada	27.52	42.31	12.78	42.29	58.78	26.01
26.	Kalahandi	31.08	46.85	15.28	46.20	62.88	29.56
27.	Rayagada	26.01	36.53	15.63	35.61	47.35	24.31
28.	Nabarangapur	18.62	28.10	9.01	34.26	47.37	21.02
29.	Koraput	24.64	33.98	15.15	36.20	47.58	24.81
30.	Malkangiri	20.04	28.24	11.69	31.26	41.21	21.28

Sources: Provisional Population Table: 1991 & 2001.

3.3 Educational Profiel of SC/St in Orissa

The State of Orissa occupies an important place in the country having a high concentration of Scheduled Tribe and Scheduled Caste population. Both Scheduled Tribe and Scheduled Caste constitute nearly 38.41% of the total State Population (STs 22.21% and SCs 16.20% as per 1991 Census). There are 62 tribal communities and 93 castes groups in the State. The rural and urban components of the SC population in the state are 89.26% and 10.74% respectively. The growth rate of population among the SCs during 1981-1991 was 32.69% as against 31.95% at the all India level. There are 15 communities in the category of sweepers/scavengers and nomadic/semi-nomadic and other de-notified communities identified as especially vulnerable groups among SCs according to East India Human Development Report (2004). The population of the Scheduled Tribes and Scheduled Castes in Orissa is as follows:

Table 3.4
Scheduled Caste and Scheduled Tribe Population in Orissa

Total Population of the State	31,659,736
Scheduled Tribes (S.T.) Population	7,032,214
Scheduled Caste (S.C.) Population	5,129,314
Percentage of S.T. Population to Total Population	22.21
Percentage of S.C. Population to Total Population	16.20
S.T. Communities (Castes)	62
S.C. Communities (Castes)	93

Sources: WWW - http://orissagov.nic.in/index.htm

Statewise Distribution of SC Population (Census-2001)

S.l. No.	*Caste*	*Population SC Total*	*Literacy % Total*	*Literacy % Rural*	*Literacy % Urban*
1.	Adi Andra	2438	58.36	50.12	72.57
2.	Amant etc.	15479	31.02	30.78	53.24
3.	Audhelie	62	38.46	38.36	0
4.	Badaik	13381	48.65	46.26	54.37
5.	Bagheti etc.	29113	42.42	41.99	55.63
6.	Bajikar	299	40.24	40.08	44.44
7.	Bari	208	61.71	54.08	71.43
8.	Bariki	19565	67.76	64.65	77.07
9.	Basor etc.	116	42.22	36.76	59.09
10.	Bauri	454150	50.15	49.88	52.34
11.	Bauti	679	56.58	53.25	87.27
12.	Bedia etc.	533	50.68	48.87	54.96
13.	Beldar	3322	50.8	49.4	65.95
14.	Bhata	6016	64.87	64.43	67.83
15.	Bhoi	98885	55.61	54.79	60.92
16.	Chachati	54	63.04	57.14	64.1
17.	Chakali	94	25.93	10.17	68.18
18.	Chamar etc.	152243	57.56	57.59	57.42
19.	Chandala	5375	49.33	48.63	69.54
20.	Cherua etc.	883	63.06	59.38	88
21.	Dandesi	60925	39.8	38.43	56.14
22.	Dewar	648907	66.33	65.12	74.58
23.	Dhanwar	1732	29.16	23.24	83.22
24.	Dhoba	583323	65.06	63.2	70.62
25.	Doma	610481	39.47	38.64	48.69
26.	Dosadha	572	71.43	82.05	70.5
27.	Ganda	565803	55.6	54.17	66.21
28.	Ghantarghada	7086	40.58	40	52.19
29.	Ghasi	105667	51.4	46.64	61.26
30.	Ghogia	79	58.46	57.81	100
31.	Ghusuria	7733	41.7	40.57	59.53
32.	Godagali	44	13.51	6.06	75
33.	Godari	195	70.37	70.89	50
34.	Godra	3663	28.21	27.82	70.37
35.	Gokha	192247	55.15	54.88	59.8
36.	Gorait	455	53.49	49.84	75.47
37.	Haddi	209701	55.82	51.11	65.71
38.	Irika	519	65.45	50.5	77.92
39.	Jaggali	4706	33.48	27.72	41.61

40. Kandra	463768	61.26	60.4	71.46
41. Karua	5298	46.16	42.82	59.68
42. Katia	8796	58.09	56.65	69.26
43. Kela	19755	51.61	52.24	43.54
44. Khadala	73101	49.58	48.94	54.78
45. Kodalo	1926	50.56	48.89	66.03
46. Kori	230	68.88	56.34	76
47. Kummari	2734	53.13	50.15	74.47
48. Kununga	4252	48.83	47.53	65.73
49. Laban	414	49.71	46.5	64.06
50. Laberi	4366	38.25	33.24	59.28
51. Madari	2843	46.02	43.54	46.43
52. Madiga	1573	42.77	31.21	44.43
53. Mahuria	5635	59.6	59.32	62.56
54. Mala	13318	53.37	47.07	63.06
55. Mang	256	54.42	52.22	63.04
56. Mangan	489	43.34	41.71	86.67
57. Mehra	22524	47.73	46.93	59.48
58. Mehtar	2035	68.43	72.74	62.2
59. Mewar	599	47.49	47.8	45.31
60. Mundapotta	1095	6.44	6.18	13.79
61. Musahar	35	35.71	45.45	29.41
62. Nagarchi	628	60.33	57.21	69.57
63. Namasudra	131645	61.93	60.43	82.13
64. Paidi	506	15.78	9.28	62.5
65. Painda	736	52.66	51.05	72.34
66. Pamidi	28	23.81	26.67	16.67
67. Pan Pano	1076180	55.48	54.65	65.95
68. Panchama	274	46.7	23.33	62.04
69. Parika	7263	47.5	45.32	61.82
70. Panka	2318	39.11	39.03	50
71. Pantanti	24674	61.38	58.74	69.97
72. Pap	9781	49.9	49.44	54.97
73. Pasi	190	76.65	60.42	83.19
74. Patial	49862	57.59	55.46	69.35
75. Rajna	82	58.9	50	67.57
76. Relli	8357	43.11	35.35	51.13
77. Sabakhia	888	33.15	33.62	23.53
78. Samasi	1667	58.1	57.44	58.85
79. Sanei	1156	58.35	53	74.19
80. Sapari	125	50	43.94	61.11
81. Sauntia	55989	41.03	39.45	64.05
82. Sidhria	213	39.78	29.14	85.71
83. Sinduria	301	49.8	45.37	68

84. Siyal	24292	72.14	71.24	88.13
85. Tamadia	1230	56.09	56.26	55.38
86. Tamudia	8281	53.76	53.49	55.99
87. Tanla	59285	50.49	49.5	64.29
88. Tiar	49675	60.15	59.22	69.95
89. Turi	8603	41.77	38.86	63.44
90. Ujia	17853	33.03	32.67	56.94
91. Valmiki	1145	45.21	41.35	73.45
92. Generic Castes	97061	53.11	50.07	63.4
All SCs	6082063	55.53	54.23	65.31

Statewise Distribution of ST Population (Census-2001)

S.l. No.	*Scheduled Tribe*	*Population ST Total*	*Literacy % Total*	*Literacy % Rural*	*Literacy % Urban*
1.	Bagata	6733	38.56	37.36	57.31
2.	Baiga	539	39.28	32.62	57.63
3.	Banjara	15868	46.4	45.84	71.28
4.	Bathuda	198296	49.56	48.8	70.82
5.	Bhottada	375845	24.29	24.01	42.17
6.	Bhuiya	277742	50.88	49.57	69.91
7.	Bhumia	103537	20.01	19.63	50.24
8.	Bhumij	248252	36.48	35.66	47.73
9.	Bhumijiia	18504	29.03	28.71	55.14
10	Binjhal	118116	41.49	41.23	56.45
11.	Binjhia	9479	4165	40.54	49.59
12.	Birhor	702	23.3	22.62	34.38
13.	Bondo Poraja	9378	14.69	14.4	32.77
14.	Chenchu	28	46.15	43.75	50
15.	Dal	15404	32.17	31.77	76.07
16.	Desua Bhumij	177	37.24	43.24	30.99
17.	Dharua	9247	19.6	18.14	64.71
18.	Didayi	7371	12.62	12.38	88.89
19.	Gadaba	72982	21.21	20.41	29.88
20.	Gandia	1345	30	24.55	63.4
21.	Ghara	275	53.59	52.76	57.89
22.	Gond	782347	46.96	46.38	69.62
23.	Ho	43113	35.18	31.85	65.64
24.	Holva	10462	35.6	35.42	38.72
25.	Jatapu	13804	32.32	31.75	54.3
26.	Juang	41339	25.35	24.78	45.53
27.	Kandha Gauda	31454	38.96	35.77	66.75

28. Kawar	7380	45.36	44.71	65.15
29. Kharia	188331	45.23	43.46	61.82
30. Kharwar	1381	57.35	57.82	53.49
31. Khond	1395643	31.87	31.16	60.35
32. Kisan	321592	50.19	48.96	64.38
33. Kol	13703	32.23	30.1	44.75
34. Kulah Loharas	9642	35.55	33.43	49.39
35. Kotha	512919	27.04	26.35	38.09
36. Koli	5366	50.69	43.2	79.98
37. Kondadora	34160	34.86	31.28	66.96
38. Kora	11340	42.48	42.22	50.51
39. Korua	1280	32.83	28.81	68.87
40. Kotia	22525	24.6	23.36	57.67
41. Koya	122535	11.73	11.48	55.2
42. Kulia	11164	70.22	69.18	76.06
43. Lodha	8905	27	25.96	62.98
44. Madia	3017	37.33	35.69	57.37
45. Mahali	17131	37.97	35.62	55.07
46. Mankidi	130	9.28	7.37	100
47. Mankidia	1050	5.56	5.14	44.44
48. Matya	17549	38.42	38.08	40.48
49. Mirdhas	32279	51.17	51	54.74
50. Munda	480252	39.69	36.85	56.78
51. Mundari	23833	46.94	43.21	61.99
52. Omanatya	23364	24.52	24.13	43.41
53. Oraon	308931	54.2	51.08	70.85
54. Parenga	12646	21.01	20.73	78.43
55. Paroja	317301	17.96	17.34	27.37
56. Pentia	7271	30.96	30.62	45.86
57. Rajuar	2803	37.93	36.55	55.56
58. Santal	777460	40.43	38.69	65.04
59. Saora	473233	41.13	40.57	57.81
60. Shabar	442537	35.4	34.62	53.83
61. Sounti	75556	47.65	47.4	50.85
62. Tharua	453	55.75	2.02	72.86
63. Generic Tribes	48080	44.42	40.52	57.41
All STs	8145081	37.37	36.13	58.12

Sources: Census Report-2001.

3.3.1 General Welfare Provisions For SC/ST Communities in Orissa

There are certain special provisions in the state provided by the Government of Orissa, Report of the activities of SC&ST Development and Minorities, Backward Classes Welfare Department (2002/03) as well as Government of India.

- ➢ According to the Constitution of India, the revised Presidential Order titled "The Scheduled Areas (states of Bihar, Gujarat, Madhya Pradesh & Orissa) Order 1977" has declared three full districts of Orissa viz. Mayurbhanj, Sundargarh, Koraput, Kuchinda tahasil of Sambalpur district, Keonjhar, Telkoi, Champua, Barbil tahasils of Keonjhar district, Khondamal, Balliguda and G.Udayagiri tahasil of Khondamal district, R.Udaygiri tahasil, Gumma and Rayagada block of Parlakhemundi tahasil in Parlakhemundi Sub-division and Suruda tahasil (excluding Gazalbadi and Gochha Gram Panchayats), of Ghumsur sub-division in Ganjam district, Thuamul Rampur and Lanjigarh blocks of Kalahandi district and Nilagiri block of Balasore district as Scheduled Areas of the state. After reorganisation of districts in the state, 7 districts fully and 6 districts partly are covered under the Scheduled Areas of the state.
- ➢ In order to provide concerted efforts to the problem of Scheduled Tribe, Schedule Caste and OBC, the Backward Classes Welfare Department was formed in 1948. Subsequently, the Department was bifurcated into Harijan Welfare & Tribal Welfare, which again was merged to be named as Welfare Department. Welfare Department was re-christened as Scheduled Tribe and Scheduled Caste Development Department since 22nd February 1999. The policies, programmes and schemes of the Department have been designed in consonance with the overall goals and objectives as enshrined in Articles 46 (Part IV), 16, 17, 19, 164, 244, 275, 330, 332,335,338,339,341, 342 and 366 of the Constitution of India and aim at improving the quality of life of ST & SC communities.

- Orissa Scheduled Castes and Scheduled Tribes Development Finance Cooperative Corporation (OSFDC)—was established during the year 1979-80 for providing financial assistance for income generating activities to ST and SC families. Livelihood support programmes for the SC and ST communities out of Special Central Assistance and Special Component Plan Schemes have been implemented under the aegis of OSFDC.
- Enforcement of the Orissa Reservation of Vacancies in Posts and Services for SC/ST Act, 1975 is a provision for reservation of 16.25% and 22.50% of posts for SC and ST communities respectively in initial appointment and promotion. There are also other special measures for the benefit of SC/ST in the state.
- Poverty Alleviation Programme for SCs and STs has been undertaken to improve the standard of living and quality of life of the poor were in operation in the state like—IRDP, TRYSEM, JRY, IAY, EAS, MWP, SFDP and DPEP etc. In 1999-2000 various individual oriented schemes were merged into a single scheme namely: Swarnajayanti Gramya Swarojagar Yojana, and Jawahar Rozagar Yojana etc.
- Efforts have been made by the State Government to provide land to the Landless Families for agricultural purposes as well as for making of houses. Emphasis has also been given for providing health care services in remote tribal areas.

3.3.2 Education Development Programme for SC/ST

Due to low standard of education achievements of the SC and ST populations the average level of literacy and other kinds of educational attainment is low for the whole state. It may be relevant to highlight some of the point's relations to the literacy level and other educational standards of SC and ST in Orissa. So the government of Orissa has been taking some special provision for them:

- Orissa was the pioneer in setting of special type of Residential Educational Institutions for the SC/ST educational development. The Department has established and manages many Residential Educational Institutions like: Residential High Schools for Boys—163, Residential High Schools for Girls—55, Ashram Schools for Boys (M.E. Standard)—112, Kanyashrams for Girls (M.E. Standard)—37, Residential Sevashrams (Primary School with residential facilities—143, Sevashrams (Primary School non-residential)—919, Primary School Hostels (1 per each Grama Panchayat of the Tribal Sub-Plan areas) —1548, Special Adivasi Hostels—7, Hostels for providing residential facilities at Post-matric and Pre-matric level—569, Residential facilities at Primary level for Tribal Girls in KBK districts—400, Teachers Training Schools—2.

- Establishment of Model Tribal Schools on the pattern of Nayodaya Vidyalaya—4, Vocational Training Centres attached High Schools facilities for the students prosecuting their studies in the Educational Institutions of the Department—17.
- Provision of Pre-matric and Post-matric Scholarships (PMS) : This scholarship are awarded at different rates for different courses as per Govt. of India Scheme at level of education. Pre-Matric Scholarship for School Level SC/ST students and Post-Matric Scholarship for the SC/ST students those who are college level and above. During 2002-2003 a total number of 80,279 student (45,493 Sc, and 34,786 St) including day-scholars receiving PMS.
- Upgradation of Merit for SC/ST Boys and Girls: The Central Sector Scheme has been introduced in the State from the current year (2002-03) at the +2 Level. The scheme is aimed at imparting special coaching to the brighter among the SC/ST students for upgrading their standards with a view to enabling them to secure admission into Medical and Engineering courses. Govt. of India has provided 100% Central assistance for the purpose @ Rs.15000/- per student per year. This programme is being introduced in 5 junior colleges.

- Pre–Examination Coaching for Civil Services & Entrance Examinations: During 2002-03, a course for coaching for the ICS Examination has been started at Utkal University for 20 st and 20 SC candidates. A course for lower services has also been introduced at Utkal University for 60 ST and 60 SC candidates. These courses are being run with the funds received from MoTA and MoSJE last year.
- Vocational Training: The Central Plan Scheme Vocational Training Centres (VTC) was introduced with a view to building capacity and marketable skills among the tribal youth for enabling them to take up new vocations. VTC will cater 5 vocational courses as per the need for a period of 6+6 months.
- OTHER FACILITIES—like Supply of Nationalised Text Books, Reading Writing materials and Garments, Excursion for students, Health measures. Provisions of School Uniforms, Special Coaching, Agricultural Activities, Drinking Water Facilities, Cash Rewards to Teachers and students, Provisions of Cots, Beds, Blankets, Mosquito nets and Utensils., Book Bank for Medical and Engineering Colleges, Provisions of Sports and Games materials, Provisions of Science apparatus, Library Books, Maps, Charts, Globes, Stipend to its students, Scholarships to SC/ ST students of those parents engaged in unclean occupation
- Special Provisions:
  - Special Employment Exchange for Scheduled Castes and Scheduled Tribes.
  - Pre-Examination Coaching and Training
  - Pre-Recruitment Training for entry into Armed and Para Military forces.
  - Provision of Legal Aid to Scheduled Castes and Scheduled Tribes persons
  - Monetary Relief to the victims of Atrocities belonging to Scheduled Castes and Scheduled Tribes as compensation.

Tribes Advisory Council constituted to advice on such matters pertaining to welfare and advancement of Schedule

Tribes in the State. Harijan Welfare Advisory Board has been constituted to advise the State Government in all matters pertaining to Harijan Welfare. Annual Adivasi Exhibition to promote lifestyle and culture of the tribal people. Promotion and development of voluntary Efforts on SC/ST are being implemented by different Voluntary Oganisations of the Central Government as well as State Government and NGO.

3.4 Department of Higher Education, Orissa

Department of Higher Education came into being in December 1992 after bifurcation of the erstwhile Education & Youth Services Department. The Department plays a vital role in promoting general education at Higher Secondary, Graduate levels in various disciplines. This department is looking after effective functioning of all 59 Government Colleges including C.A.M.S., Cuttack renamed as Institute of Management and Information Technology, imparting general and professional education and. Now it has 9 Universities, 15 Autonomous colleges and more than 1300 General colleges, Medical, Engineering, Management, Ayurvedic, Homeopathic, Law, Dance & Music Colleges, B.Ed. training Centers, C.T. and Hindi training Centers etc. The autonomous colleges and universities in Orissa have a numbers of undergraduate departments with Hons. and some P.G. Depts in Humanities, Science and Commerce faculties and M.Phil. in some subjects. The U.G.C. conferred autonomy to the Universities and Autonomous Colleges for their overall development for the local needs of the students. In keeping with the increasing demand of the time M.C.A. course has been introduced from the session 1997-98 in some higher institutions in Orissa. Due to the high standard of education in Orissa Students from all over India are coming for higher studies. Now there is a tremendous growth of different educational institutions in the state. Numbers of institutions in Orissa with its student enrolment and percentages of boys and girls are given below.

Table 3.5
Selected Educational Statistics of Student Enrolments, Institutionwise
During 2000-2001 [See also Figs. 3.5 (i-ii)]

Type of Institution	*No. of Institute Enrolment*	*Enrolment of Boys (%)*	*Enrolment of Girls (%)*	*Total Enrolments*
Universities	8	7851 (68.00) (6.17)	3696 (32.00) (8.37)	11547 (6.73)
Art/Science/Com. Colleges	567	112122 (74.26) (88.08)	38861 (25.74) (87.95)	150983 (88.05)
Engg & Tech and Arch. Colleges	19	3366 (91.82) (2.64)	300 (8.18) (0.68)	3666 (2.14)
Medical Colleges: D/ Al./Ay./Ho	16	2700 (81.82) (2.12)	600 (18.18) (1.36)	3300 (1.92)
Teachers Training Colleges	13	1253 (63.28) (0.98)	727 (36.72) (1.65)	1980 (1.15)
TOTAL	623	127292 (74.23)	44184 (25.77)	171476 (100%)

Sources: Directorate of Higher Education, Orissa, Bhubaneswar.

The percentages of student's enrolment in each level institution are provided in the parenthesis bottom of each number and percentages of boys and girls are provided in right side of each number institution wise. There are total 623 higher-level academic institutes in all fields, out of which there are 567 (highest) general colleges and only 8 universities in Orissa as per the year 2000/01. The above table shows that the percentages of girls in all level of institutions are less than boys, there are little deviations in Arts, Science and Commerce streams, where boys—88.08% and girls—87.95%. Similarly, in engineering/technical colleges, boys (91.82) percentages is much higher than girls (8.18). Again, as a whole institution wise percentages of boys (6.17%) are less than girls (8.37%), it means more girls are having enrolled in higher education, but on the other hand, in universities level out of a total number (11547), boys—68.00% and girls are only 32.00%, similarly, in engineering and technologies percentages of boys (91.82) are much ahead than girls (8.18), At last it shows that there are 74.3% boys and 25.77% girls in all.

Teacher education institutes of Orissa are of basically of three levels—Post Graduate, Graduate and Elementary. In higher level, three institutions of advance studies in education and one college of teacher education are running, Master Degree in Education (M.Ed.) programme with the combined intake of 96 students. Regional Institute of Education (RIE) also taking 32 students. Only one institution i.e. Government College of Physical Education, Bhubaneswar is running the Master Degree in Physical Education (M.P.Ed.) with an intake of 16 students. However, the MA Education which is considered an equivalent qualification to M.Ed. as per NCTE regulations.

3.4.1 SC/ST Education at Higher Level

Despite last five decades of experiments through the policy of Affirmative Actions, the representation of the Scheduled Castes and Scheduled Tribes in higher education remains insignificant. This is a matter of serious concern since higher education is closely linked to higher and better jobs and thereby to higher income and social mobility. Therefore, it is pertinent to understand and analyse their situation at higher level of education. The below mentioned table gives a comparative picture among SC and ST and NON-SCST (General) pertaining to their enrolment at different level of higher education during 2000/01 and detail analysis of data for the last five years (1996/97-2000/01) are given in the preceding chapter.

The above table reveals that in different courses there are 12559(6.79%) SCs, 8206(4.44%) STs and others 164125 (88.77%) students in all during the year 2000/01. Course wise percentages shows that SC community prefer arts in graduate level 7864 (62.62%), ST students 4900 (59.71%) and others 86318 (52.59%) out of there total percentages and it also shows that they are not daring to take technical/ professional courses, which are prevailed more among non-SC/ST students.

Table 3.6

Selected Eductional Statistics of College Level and Above

Enrolment During 2000/2001

	Total Enrolment Inclding SC/St			*Scheduled Caste*			*Scheduled Tribe*		
Degree/Above Courses	Boy	Girl	Total	Boy	Girl	Total	Boy	Girl	Total
Ph.D/D.Sc./D.Phil/M Phil	400	130	530	35	14	49	23	7	30
M.A.	4623	2536	7159	361	117	478	166	52	218
M.Sc.	1990	874	2864	127	44	171	57	10	67
M.Com.	1427	97	1524	30	7	37	13	9	22
B.A. & B.A. (H)	70899	28483	99082	6502	1362	7864	3890	1010	4900
B.Sc. & B.Sc.(H)	22600	6067	28667	1066	367	1433	987	159	1146
B.Com.&B.Com. (H)	19748	3486	28234	876.	193	1064	727	182	909
B.Ed./E.T.	1253	727	1980	206	51	257	219	24	238
Med./MBS:Al,,Ho,Den	2700	600	3300	233	95	328	172	92	264
Teacher Training Sch.	1721	1629	3350	139	35	174	108	12	120
Polytechnic/Deploma	300	600	900	44	60	104	30	20	50
Tech. Indust.: Art/Craft	6300	1000	7300	480	120	600	229	13	242
TOTAL	133961	46229	184890	10099	2465	12559	6621	1590	8206

Sources: Directorate of Higher Education of Orissa, Bhubaneswar

Table 3.7
Cource-Wise Distributions of SC/ST Percentages

Degre/Above Courses	*SC*	%	*ST*	%	*Other*	%
Ph.D / D.Sc./D. Phil/ M. Phil	49	0.39	30	0.37	451	0.27
M.A.	478	3.81	218	2.66	6463	3.94
M.Sc.	171	1.36	67	0.82	2626	1.60
M.Com.	37	0.29	22	0.27	1465	0.89
B.A. & B.A. (H)	7864	62.62	4900	59.71	86318	52.59
B.Sc. & B.Sc.(H)	1433	11.41	1146	13.97	26088	15.90
B.Com. &B.Com. (H)	1064	8.47	909	11.08	26261	16.00
B.Ed./B.T.	257	2.05	238	2.90	1485	0.90
Medicine/MBBS:Al,Ay,Ho,Den.	328	2.61	264	3.22	2708	1.65
Teacher Training School	174	1.39	120	1.46	3056	1.86
Polytechnic/Deploma	104	0.83	50	0.61	746	0.45
Tech. Indust.: Art/Craft	600	4.78	242	2.95	6458	3.93
Total	12559	100.00	8206	100.00	164125	100.00

So far, different studies conducted by Mohanty, (1983), Chakraborty(1997), Pandey(1993) etc. have revealed that non-SC/ST communities are having more educational advancement and positions in the state. But, due to some governmental facilities/effects SC/ST communities are doing better advancement in education in urban areas, not in rural areas. Yet, there are some limitations for the SC/ST communities—higher education and good quality education is available in urban centres that are very expensive. Instruction is done mainly through English language. It is highly inaccessible to girls due to existing social traditions and customs. Further, it is also revealed by various studies by Debi (1987, 1984), Bal (1999) that very few of them get into higher education. Mostly they cluster around substandard institutions, enroll into general education. This is because it is less expensive and does not require special skills, guidance. They perform poorly and take longer time to complete. As per the New Education Policy, which is being implemented since 1986, the pattern of 10+2+3 years of education is being followed across the country along with new and modern contents of education. The subjects of New Math's, Modern Science and English language are the three subjects the majorities are unable to clear at 10th standard. At XIth they can choose Science, Commerce or Arts stream. Higher education is considered from XIth standard onwards. Moreover, they need to migrate to cities or towns where higher education is available but in Orissa which is a backward state in every sphere find it very difficult to access lodging, boarding and LIS facilities since most of the educational institutions do not provide these facilities.

3.5 Academic Library System in Orissa

Prior to our independence, a library in the university was usually established much after its incorporation. It was because the university then was only an examining body with no teaching and research functions. There was as such no need for the university library. But with the passage of time, teaching and research came to become the basic functions of the universities. Under these changed circumstances, the role of the university libraries became crucial, intrinsic and academic in nature. Realizing this, the UGC, ever since its inception, has been providing necessary funds for the growth and development of university libraries. As a result, a number of university libraries in India are now housed in large and functional buildings with big collections and adequate staff. But still there are wide variations among these libraries. Orissa the most disadvantaged state of India is suffering more LIS challenges then any other state in the country, there are rapid growth of different educational institutions as well as libraries without quality and value of education, where an increasingly large number of students attempt to continue their studies beyond compulsory education for qualifications in the employment market. Orissa academic library system consists of three levels of libraries—school, college and university. There are at present 9 universities, 15 autonomous colleges, 567 degree colleges and more than 800 junior colleges and nearing about 42 thousand schools having its own libraries in its institute campus.

In the case of Academic libraries, while there has been an overall improvement in University Libraries, the number of good college libraries is still quite limited. Most of them continue to face various problems such as paucity of funds, physical facilities, shortage of staff, etc. Lending service is the major activity of most of the Academic libraries and special services such as current awareness, SDI are usually not provided. The students opting for the paper on these libraries and teachers teaching this paper would like to study the university libraries in their entirety. A few books on the university libraries, which are available, are now out of date. Libraries attached to the colleges are suffering more then university libraries in Orissa. College's libraries are very small in size, limited staff and less service. Most of the colleges' libraries are managed by non-professionals with limited collection and staffs within a room, but certain cases there are some deviation to it, especially in city or towns. Among the college libraries Ravenshaw College (Konika) Library is the biggest one, then S.C.S. colleges library, N.C. College library, B.J.B. Colleges etc. are also most reputed libraries in the state. On the other hand, University libraries, like Utkal (Vanivihar), Sombalpur (Jyotivihar), Berhampur (Bhanjavihar) and OUAT have good library collections with professionals, then other four Universities in Orissa. Again, libraries are growing in each school without any proper guidance or standard. The school libraries in general have lagged behind in the development process. Numbers of academic libraries in Orissa estimated during 1996-1997 has been given as follows.

Table 3.8

Number of Academic Libraries in Orissa (Estimated Figure: 1996/97)

Category	*Types of Academic Institutions*	*Numbers*
Cat.-A	Higher Education Level: Uni. and Auto. Colleges	24
Cat.-B	Science & Technological Libraries	49
Cat.-C	College Libraries: +3 above Level	567
Cat.-D	Senior Basic School /Junior College (+2 Level) Libraries	11,510

Sources: Annual Report: 1996/97, Government of India, Ministry of HRD, with NIC.

Findings from the above studies reveals that, there are only 11510 libraries in the school level (upto +2) and there are only 640 libraries in the higher level of education. It means the academic library system in Orissa is very poor in comparison to the Educational statistics—1999/00 given in preceding chapter. Again, it was studied that in most of the areas (particularly in the tribal districts) there are no libraries (Public or Academic) and no schools within 10 km radius in Orissa, this causes illiteracy and under development among the tribal people. There are widespread illiteracy is the greatest handicap for developing library service and its uses in some urban and rural areas in the traditional pattern in the state. It is true that some dedicated people nowadays live in villages but by and large the village dwellers are crippled with illiteracy or limited education especially in the tribal areas. The SC/ST communities generally lives in such backward areas, have to work hard to earn their living. At times all the members of a family remain unchanged in the productive process. Reading books, they feel, does not increase their professional efficiency or productivity. There is, therefore, no motivation for learning and using library. There are many other problems linked with library and information field in the rural to urban are:

- Lack of resource is another serious bottleneck in developing library services in the academic environment. The condition of the majority of educational libraries, particularly, in the tribal/hill areas of Orissa, is extremely miserable. Many of them do not have their own house, some are located in small thatched huts and some share a room in the school and time with their institutions. Very few libraries in the colleges can provide reading-room facilities even. Storage facilities are also very poor. Stock of reading materials is insignificant. Moreover, the service is highly irregular and uncertain. All these do not encourage people to use libraries. There is also the dearth of suitable reading materials in their regional languages. The demand for books in rural libraries is mainly limited to light literature in regional language.
- The quality of library service depends to a great extent on the quality of a person rendering the service. It is the librarian who can make or unmake the services. While his imagination, initiative, resourcefulness and dedication can make the library an ideal public institution, is apathy inertia and lack of dedication will make it a dull and dreary organization. What is therefore, needed most is a competent librarian who can organise the services in a balanced manner for all sections of the community served by the library. In order to attract the right type of persons to the library profession, the service condition of the library professionals need improvement.
- The absence of a Public Library System in most of

the districts, blocks and village panchayats are also responsible for the haphazard growth of libraries in rural areas. This system can be devised by state government authority or administrative sanction. Need of the hour is to open more libraries. According to International Federation of Library Associations & Institutions (IFLA) standards, there should be one public library for every 3000 people with every 1 billion people. In order to keep pace with the growth in population and the explanation in knowledge, almost every other village will have to be provided with library facilities. One of the IFLA standards stipulate with the nearest library unit should not be more than a mile away from the residential areas.

- The problems of developing economy have strained library services in many ways. Inflation has depleted the resource of the libraries. As the purchasing power of the rupee is being reduced, the quantum of reading materials that can be acquired also gets reduced. The constant increase of price, inadequate collection of subscription from the readers is not sufficient to maintain the libraries. The information explosion, impact of information technology and growth in electronics resources etc are also limiting the conventional libraries in its developmental activities in the state.
- The challenge posed by the electronic media or television is real and its impact on reading habit or library use has been very negative. Witnessing television programmes has made great in roads on reading books for pleasure.
- The need of the hour to provide better library services is to make provision of free and compulsory library service to the disadvantaged community. In the wake of the slogan "Education for All" comes in the complementary battle cry of "Books for All". As a consequence of making "right to education" a fundamental right, as published in daily newspaper, *The Hindu* (2002) free unhindered easy access to books

and libraries also becomes essential. The right to have easy access to books is to be ensured.

3.5.1 LIS for SC/ST Communities

It is recognized that information is most vital to human existence and more critically essential to all activities relating to research and development. It is also; regarded as the 6th basic need of human beings, so there should be "right to information" for all. Our country should adopt this and make policy for the deprived section; every state should follow some special guidelines on this for the betterment of the state. "Right to information" leads to education, education is considered as an important mechanism for the development of deprived communities that is directly linked to better jobs and economic development. However, it is not possible for disadvantaged communities to access or to possess information, for sustain and perform better in education due to their poor social and stigmatized background without governmental support. That is why, they have been provided with various material and non-material library and information facilities including at all levels of education.

However, during last five decades of the experimentation of the policy; studies have revealed that their progress in higher education is unsatisfactory due to the education system itself followed by the unfavorable socio-economic conditions and biased attitudes of the upper castes. However, this does not mean that facilities do not help them improving their plight. The education system has provided great access to all sections of the society, including children, but our state due to the above mentioned constraints the benefits of expansion of educational facilities have not fully reach the Scheduled Castes and Scheduled Tribes to bring them at par with other Communities. To appreciate the special efforts made in this direction and to know the size of the remaining task, it is necessary that data on progress of education and information needs of these communities be complied and made available to public at large. The present study is an attempt to present the information needs related to various socio-economic and educational development of

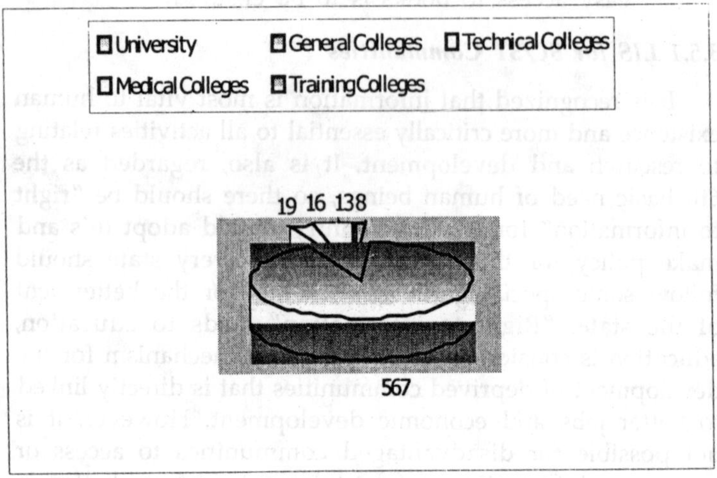

Fig. 3.5(i)

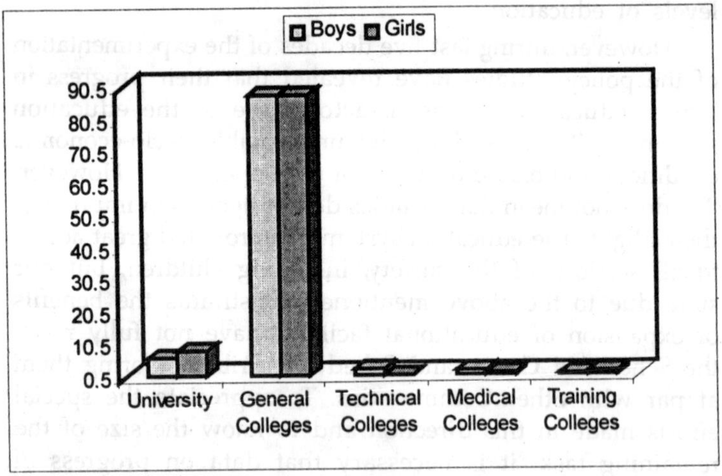

Fig,3.5(ii)

Scheduled Castes and Scheduled Tribes communities in the state. The Dept of Education, Government of Orissa should enact some special privilege based on library and information facilities from their local level to higher level, for the all-round development of the disadvantaged communities.

3.6 Objectives of the Study

This study is primarily designed to reflect the reading interests, various needs, behaviors and use pattern of the various information sources by the Scheduled Caste and Scheduled Tribe: students, research scholars and faculties within the higher academic field in Orissa. It also depicts to investigate what kind of information are there in the universities and autonomous college libraries in Orissa, and how students' information behavior is affected by their needs. A model for information behavior of university students will be the result of the study. The model will be developed on the basis of existing theories of information behavior, learning, and empirical studies. But especially in the present topic an attempt has been made to highlight various dimensions of information needs of SC & ST communities in the Universities and autonomous colleges of Orissa and also:

(a) To assess the information needs of SC & ST students i.e. +3 Graduate Level, M.A., M.Com., M.Sc. etc. and research scholars of different departments in the Autonomous Colleges and Universities of Orissa

(b) To identify the sources of information, which they usually make use in getting the required information and type of materials that, are preferred by them

(c) To assess the inter-personal higher education of SC & ST student communities in Orissa.

(d) To reveal the areas of inadequacy in the libraries resources so that efforts may be made to satisfy them.

(e) To evaluate the services presently provided by the library and to assess what more services they really need.

(f) To assess the SC & ST students needs, requirements and opportunities available for higher education in India with specific reference to Orissa.

(g) Participation of the SC & ST community students in uplifting their community socially, economically and educationally.

(h) To determine the extent to which they are aware about the different information of the government as well as future plan.

(i) To obtain suggestions for further improvement of there communities.

3.7 Methodology

The primary goal of the study is to find out the information needs of the SC/ST students, researchers and faculties in autonomous colleges and universities of Orissa, first the different higher educational institutions like autonomous colleges and universities in the state are identified. List of different subjects/course in Graduate level and Post Graduate levels prepared, then number of student enrolment, research scholars and faculty members in the universities and autonomous colleges are listed.

A structured questionnaire, with both closed and few open options, was administered to elicit both quantitative as well as qualitative information from the respondents relevant to the study in the light of their observations and experiences. In the front page a request letter from the investigator was attached with assurance to be strictly confidential was prepared. The entire questionnaire was divided with three parts—Part A, Part B and Part C with all total 58 different questions. After obtaining the name and address of the institutions, the investigator or his representative were visited the concerned institute and delivered the questionnaire with a kind request of early return of the filled in questionnaire. There are 500 questionnaire were distributed in all, where 324 were received. The data collected through the questionnaire were then scrutinized and their consistency was checked.

Identification of information needs is essential to the design of information systems in general and to the provision of effective information services in particular. But it has been found to be a difficult task as it is almost an investigative or detective work. In order to identify information needs one should adopt various methods to gather information on the various factors that influence the information needs. No single method or tool will serve entirely. A careful selection and blending of several techniques depending on the user whose need is being studied is necessary. In fact, the "information needs identifier" should study, prepare and equip himself thoroughly to perform the task of identifying information needs. A formal step-by-step procedure, which can be adopted to study the information needs of a majority of users, is proposed in this paper. Besides gathering and recording the information needs, a careful analysis is to be made to distil actual needs from the data gathered. It is hoped that the methodology discussed here, would be easy to perceive and be translatable into practice. It is to be noted that the methodology would become clearer and clearer as each step is put into practice enhancing the understanding of the scenario and help in fine-tuning the procedure to suit particular situations. Moreover it has been found that the proposed methodology is not only useful in identifying the information needs, but also has a profound impact on finding ways and means of satisfying such needs. In other words, the information needs identifier would discover, as a bye product, several ideas, tools, methods and techniques of satisfying the users in meeting their needs.

3.8 The Design of the Study

Since, the existing library and information System in the state generally ad-hoc, un-related to one another, it is highly essential that future development of the library and information resource would occur in a cohesive manner according to a plan based on a National Policy for Library and Information Service (I&IS), which will serve as guidelines for the development and improvement of L&IS in the State. In view of the vital role in research, education, industrial growth and socio-economic development of the state the need for their establishments and developments of a LIS have duly been well accepted for the state. In addition Information technology is also an area of fundamental importance to the economic development of the state.

The present study represents an exploratory-cum-descriptive research design. The idea is to enquire into the phenomena with 'care' i.e. scrutinizing the existing materials related to phenomena under investigation so as to gain new insight into it. Descriptive studies are oriented towards finding out what has occurred. While the basic purpose of the present study is to explore the information needs of SC and ST Students, Scholars and Faculty Members of the Universities and Autonomous Colleges of Orissa, an attempt is also made to give a model of WAN for the academic library system in Orissa as a whole.

3.9 The Universe and Sample

The Universe in the sense in which it is used in the sampling statistical parlance constitute of all the individuals or things or events or documents or observations confirming to a designated set of specifications, which the particular study principally covers. A careful definition of the universe and the observations and of the significant relationship between them is the cornerstone of planning the representative ness. The Universe of the study covers of all the SC/ST student/researcher/faculties working in the Universities and Autonomous Colleges of Orissa. The sample for the present study comprises of 8 Universities and 12 Autonomous Colleges Of Orissa.

Table 3.9

Districtwise Institutions Taken for the Sample Study

Districts	*No. of Universities*	*No. of Auto. Colleges*	*Total*
Balasore	1	1	2
Bhadrak	-	1	1
Cuttack	-	1	1
Dhenkanal	-	1	1
Gajapati	-	1	1
Ganjam	1	1	2

Jajpur	-	1	1
Khurda	3	2	5
Mayurabhanja	1	1	2
Puri	1	1	2
Sambalpur	1	1	2

3.10 The Pilot Study

The pilot study was undertaken in Orissa state, one of the 28th states of the country. Its Capital Bhubaneshwar, Area: 155,707 sq km, Population: 36,706,920 (Census-2001), Language: Oriya, Bengali, Hindi, English, No. of Districts: 30, Orissa lies along the eastern seaboard of India, south of Bengal. Their main attractions are the temple towns of Puri and Bhubaneshwar and the great Sun Temple at Konark and the state is mineral rich and a big exporter of iron ore with a large factory at Rourkela. Literates' rate of the State: Total Persons-20,053,785, Males-12,118,256, Females-7,935,529. Percentage of Literates rate to total population: Persons: 63.61 % Males: 75.95 % and Females: 50.97% as per 2001 census Govt of India. We have mentioned on its various limitations based on its social, educational and economic conditions, with this chapter. As the present research is based on information needs of sc/st; students, research scholars and faculties of autonomous colleges and universities of Orissa, the pilot study for the same is mentioned below.

In order to find out the information need, the survey method has been followed for the collection of data required. A questionnaire was designed keeping in view the objectives and hypothesis of the study and it was distributed randomly to 500 student/research scholars/faculties in 20 higher-level academic institutions all over Orissa. A combination of questionnaire and interviews were the major instruments used by the researcher to elicit information from the individual student/research scholars/faculties of 8 Universities and 12 Autonomous colleges. The questionnaires were distributed to the them after several personal visits by the researcher to their respective institutions and on site to collect the filled questionnaire and to interview them, respondents were asked to answer different questions. Most of the Universities are taken all the faculties having P.G Level (Science, Commerce and Arts) including SC/ST boys and girls. Similarly, all the 12 Autonomous Colleges are taken including boys and girls starting from +3 Degree Level and some of the P.G.Level Departments in the institute. There are very few SC/ST researchers and faculties taken to the survey.

3.11 The Database

The database of the study is collected primarily through questionnaire and is also drawn from a wide variety of secondary sources. The major part of the secondary data has been collected from Annual Reports, College Calendars, Academic Libraries, broachers, syllabus, advertisements of respective Institutes, and Government of Orissa Information Cell, welfare departments, NGO's in Orissa, SC and ST Cell, Government Reports on special educational meetings, Dept of Education, Govt of Orissa, Directorate of Higher Education, Govt. of Orissa, Bureau of Statistics, SC/ST R.T.I Nabakrishna Chouduri Centre for Development Studies (NCDS) and Orissa Ganaganana Bhawan etc. The time period for the purpose relates to the financial period between 1997-2002. Every possible care has been taken to keep abreast the latest references on the topic for the purpose of review of literature in order to find the gaps in the research from different current journal articles, books, Internet sources etc.

3.12 The Questionnaire

The questionnaire method has been used for collection of data for the present study. However by keeping in view the various advantages and disadvantages of the survey methodologies, a combination of Questionnaire and Interview method has been adopted for the survey. Designing an appropriate questionnaire for a survey is of great importance since the analysis and results of data acquired depend to a very large extent on the questions asked and answers sought. A great deal of careful thought has been given to the structure of questions, arrangement of topics and choice of response method. Accordingly, the present questionnaire (See Appendix-A) has been designed.

The questionnaire consists of 3 parts, having 58 questions in all. Part–A constituent's personal data of student/researcher/faculties. Part-B constitutes academic and social needs student/researcher/faculties. Part-C consists about the information seeking behavior of the student/researcher/faculties. The first part constituted personal–data, which contains 17 questions and the second, part the 'questionnaire paper consists of all total 16 questions about there academic and social need and Part-C contains 25 questions. There are three types of questions:

(a) Objective type questions–Yes/No and Please Tick from the options given
(b) Single line answer questions
(c) Questions with descriptive type answers.
(d) In the personal-data section, information relating to name, address, sex, category, profession, institution, education, subject area of specialization, language, reading interest, general information need and some questions about family member has been asked. In the second part of my questionnaire the information is based on academic and social need of the respondent. In its final part some questions has been made on their information seeking behavior towards library as well as their information demands.

After designing the questionnaire, the distribution of the same to the right persons becomes a major activity in the survey. Proper record has to be maintained of the persons to whom questionnaires are distributed. A number of follow up visits to the institution are made The response in a survey depends upon several factors such as the target group chosen accessibility to the group, the questionnaire-designed etc. About 500 questionnaires were distributed among the student/researchers/faculties in 6 universities and autonomous colleges of Orissa, among all only 396 were responded out of 500.

3.13 Limitation of the Study

In the previous studies in educational field there are studies, which are based on students not researcher, or faculties, but in this study it covers all. Again, it also studies in higher-level education field i.e. autonomous colleges and universities and our limitations are specially meant for scheduled caste and scheduled tribe in both the institutions. We have identified three main points of SC and ST student/researchers/faculties as: there social status, activities and information demands for there upliftment. This is not a participative user research and hence respondents are asked to present their community needs, government assistance and their institutional library services etc. Nevertheless all possible care has been taken to give this present work, its designed shape with a hope that this exercise within its limitations can enable other scholars to make further extensive and intensive studies on the information needs of student/researchers/faculties working various educational institutions of Orissa.

In order to identify information needs of this to have some insight into the actual information needs one should adopt various methods to gather information on the various factors that influence the information needs. No single method or tool will serve entirely. A careful selection, library users education programmes and blending of several techniques depending on the users actual need whose need is being studied is necessary. A formal procedure, which can be adapted to the study of the information needs of the SC/ST users, is proposed in the following sections. Besides gathering and recording the information needs, careful analysis is to be made to distil actual needs from the data gathered. To derive the advantages of a combination of 'a priori' and 'pragmatic' approaches, the methodology proposed in the thesis involves the conceptual and empirical survey of user information needs. The major steps in the process of identifying information needs is as follows: Study of subject(s) of interest to the institution/User(s), Study of the institution and its environment, Study of the immediate environment of the User(s), Study of the User(s) social economic background, Formal interview with the user identification and recording of information needs, analysis and refinement of the identified information needs etc.

4

Analysis and Findings

This chapter consists of two parts: primary data analysis and secondary data analysis. Before going to primary part, secondary data analysis is presented here, which deals with various academic institutions and libraries in Orissa. The study population surveyed included exclusively the scheduled caste and scheduled tribe student, researchers and faculties in the universities and autonomous colleges of the state. The study enumerates their percentages of enrolment, level of education, specialization, socio-economic profile, various subject interests, library collection, library service, information needs etc. in the primary data. The study uses the secondary sources of information from the Annual Reports and College Calendars of the respective academic institutions and its libraries, Directorate of Higher Education, Government of Orissa, Report of the Commissioner for SC/ST, Economic Survey Government of Orissa, Dept. of Personnel & Training. Quoted in National Commission, Census Report, Report on the Activities of SC/ST Development Department and Minorities & Backward Classes Welfare Department, Government of Orissa, Orissa Educational Statistics, Data Collected by Orissa College Library Association (OCLA), Directorate of SC/ST Research Training Institute Orissa. The study highlights educational variation of SC/ST and non-SC/ST, the possible causes for these, and helps to draw certain inferences. This may aid the formulation of more relevant and equitable development policies and programmes. The time period for the purpose related to the financial years between 1997–2002. The main purpose of such an analysis is to take stock of the activities and the trends thereof with a view to review the scheduled caste and scheduled tribe educational development and information needs of 20 educational institutions of Orissa. Such an analysis is very much necessary as the evaluation of educational developmental programme and policies and eradication of illiteracy in Orissa as well as India. The government and policy planners are always concerned with, as to how one can improve the level of education of the SC/ST Communities and bring them towards national mainstream. The information needs of the students, researchers and faculties can appropriately be assessed only after a due stocktaking of their place of living, sex, age, category they belong, profession, educational background, media they use, family status, study condition, problem they are facing in study, governmental assistance and their information seeking behaviors etc.

4.1 Educational Statistics of Orissa

Literacy is considered important as it plays or should play a crucial role in the process of social transformation as it paves the way for attainment of the objectives of social development. There were historically determined constraints on the universal spread of literacy and of education in Indian society even before independence. Spread of literacy stemmed from the primary edifice of social stratification inherent in caste prejudices. The social system based on caste was responsible for the birth of the principle of segregation and was so deterministic that it forced an individual to subordinate his individuality to "the institutionalized framework of social inequality and discrimination in conjunction with variation in income distribution engendered vast disparities not only in access to the institution of formal learning but also in the levels of educational attainment of the different segments of the Indian people", quoted by Ahmad (1983). Although Orissa is not known for much caste conflict, this it self is an indication of their pitiable condition, which has not permitted it to develop into an organized class. However, there is wide variation of literacy among SC/ST and general, male and female, SC and ST, district and districts, urban and rural etc. An article of The Hindustan Times (2003) mentioned that, the Orissa government's task force on education, set up to prepare its Vision-2020 document, presents a gloomy picture of prevailing conditions in tribal-dominated areas of Orissa. The task force on education, set up by the Orissa government to prepare its Vision-2020 document, notes in its report that for three years, 27 high schools in the state have showed 'Nil' results. All 27 schools are located in tribal-dominated areas. An ongoing nation-wide enrolment drive—Sarva Siksha Abhiyan—whose slogan is 'School-Chale-Hum' (Let's Go To School), may be having the desired impact, but there are schools in Orissa where, for several years, not a single student has managed to pass the high school certificate (Class X) examination. For example Gopalpur Girls High School in Kalahandi district is one such school, where not a single student has passed the HSC (Higher Secondary Certificate) examination between 1996 and 2000.

Again, out of 27 schools in the backward areas, eight schools in Koraput, eight in Rayagada, two each in Malkangiri and Nawarangapur districts, four in Kalahandi district and one each in Phulbani, Gajapati and Sundargarh. Officials at the school and mass education department and the SC and ST development department blame each other for the dismal state of education in Orissa's tribal areas. A task force member said: "A kind of double administration by the welfare officers of the SC and ST department and the inspectorate of schools has ruined these special schools. No one is bothered about teacher absenteeism, lack of mid-day meals and the absence of facilities." Officials at both departments agree that the objective of promoting primary and secondary education in tribal areas has not been achieved.

According to an umbrella body of tribal legislators, Adibasi Bidhayak Parishad, the issue of education for tribal children has not been seriously dealt with. MLAs claim that not a single school has an adequate number of teachers. The government still has to provide books to the tribal students, they say. In Orissa, 10,000 of the 40,000 schools have no school buildings, and 40% of classrooms do not possess a blackboard. Three thousand schools are single-room schools with just one teacher. Fifty-five per cent of schools do not have drinking water facilities.

A general educational scenario is mentioned in the previous chapter (Chapter-III). The following table mentioned below provides the educational statistics of Orissa from primary level to higher level.

Table 4.1
Orissa Education Statistics 1998-99

Types of Institutions	*No. of Institutions*	*No. of Student*	*No. of Scholars*	*No. of Teachers*
1. Primary Schools (Formal)	42104	5232000	-	111040
2. Middle Schools (Formal)	11510	1412000	-	35914
3. Secondary Schools	6094	1076000	-	51568
4. General Colleges	1367	555000	-	23003
5. Higher Education	591	171476	1682	8934

Sources: Department of Education, Govt. of Orissa

The above table shows the educational institutions, student enrolment, numbers of scholars and teachers available in Orissa during 1998/99. The numbers of general colleges are 1367 with 555000 students and having 23003 teachers in all and there are 171476 students in 591 institutions (higher level) having 8934 teachers. The teacher student ratio is 1:19 in our higher education system. The distribution of student enrolment as per their level of education in higher academic system during 1996/97 to 1999/00 is given below.

4.1.1 Institutions of Higher Education

In higher educational level the state has nine universities and fifteen autonomous colleges at present, namely—Utkal University, Sambalpur University, Berhampur University, North Orissa University, Fakir Mohan University, Sri Jagannath Sanskrit University, Orissa University of

Agriculture and Technology, Utkal University of Culture and Biju Pattanayak University of Science & Technology (all engineering & technical colleges in Orissa). Apart from these Universities, it is proposed to open an Adivasi University at Koraput to expand higher education in tribal districts of southern Orissa. By 2001-02, fifteen colleges have been conferred with autonomous status namely B.J.B. College, Bhadrak College, Dhenkanal College, F.M, College, G.M. College, Govt. College Bhawanipatna, Govt. College Rourkela, Khallikote College, M.P.C. College, N.C. College, R.D. Womens College, Rajendra College, Ravenshaw College, S.C.S College and S.K.C.G. College. Besides Government have also recommended the name of two Government Colleges located in backward and KBK areas namely Vikram Dev College, Jeypore and Government College, Phulabani to the University Grant Commission for grant of autonomous status, Economic Survey, Orissa (2002/03).

Among the higher academic institutions, North Orissa University at Baripada, Fokir Mohan University at Balasore and Biju Pattanayak University of Science & Technology at Rourkela started functioning form 2002/03. However, OUAT is the second oldest agriculture university in the country, made its humble beginning in the 1962 with two colleges, i.e. college of agriculture and college of veterinary science and animal husbandry. Now it has grown into a full-fledged institution having eleven constituent colleges imparting education and training in various aspects of agriculture. Animal Husbandry and Veterinary sciences, agriculture engineering and technology, home science, fisheries, forestry, general engineering and basic science. The University has developed a strong research base for generation of technology capable of improving productivity. Stability, profitability and sustainability of the major farming systems under varied agro-climatic situations of the State. Dissemination of the latest technology covering different areas of agriculture and allied discipline is one of the major responsibilities of the university. This is achieved through various types of training, distance education programmes, on farm trials and demonstration in farmers field, farmers' fairs and various mass communication programmes. The total intake capacity of all these constituent college under OUAT is 1,250 and during 2001-02. The university has so far produced 11,042 graduates, 3206 postgraduates and 180 PhDs in different disciplines. An amount of Rs.66.24 lakhs assistance has been proposed in the Annual Plan, 2002-03 for continuance of higher secondary, +3 courses in science and postgraduate courses in Microbiology under OUAT.

For the above institutes, the State Government provides development grants and special development grants to the universities in the state, besides OUAT, which is assisted under the agriculture budget is also provided grants in the education budget to conduct higher secondary and +3 courses in science and post graduate course in micro-biology. An outlay of Rs. 95.00 lakh has been proposed for providing recurring and non-recurring expenditure during 2002-03 to the North Orissa University and Fakir Mohan University. Except, theses, UGC also providing various other grants to the institutions for there developmental activities. Colleges provide Degree teaching and PG teaching facilities are available in 24 Government Colleges in 27 subjects.

There are three principal levels of qualifications within the higher education system in Orissa There are Bachelor/ Undergraduate level, Master's/Post-graduate level and Doctoral/Pre-doctoral level. Diploma courses are also available at the undergraduate and postgraduate level. At the undergraduate level, it varies between one to three years in length; postgraduate diplomas are normally awarded after one year's study. Bachelor's degree in arts, commerce and sciences is three years of education (after 12 years of school education). In some places there are honors and special courses available. These are not necessarily longer in duration but indicate greater depth of study. Bachelor degree in professional field of study in agriculture, dentistry, engineering, pharmacy, technology and veterinary medicine generally take four years, while architecture and medicine, it takes five and five and a half years respectively. There are other bachelor degrees in education, journalism and librarian-ship that are second degrees. Bachelor's degree in law can either be taken as an integrated degree lasting five years or three-year course as a second degree. Master's degree is normally of two-year duration. It could be coursework based without thesis or research alone.

Admission to postgraduate programmes in engineering and technology is done on the basis of Graduate Aptitude Test in Engineering or Combined Medical Test respectively. A pre-doctoral programme—Master of Philosophy (M.Phil.) is taken after completion of the Master's Degree. This can either be completely research based or can include course work as well. Ph.D. is awarded two year after the M.Phil. or three years after the Master's degree. Students are expected to write a substantial thesis based on original research, generally takes longer. Professional courses like Computer Application, Industrial Chemistry, Mass Communication, Tax Procedure and Practice etc. have been introduced through UGC assistance. Apart from these, all the Universities are providing PG teaching facilities on art, science and commerce oriented subjects like and emphasis is also put on professional and vocational courses like Management courses, Computer education, Law, Physical education and UGC sponsored vocational courses on Agriculture, Dairy farming etc.

There are different courses provided in the higher education institutes of Orissa, i.e. Ph.D, D.Sc, D.Phil, M.Phil, Post Graduate level—M.A., M.Com., M.Sc., Graduate level—B.A.,B.Sc., B.Com. in both hounors & pass and in professional levels there are also graduate and post graduate level M.Tech.,B.Tech., M.B.B.S, in Allopathic/Ayur/Hemeo/Dental, M.Ed,.B.Ed. LLM, LLB, MLIS, BLIS by Dept of Education Govt. of Orissa (2003). Refer Chapter-III (Table-3.5) for detail higher educational institutes and enrolment in Orissa.

The above table gives distribution of SC, ST and General students enrolment in the higher academic institutions of Orissa during the period of 1996 to 2001. This also distribute them as per their levels of education within the years, shows that the numbers of general students are more than the SC/ST's and also pointed the increasing numbers of SC/ST in recent past. Details of their percentages are given in the proceeding tables.

Table 4.2

Distribution of SC/ST and General in Level of Education During 1996-2001

Level of Education	*Ph.D/D.Sc./D.Phil/ M. Phil*			*Post Graduate*			*Graduate*			*Professionals: Graduate &P.G*		
Categories	*SC*	*ST*	*GEN*	*SC*	*ST*	*GEN*	*SC*	*ST*	*GEN*	*SC*	*ST*	*GEN*
2000/01	49	30	451	686	307	10554	10361	6955	154990	585	502	4193
1999/00	43	30	433	654	292	9545	9942	6644	139520	612	620	5489
1998/99	42	29	428	643	286	9878	9913	6714	138003	563	496	4314
1997/98	35	19	377	619	227	9280	9233	5129	117044	538	418	3908
1996/97	21	12	284	539	175	8643	8991	5100	100526	532	299	2885
Total	190	120	1973	3141	1287	47900	48440	30542	650083	2830	2335	15509

Sources: Directorate of Higher Education, Orissa

4.1.2 Institutions of Technical Education

Owing to the changing need of the State for exploitation of its vast natural resources in diversified and emerging high-tech areas, it requires sustainable improvement in the overall quality and growth of technical education to meet the changing scenario of the future of the State as a whole. Keeping in view the demand for manpower in the field of technical education, subjects such as Information Technology, Electronics & Computer Application, Metallurgy, Chemical Engineering, Pharmacy etc. have been introduced in different institutions. By the end of 2001-02, there were thirty-five Engineering Colleges including six Govt. Engineering Colleges and twenty-nine private Engineering Colleges with a total intake capacity of 8,749 students in different faculties.

In the Govt sector, there are 13 Engineering Schools/ Polytechnics including the Film and Television Institute of Orissa. These institutions offer diploma courses in both engineering and non-engineering disciplines as per the guidelines, norms and standards prescribed by the All India Council for Technical Education (AICTE), New Delhi. Out of the above institutions, four Polytechnics, at Rourkela, Dhakanal, Bhubaneswar and Berhampur with an intake capacity of 220 are meant exclusively for women,. In addition to the above institutions, 13 private polytechnics/Engineering schools were engaged in imparting technical education during 2001-02. The total intake capacity of the 26 Engineering Schools/Polytechnics is 4,955.

It has been proposed to establish Orissa University of Technology to maintain and improve standard of education in Engineering Colleges and to upgrade the infrastructure and other facilities in the State for technical education. The scope of the proposed Technology University will include institutions imparting education in engineering and technology, industry, management and applied sciences. Computer and Business Management Programmes are proposed to be included in the curriculum of the proposed university. Besides, the state Govt. is actively considering to set up an Indian Institute of Information Technology (IIIT) at Bhubaneswar with active collaboration of industrial leaders, Economic Survey, Government of Orissa (2002/03).

4.1.3 Institutions of Medical Education

In the field of medical sciences, the State has three Medical Colleges, one Dental College, one Pharmacy College, three Ayurvedic Colleges, four Homoeopathic Colleges and one Nursing College in the Government sector. There are also two Ayurvedic Colleges and two Homoeopathic Colleges and thirteen Pharmacy Colleges in the private sector. The intake capacity in the Government sector of the three Medical colleges was 321, of the Dental College 20, and of the fourteen Pharmacy colleges including 13 in the private sector was 780 during 2001-02. Besides, 3 Nursing schools were functioning in the state with intake capacity 200.

4.1.4 SC/ST's Percentages in Higher Education in Orissa

A profile of literacy in general for the Scheduled Castes (SC) and Scheduled Tribes (ST) population in Orissa during census—1991 shows that the literacy rate in the state was 36.8 per cent—52.4 percent for males and 20.7 per cent for females. Rural female literacy is as low as 19.4 per cent. Across districts, it is alarmingly low at 9.9 per cent in Ganjam, followed by 10.4 per cent in Kalahandi, and 10.7 percent in Koraput. In more than 50 percent districts of the state, rural female literacy is less than 15 per cent. Across districts, urban literacy ranges between 54.6 per cent in Cuttack and 37.2 per cent in Koraput. The male literacy rate is higher than the female literacy rate in rural and urban areas in all the districts. But, for the higher-level education different data was collected from different secondary sources all over Orissa is given. Selected educational statistics of five years starting from 2000/2001 to 1996/1997 is provided under the following table below.

The above table shows that percentages of higher-level education have been increasing every year during last five years. But in PG level, there are little differences during 1998/99 (20.69%) and 1999/00 (20.05%), in professional level more student enrolled during 1999/2000 (32.5%) than others. All this reveals that in higher level there are some developments. This may be due to government's role played for the same or people are more aware about higher

Table 4.3

Year Wise Distribution of Enrolments in Different Levels of Education During 1996-2001 [See also Fig. 4.3]

Years	*PhD+*	%	*P.G.*	%	*Graduate*	%	*Profesion*	%	*Total*	%
2000/01	530 (0.28%)	23.22	11547 (6.09%)	22.07	172306 (90.85%)	23.63	5280 (2.78%)	25.54	189663 (100%)	23.58
1999/00	506 (0.29%)	22.16	10491 (6.04%)	20.05	156106 (89.81%)	21.41	6721 (3.87%)	32.51	173824 (100%)	21.61
1998/99	499 (0.29%)	21.86	10807 (6.31%)	20.65	154630 (90.26%)	21.21	5373 (3.14%)	25.99	171309 (100%)	21.30
1997/98	431 (0.29%)	18.88	10126 (6.90%)	19.35	131406 (89.50%)	18.02	4864 (3.31%)	23.53	146827 (100%)	18.25
1996/97	317 (0.25%)	13.89	9357 (7.31%)	17.88	114617 (89.54%)	15.72	3716 (2.90%)	17.97	128007 (100%)	15.91
TOTAL	2283 (0.28%)	100.00	52328 (6.51%)	100.00	729065 (90.64%)	100.00	20674 (2.57%)	100.00	804350 (100%)	100.00

Table 4.4

Level Wise Distribution of SC/ST and Non-SC/ST Enrolments During 1996-20/01

Years	*2000/2001*		*1999/2000*		*1998/1999*		*1997/1998*		*1996/1997*	
CAT.	*SC/ST*	*GEN*	*SC/ST*	*GEN*	*SC/ST*	*GEN*	*SC/ST*	*GEN*	*SC/ST*	*GEN*
Ph.D. /D.Sc.	79 0.41%	451 0.27%	73 0.39%	433 0.28%	71 0.38%	428 0.28%	54 0.33%	377 0.29%	33 0.21%	284 0.25%
Post Graduate	993 5.10%	10554 6.20%	946 5.02%	9545 6.16%	929 4.97%	9878 6.47%	846 5.22%	9280 7.11%	714 4.56%	8646 7.70%
Graduate	17316 88.91%	154990 91.07	16586 88.05%	139520 90.02	16627 88.98%	138003 90.42%	14362 88.56%	117044 88.61%	14091 89.93%	100526 89.48%
Professionals	1087 5.58%	4193 2.46%	1232 6.05%	5489 3.52%	1059 5.67%	4314 2.83%	956 5.89%	3908 2.99%	831 5.30%	2885 2.57%
Totals	19475 100%	170188 100%	18837 100%	154987 100%	18686 100%	152623 100%	16218 100%	130609 100%	15669 100%	112341 100%

educational benefits or student may not having employment during there educational period hoping for it.

Above table reveals that in all the four level of education non-SC/ST enrolment are higher than SC/ST and it also shows year wise educational enrolment is developing since 1996, perhaps this is for more awareness and attention of education department government of Orissa and middle class people, but it reveals SC/ST enrolment is not so increased as non-SC/ST in all the five years except 2000/01. During the year when a comparison has made it shows that in PhD SC/ST (79) 0.41% and non-SC/ST (451) 0.27%, in professional level SC/ST (1087) 5.58% where as non- SC/ST (4193) is only 2.46%. The year wise distribution of only SC/ST shows that in all level of education the percentage is increasing better except professional levels (23.85%) during 1999/00. The year wise comparison table of SC/ST is as follows.

Table-4.5 states that, during the mentioned five years SC/ST's are advancing in all the levels in higher education, but there are little deviations in professionals and non-professional courses, where these students are now taking interest in professional rather than non-professional. In comparison with graduate and postgraduate: there are more percentages of PG than Graduate.

The year wise percentages of SC, ST and NON –SC/ST are found from the above table, shows NON-SC/ST percentages are more than SC/ST, and between SC and ST percentages of SC is much higher than ST. Educational level of SC/ST and NON-SC/ST shows that percentages of SC/ST increasing year after year than NON-SC/ST, it is more in professional courses. Thus credit goes to the governmental actions for their overall development and different educational facilities provided time to time during the year.

4.2 Status of Academic Institutions

The information collected for the theses and the coverage of institutions for the purpose including the streams in which courses are important and information of the like have been done. However, the aspects, which were considered under

Table 4.5

Yar Wise Distribution of SC/ST Percentages During 1996/97-2000/01

[See also Fig. 4.5]

Year	*Ph.D/D.Sc./D.Phil/ M. Phil*		*Post Graduate*		*Graduate*		*Professionals: Graduate & P.G.*	
	SC/ST	%	SC/ST	%	SC/ST	%	SC/ST	%
2000/01	79	25.48	993	22.43	17316	21.92	1087	21.05
1999/00	73	23.55	946	21.36	16586	21.00	1232	23.85
1998/99	71	22.90	929	20.98	16627	21.05	1059	20.50
1997/98	54	17.42	846	19.11	14362	18.18	956	18.51
1996/97	33	10.65	714	16.12	14091	17.84	831	16.09
Total	310	100.00	4428	100.00	78982	100.00	5165	100.00

Table 4.6: Distribution of Categories of Enrolments-1996/97 to 2000/2001

Categories of Enrolment	*Ph.D/D.Sc./ D.Phil/M. Phil (%)*	*Post Graduate (%)*	*Graduate (%)*	*Professionals: Graduat & P.G (%)*	*YEARS*
SC	49(9.25)	686(5.94)	10361(6.04)	585(11.08)	
ST	30(5.66)	307(2.66)	6955(4.05)	502(9.51)	
NON-SCST	451(85.09)	10554(91.40)	154990(90.33)	4193(79.41)	
TOTAL	530(100%)	11547(100%)	172306(100%)	5280(100%)	2000/01
SC	43 (8.50)	654(6.23)	9942(6.37)	612(9.11)	
ST	30(5.93)	292(2.78)	6644(4.26)	620(9.22)	
NON-SCST	433(85.57)	9545(90.98)	139520(89.38)	5489(81.67)	
TOTAL	506(100%)	10491(100%)	156106(100%)	6721(100%)	1999/00
SC	42(8.42)	643(5.95)	9913(6.41)	563(10.48)	
ST	29(5.81)	286(2.65)	6714(4.34)	496(9.23)	
NON-SCST	428(85.77)	9878(91.40)	138003(89.25)	4314(80.29)	
TOTAL	499(100%)	10807(100%)	154630(100%)	5373(100%)	1998/99
SC	35(8.12)	619(6.11)	9233(7.03)	538(11.06)	
ST	19(4.41)	227(2.24)	5129(3.90)	418(8.59)	
NON-SCST	377(87.47)	9280(91.65)	117044(89.07	3908(80.35)	
TOTAL	431(100%)	10126(100%)	131406(100%)	4864(100%)	1997/98
SC	21(6.62)	539(5.76)	8991(7.84)	532(14.32)	
ST	12(3.79)	175(1.87))	5100(4.45)	299(8.05)	
NON-SCST	28489.59)	8643(92.37)	100526(87.71)	2885(77.64)	
TOTAL	317(100%)	9357(100%)	114617(100%)	3716(100%)	1996/97

the study for procuring information an academic status of institutions from the libraries of Universities as well as Colleges of the state, are as follows

Table 4.7

Institutionwise Students, Scholars & Faculties Under Study 2000/2001

	Name of the Institutions	*Students*	*Scholars*	*Faculties*
1.	B.J.B. (Auto) College, Bhubaneswar	2500	-	170
2.	Berhampur University, Berhampur	4810	156	234
3.	Bhadrak (Auto) College, Bhadrak	4782	-	165
4.	Dhenkanal (Auto) College, Dhenkanal	2837	-	116
5.	F. M. University, Balasore	3205		175
6.	F..M., (Auto) College, Balasore	3600	-	105
7.	G.M. (Auto) College, Sambalpur	2868	-	192
8.	Govt. (Auto) College, Bhawanipatana	3119	-	86
9.	Khalikote (Auto) College, Khalikot, Berampur	4872	25	174
10.	M.P.C. (Auto) College, Baripada	4200	74	150
11.	N.C. (Auto) College, Jajpur	3439	-	124
12.	North Orissa University, Takatpur, Baripada	3109	35	125
13.	Orissa University of Agri & Tech, Bhubaneswar	4837	197	223
14.	R.D.Womens (Auto) College, Bhubaneswar	1632	-	77
15.	Ravenshaw (Auto) College, Cuttack	5789	22	191
16.	S.C.S. (Auto) College, Puri	3568	13	133
17.	Sambalpur University, Sambalpur	4723	164	216
18.	Shri Jagarnath Sanskrit University, Puri	2198	230	92
19.	Utkal University of Culture, Bhubaneswar	600	15	32
20.	Utkal University, Bhubaneswar	4950	264	254
	Total	71638	1195	3034

Sources: From Concerned Institute's: College Calender/Annual Report/ Library Records, During 1998-2003.

4.3 Status of the Academic Libraries in Orissa

The academic community appears to be the largest consumer of information. Their job of teaching, learning and research involves generating, collecting, processing, storing, disseminating and using information in several forms for different purposes. A continuous effort needs to be taken up for developing system approach within the institution to improving an information environment. Thus academic institutions are information intensive organizations. The concepts like knowledge management, best practices, intellectual control, business intelligence, process innovation are coming up to the mainstream of academic environments because of the widespread use of information technology which has a direct bearing on organizational change. In order to undertake a successful knowledge management initiative, there is need for technological and behavioral change of the government as well as library professionals. This phenomenon of information behavior within the academic institution is not only supportive of educational missions but also serves to sustain motivation towards an effective outcome of objectives of the institution.

Higher academic information system works according to the collected information and by the objectives of its parent institution. It deals with its internal and external information. The internal information is required for it's internal functioning, and it is used for internal administrative and academic procedures. This information persists only in the internal domain of the university. The external information is required in public domain for various types of queries and know-how about the university, research activities and social missions. Universities and colleges always try to maintain access of its information for its administrators, faculties, students and other staff related with the institution. It also provides its information to local, national and international users and partners. The openness of the information leads towards efficient, transparent and effective administrative procedures within and outside the campus.

Orissa academic library system comprises in three levels

i.e. school and college and the university libraries. Excepting very highbrow private schools, most schools in Orissa do not have a library per se in the present situation. This area of librarianship is very neglected and needs immediate and continuous attention. As regards to college libraries, most colleges have libraries but other than very well known colleges in city areas, the ordinary colleges do not run libraries of any consequence. There is some library development in costal area institutions. But on the other hand universities are having there own libraries within there campus. For all these higher academic libraries the budgetary provision available from state government, UGC and ICSSR through grants, aid etc, sometimes-special grant, and donation are also received for library infrastructure. Thus there is no separate budget for the libraries. Therefore, Orissa faces the challenges of actually preparing a perspective plan from scratch i.e., from collection development to networking through IT solutions, and will need a complete blueprint to develop higher academic libraries during the coming centuries.

4.3.1 Collection Development

Document collection is considered as the foundation of any library. College and university libraries cannot respond to the rising needs of its numerically increasing users unless it has the materials required by them. For supporting education and research programmes of the university. The state of Orissa is having more than 10000 academic institutions and libraries in each institution. Academic libraries serving more than 750,000 students and faculty. The Orissa Higher Education library system having a good collection development for the benefit of the statewide academic community. The goal of this initiative is to provide a high quality collection of different sources of document based on the syllabus as per the Government of Orissa., and it has many more resources that supports instruction, study, and research by students, faculty and staff in all eligible Orissa higher education institutions. The present scenario of the document collections of the libraries of higher education in Orissa is presented in Table 4.8.

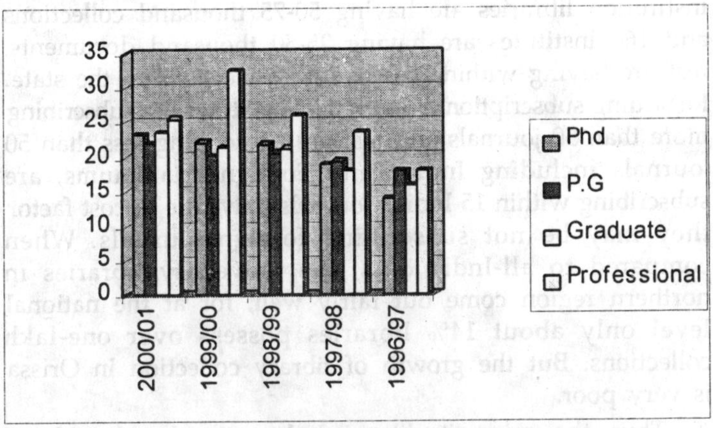

Fig. 4.3: Year Wise Distribution Level of Education During 1996-2001

Table 4.8

Academic Libraries Document Collection in Orissa

Sl.	*Ranges of Library Collections*	*No. of Lib. in Higher Education (+Govt. & Pvt).*
1	Library Collections (including bound periodical) Within - 1000-25000	359
2	Library Collections (including bound periodical) Within - 25,000-50,000	166
3	Library Collections (including bound periodical) Within - 50,000-75,000	48
4	Library Collections (including bound periodical) Within - 75,000-100,000	12
5	Library Collections (including bound periodical) Within -100,000 - Above	7

Sources: Orissa Educational Statistics, 2001-2002.

Data presented in the above table reveals that 4 universities and 3 autonomous colleges in the state have document collections above one lakh are in the city areas basically old institutes, there are 12 institutes in the state having their collection within 75–1 lakh collections, 48 institution libraries are having 50-75 thousand collections and 166 institutes are having 25-50 thousand documents, rest are having within 25 thousand collections in the state. Regarding subscription of journals 7 institutes are subscribing more than 50 journals and rest are subscribing less than 50 journals including Indian and Foreign. Maximums, are subscribing within 15 Indian journals only, due to cost factor they may be not subscribing foreign journals. When compared to all-India data, the university libraries in northern region come out fairly well, for at the national level only about 14% libraries possess over one-lakh collections. But the growth of library collection in Orissa is very poor.

Thus, the university librarians have to play the role of modern managers, and therefore, require "adaptability, willingness to accept changes, a stable temperament, emotional balance and endure ness". It is rightly observed that the library managers of the 21st century need to redesign and restructure their organization to eliminate the positions that encourage the powerlessness and ineffectiveness of bureaucracy. Then librarians in those positions can delegate tasks and responsibilities more easily, accomplish results and become leaders. Orissa academic librarians should be aware of the above facts as well as the information explosion due to growth of IT industry, which have direct effect on information sources and thus have impact on the information management. Information resources are today available in different formats and media like: printed sources, online databases, CDROM databases, Internet sources etc. It is now important question on part of the Orissa academic librarians to predict present situation as well as future use of different types of information sources and then make proper selection for the collection development. It is a good sign for Orissa LIS that the 11th Public Library Act has been passed in 2001 and published in Orissa Gazette on 11th March 2002 for general information of the public.

The library and information manpower plays the key role in making the library resources available to the users. There has been wide discussion on the need to accord them the academic status studied by Parida (1992 and 1999). Long back, the Kolkata University Commission (1917-1919) recommended for the first time that the university should have the services of a librarian who "should have salary and status of a Professor...." Later, all the commissions and Committees put forward similar recommendations so that "the status and salary scale of library staff should be the same as that of teaching and research staff". But at present there is parity in the salary scales of the University Librarian with that of the Professor. Thus, this may affect the job satisfaction of any academic libraries. On the other hand the effectiveness of any library depends on the quality and quantity of the personnel. It is necessary that the staff provided in the academic libraries should be properly trained and quailed; it is also necessary that the staff sanctioned to work should also be adequate. But the data collected from the academic libraries of Orissa that there is no guidelines on standards prevailed in the libraries and there are professionals, non-professionals, binders, clerical staff, sweepers, attendant, peons, contact workers etc.

Table 4.9

Collection Development of Academic Institutions Under Study

	Name of the Institution Libraries	*Books and Bound J.*	*Current J. Sub. FGN/IND*
1.	B.J.B. (Auto) College, Bhubaneswar	65,000	18
2.	Berhampur University, Berhampur	123,000	38
3.	Bhadrak (Auto) College, Bhadrak	70,000	12
4.	Dhenkanal (Auto) College, Dhenkanal	53,000	4
5.	F. M. University, Baleswar	1,13,000	21
6.	F..M. (Auto) College, Balaswar	149,000	15
7.	G.M. (Auto) College, Sambalpur	64,000	9
8.	Govt. (Auto) College, Bhawanipatana	59,000	4
9.	Khalikote (Auto) College, Khalikot, Berhampur	125,000	15
10.	M.P.C. (Auto) College, Baripada	71,000	6
11.	N.C. (Auto) College, Jajpur	106,000	7
12.	North Orissa University, Takatpur, Baripada	62,000	11

13. Orissa University of Agri & Tech, Bhubaneswar	75,000	195
14. R.D.Womens (Auto) College, Bhubaneswar	34,000	11
15. Ravenshaw (Auto) College, Cuttack	181,000	45
16. S.C.S (Auto) College, Puri	107,000	19
17. Sambalpur University, Sambalpur	134,000	47
18. Shri Jagarnath Sanskrit University, Puri	85,000	19
19. Utkal University of Culture, Bhubaneswar	3230	5
20. Utkal University, Bhubaneswar	1,97,000	130

4.3.2 Library Manpower

From among the 20 libraries in the state, 8 libraries belonging to university libraries and 12 libraries are autonomous college libraries. And, it was shocking to find out that some of the libraries there is no permanent librarian appointed, and a bad tradition of having teachers from teaching departments other than library and information science as Acting/Officiating Librarians. This is unfortunate not only for the library but also the library profession.

4.3.3 Library Budget

Budget is the most important part of any activities; adequate fund is necessary for effective and efficient work. If sufficient fund are not provided to the libraries the standard of library services are supposed to be disrupted, poor and ineffective. But, in Orissa academic environment every year there is budget cut for the education and there is no separate grant or aids for libraries, again, the budgetary position of the autonomous college and universities libraries in the state varies considerably. The University Grant Commission and the State Government provide fund to the libraries. Which the former have to depend upon their parent institutions, the state governments, and the UGC. The University Libraries in the state are financially better than the college libraries.

4.3.4 Library Services

In general libraries in the educational institutions have to serve all their students, researchers and faculties. So, there is a great role to play on the part of library professionals to properly select and manage its various sources for use. It includes all methods and procedures for collecting and processing information resources and formatting the documents in a manner, suitable for the users. In case of Orissa, which is a backward state in the country, is suffering in many ways—lack of cooperation within universities, proper library building, furniture equipment, fund, trained staff, and use of poor library technique, lack of information technology and motive of the State Govt. etc. Almost all the university libraries and college libraries in Orissa have been providing the traditional library services such as circulation of books, references services, reprographic services etc. Some libraries are providing Current Awareness Services, SDI services and conducting user education programme. But it may be pointed out that some of these services are not given with efficiency and effectiveness. There is a need to gear up not only the old ones, but also to initiate new services with the assistance of computer technology so that total library operations and services can be modernized, Seth (1992). In this area much remains to be done as the image of the university library is directly linked with the quality of services it provides to its ever-rising number of users with diverse requirements.

An information system exists for the user, and thus the users are the most important element in an information system. How to provide better and more effective information services to the user, is the main concern of every good information system. To achieve this end planning of user education is very important particularly in academic libraries. As many libraries suggested many methods for planning of user education, these can broadly be grouped in the following heads: Guiding by signs and boards of different sources in reasonable places, User orientation services of the library (different services, sources, techniques in the library), distribution of brochures/leaflets (about the collection, services), Literature search techniques (use of indexing/ abstracting, thesaurus, citation indexes, style manuals, bibliographies etc.) and lastly educating the user about information skills, outreach programmes, reference tools etc.

Table 21, reveals that all the 20 libraries have reprographic services where in no libraries have translation and document delivery services, none of the libraries are having internet browsing facilities except OUAT, which has trying for automate there library. Some of the University Libraries are having giving ILL, DD and CAS/SDI services.

4.3.5 Status of Infrastructure Available in Academic Libraries in Orissa

There have been attempts in the last 2-3 years to introduce computer application to library and information activities in Orissa. However, it is only during the recent period some institutions have become more earnest to computerize their operations and services. Most of the libraries have either installed one or the other computer systems, or are in the process of computerizing their housekeeping functions only. The library and information activities, which can be computerized, include circulation, acquisition, serials control, catalogues, documentation lists, management, bibliographic databases, budgeting, information retrieval etc. Seth and Others (1997). The study revealed that majority of the library professionals in the higher academic libraries have knowledge about library software like—CDS/ISIS, SANJAY, LIBSYS, GRANATHALAYA etc. There is also enthusiasm among the library and information professionals to get training in library computerization from different institutions like INSDOC, DRTC, IASLIC, SIS, ILA, and INFLIBNET etc. have been offering various short-term programmes on computer application to library and information activities. There have been more centers recognized by the National Information System for Science and Technology to import training on manpower development on information technology. In this context a multi-pronged approach be adopted to reform human capital in higher academic libraries. In-service training for library professionals be promoted to increase efficiency and effectiveness in library services in the new automated library environment.

An exercise was made to find out the library budget total numbers of professionals working in the libraries, the analysis of data reveals that all the universities are having more than ten professionals except Utkal University of Culture which is having only 2, regarding library budget Utkal University is getting fund then all. The analysis also reveal that 5 institutions are having direct telephone and internet connection and others are not having.

Although information technology (IT) is extremely essential for maximizing the utilization of the existing libraries so that it can reach out to the remote areas for the vast disadvantaged community and benefit the reader at large, it is incumbent to know that the institution and library personnel are facing lot of constraints to implement the same. Some of the major problems being faced by Orissa Academic Libraries Systems, as discussed in this studies may be summed up as follows:

1. Bureaucratic bottleneck and fixed mindset of the government.
2. Insufficient document resources to meet the needs of their users potential demand,
3. The information explosion and increasing cost of library materials and organizing them for use,
4. The growth of knowledge, with the consequent demands, particularly in university libraries
5. The varying levels of financial resources and funding provisions must be separate for the Library.
6. The cost of storing infrequently used materials that accumulate when a library tries to be self-sufficient and space problems due to growth of collections.
7. The requirement to serve the disadvantaged communities and users that are not being served, in colleges, particularly in rural area.
8. Lack of physical facilities in terms of space, furniture, equipment and information technology with electronics facilities,
9. The difficulty in attracting and recruiting right type of professional staff to meet the changing and complex information needs of users, .
10. The need for developing cooperation and resource

Table 4.10

Services Rendered in the Academic Institutions Under Study

Name of the Institutions	*Reprog-raphic*	*Trans-lation*	*Document Delivery*	*Inter Library Loan*	*Cas/ SDI*	*Cdrom/ online*	*Internet Browsing*
Berhampur University	Yes	No	No	No	No	No	No
F. M. University	Yes	No	No	No	No	No	No
North Orissa University	Yes	No	No	No	No	No	No
Orissa University of Agri & Tech	Yes	No	Yes	Yes	Yes	Yes	Yes
Sambalpur University	Yes	No	No	No	No	No	No
Shri Jagarnath Sanskrit University,	Yes	No	No	No	No	No	No
Utkal University of Culture,	Yes	No	Yes	No	No	Yes	Yes
Utkal University, Bhubaneswar	Yes	No	Yes	Yes	No	Yes	Yes
B.J.B. (Auto) College	Yes	No	Yes	No	No	No	No
Bhadrak (Auto) College	Yes	No	No	No	No	No	No
Dhenkanal (Auto) College	Yes	No	No	No	No	No	No
F..M., (Auto) College	Yes	No	No	No	No	No	No
G.M. (Auto) College	Yes	No	No	No	No	No	No
Govt. (Auto) College	Yes	No	No	No	No	No	No
Khalikote (Auto) College	Yes	No	No	No	No	No	No
M.P.C. (Auto) College	Yes	No	No	No	No	No	No
N.C. (Auto) College	Yes	No	No	No	No	No	No
R.D.Womens (Auto) College	Yes	No	No	No	No	No	No
Ravenshaw (Auto) College	No	No	No	No	No	No	No
S.C.S (Auto) College	No	No	No	No	No	No	No

Sources: Annual Report and College Calendar of the concerned Institute during 1997-2003

sharing, network among libraries in Orissa.

11. The need for improving and diversifying the educational training programmes in Library and Information Science (L&IS) and innovative attitude for the library professionals.

Many external factors, such as new teaching methods, growth in research activities, intensified postgraduate training and improved IT services, set special challenges to libraries today. The significant growth in electronic content production requires critical evaluation of present library procedures, new expertise and cooperation as well as ability to react to the changes in user needs.

4.4 Summary and Findings of the Secondary Data

Major findings of the study based on the secondary data are presented below:

> The first and foremost indicator of educational progress of the state or the disadvantaged community in the field of higher education is the number of standard institutions, its faculties and student enrolment. The secondary data provided on Orissa educational scenario shows there has been a spurt in the enrolment of SC/ST students in higher education in autonomous college level. The SC students are better placed as compared to STs. The majority of disadvantaged students are in the Arts stream and as such the goal of economic empowerment of this population in the state seems to be illusive. The state is far behind as compared to the national average literacy as per the census of India during entire census since independence, again the literacy levels, particularly female literacy are extremely low for landless wage earners, marginal landholders SC/ST. The gender disparities are also wide especially among this category. Higher dis-continuation rates as well as enrolment rates further investigation to find out the casual factors. However, the performance of the state regarding SC women's higher education seems to be satisfactory in

Table 4.11

Manpower, Budget and Infrastructure Available in Higher Education Libraries

Name of Institutions	*Library Budget*	*Library Manpower*	*No. of Comp.*	*Direct Tel. Connect*	*Internet Connect*
Berhampur University	45,00,000	19	6PCs	Yes	Yes
Fakir Mohan University	2,00,000	10	1PCs	NA	NA
North Orissa University	3,00,000	12	1PC	NA	NA
Orissa University of Agri. & Tech	36,00,000	21	10 PCs	Yes	Yes
Sambalpur University	43,00,000	17	10PCs	Yes	Yes
Shri Jagarnath Sanskrit University	2,00,000	11	1PCs	NA	NA
Utkal University of Culture	50,000	2	Nil	NA	NA
Utkal University	75,00,000	52	10 PCs	Yes	Yes
B.J.B. (Auto) College	2,00,000	14	1PC	Yes	NA
Bhadrak (Auto) College	30,000	8	Nil	NA	NA
Dhenkanal (Auto) College	25,000	5	Nil	NA	NA
F..M., (Auto) College	50,000	9	Nil	NA	NA
G.M. (Auto) College	50,000	5	1PC	NA	NA
Govt. (Auto) College	34,000	3	Nil	NA	NA
Khalikote (Auto) College	1,00,000	12	1PC	Yes	NA
M.P.C. (Auto) College	75,000	7	Nil	NA	NA
N.C. (Auto) College	1,00,000	15	1PC	Yes	NA
R.D.Womens (Auto) College	1,00,000	6	1PC	Yes	NA
Ravenshaw (Auto) College	13,00,000	20	4PCs	Yes	Yes
S.C.S (Auto) College	12,00,000	16	4PCs	Yes	NA

terms of number and percentages, but it is only in urban areas. It could be said that in spite of constitutional obligations, legal provisions, central and state level policies and programmes affirmative action's the benefits of higher education are availed of by a small number of SC/ST communities only.

The type of higher institution shows during 1998/99 that the educational institutions, student enrolment, numbers of scholars and teachers available in Orissa are very poor. The numbers of general colleges are 1367 with 555000 students and having 23003 teachers in all and there are only 171476 students in 591 institutions having 8934 teachers in all. The teacher student ratio is 1:19 in our higher education system, which is much less than the national average. The distribution of student enrolment as per their level of education in higher academic system during 1996/97 to 1999/00 gives the percentages of SC/ST students in higher-level education have been increasing every year during last five years. But in PG level, there are little differences during 1998/99 (20.69%) and 1999/00(20.05%), in professional level more student enrolled during 1999/2000 (32.5%) than others. In the mentioned four levels of education non-SC/ST percentages of enrolment is lesser and lesser during 1996/97 to 2000/01, perhaps this is for more awareness and attention of education department government of Orissa and middle class people, but it reveals SC/ST enrolment is not so increased as non-SC/ST in all the five years except 2000/01. During the year when a comparison has made it shows that in Ph.D SC/ST-(79) 0.41% and non-SC/ST-(451) 0.27%, in professional level SC/ST-(1087) 5.58% where as non-SC/ST (4193) is only 2.46%. The year wise distribution of only SC/ST shows that in all levels of education the percentages are increasing better except professional levels (23.85%) during 1999/00. Thus, credit goes to the governmental actions for their overall development and different educational facilities provided time to time during the year. All this reveals that in higher level there are some developments. This may be due to government's role played for the same or people are more aware about higher educational benefits or student may not having employment during there educational period hoping for it.

Status of the higher academic library system shows that the libraries are facing development challenges in many angles: like financial, collection building, man power development, separate building for libraries and no electronics infrastructure for library automation etc. There is no separate budget for the libraries. Budgetary provision available from state government, UGC and ICSSR through grants, aid etc., sometimes special grant, and donation are also received for library infrastructure. Thus. Therefore, Orissa faces the challenges of actually preparing a perspective plan from scratch i.e., from collection development to networking through IT solutions, and will need a complete blueprint to develop higher academic libraries during the coming centuries.

4.5 Analysis and Findings of Primary Data

Primary data for the present study was collected largely through questionnaire and at times also through personal interviews. In order to find out the information use pattern among the students faculties and researchers in autonomous colleges and university environment, the survey method has been followed for the collection of data required. A questionnaire was designed keeping in view the objectives and hypothesis of the study and it was distributed randomly to the student faculties and researchers in the various autonomous colleges and universities of Orissa. The questionnaire was distributed among 480 students/ researchers/faculties of 8 universities and 12 autonomous colleges of Orissa, out of which 324 only collected and 7 questionnaire are rejected and remaining 324 questionnaire are treated as primary data for the entire research work. The questionnaire were distributed in various institutions by hand and post, to individual institutions in all over Orissa specially Scheduled Tribes and Scheduled Castes students/researchers and faculties particularly and there is information famine to these people. These groups are listed below in order to discuss elaborately about each group.

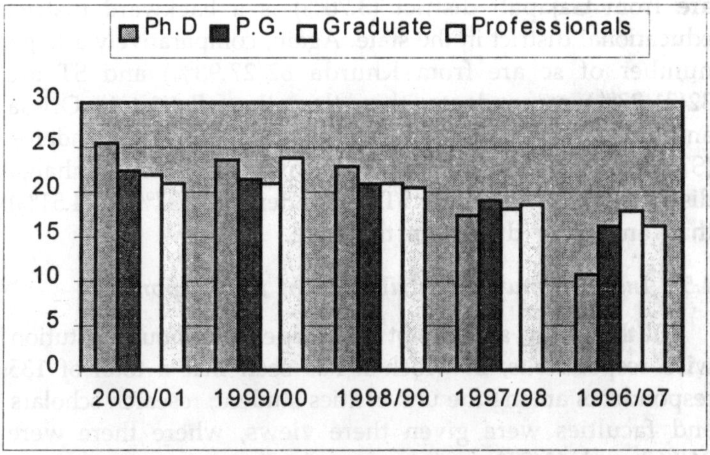

Fig. 4.5: Yearwise Distribution of SC/ST Percentage During 1996/97-2000/01

4.5.1 District Wise Academic Institution Under Study

The present study was conducted in the academic institutions of the 11 districts of Orissa, mostly covering with SC/ST - students, researchers and faculties. Among the district, Khurda district (state capital) has three universities and two autonomous colleges to its credit. All total 20 numbers of institutions are taken for the study, out of which equal numbers of questionnaire were distributed among SC/ST students/researchers and faculties of eight universities and twelve autos. Colleges. Collection of data was made as per the following tables.

The above table shows the district wise distribution and collection of data from various institutions in Orissa. The study population consists of specially the SC/ST students, researchers and faculties in various autonomous colleges and universities of Orissa; A sample study was conducted having total collected data of 324 respondents. Among 324 respondents it is observed that a highest majority of the respondents are from Khurda district (29.01%), followed by Puri district (10.49%), it is only due to more institute taken from Khurda (3+2) which is also the capital city (Bhubaneswar is coming under the district of Khurda) of the state and the same time a poor number of respondents are from Gajapati district (3.70%) is a backward district educational district in the state. Again, comparatively a large number of sc are from Khurda 62(27.93%) and ST are 32(31.37%) respondents, than the other district in Orissa and the least (SC) are from Gajapati(1.35%) & no respondents (ST) from Denkanal. Similarly, Korda and Mayurabhanja districts are having more ST respondents (31.37% & 24.51%) than any other district in the state.

4.5.2 Institutionwise Distribution of the Respondents

In this study, an attempt was made to find out institution wise respondents, in which it has seen that a total of 135 respondents among the universities student, research scholars and faculties were given there views, where there were 94(SC) and 41(ST).

Table 4.13, indicates the University wise respondent of Orissa, and 8 universities were taken for the study. Among all the 8 universities the researcher received only 135 questionnaire s of the respondents both from SC and ST where SC candidates are more than ST and also come to find that highest number of SC's are from Sri Jagannath Sanskrit University (17.02%), lowest number in North Orissa University at Takatpur (5.32%), Similarly, highest ST are in North Orissa University at Takatpur (29.27%) and only 1 person from Utkal University of Culture (2.44%), ranking to the same OUAT and Utkal University are coming under rank 1 (14.81%) position among the SC/ST respondents among the 8 universities at the same time, Sombalpur University and Utkal university of Culture are having least respondents (rank-5) among all.

It is found from the above table that out of 189 respondents, only 128 SC and 61 ST are in the 12 autonomous colleges. Ravenshaw College, B.J.B College, N.C. College and Ramadevi Womens Colleges are having 10% above respondents of SC & ST than the other colleges. The number of SC (128) are more than double of ST(61) in this institutions. ST is minimum compared to SC in MPC College (21.31%), SKGC College (14.75%), Ramadevi Women's College (11.48%), BJB college (14.75%), whereas it is maximum in MPC College (21.31%), Baripada.

It is found from the above Table 4.15, that out of total respondents of SC/ST, student researchers and faculties, only 256 are students, 44 researchers and 24 respondents are fron faculties in 20 different academic institutions. Students' percentages are more than other two, OUAT and Utkal Universities have more number of students than the other institutions. There is no SC or ST teachers in Sri Jagannath Sanskrit University, Puri and Utkal University of Culture, Bhubaneswar. There is not much SC & ST in Sambalpur University although it was one of the oldest university of Orissa. The number of SC is more than double of ST in the universities. ST is minimum compared to SC in Utkal university of Culture where as it is maximum in North Orissa University, Baripada. There is no SC or ST teachers in Sri Jagannath Sanskrit University, Puri and Utkal University of Culture, Bhubaneswar. There is not much SC & ST in Sambalpur University although it was one of the oldest university of Orissa.

4.6 Analysis of Personal Data of the Respondents

The very idea of human resources development establishes a permanent link between education and profession. The role of education is to place the right person at the right place. The relevance of education and different level of profession further increase the purpose of the present study among the less advantaged communities. Here, the present study is related to the personal data of the respondents, include-profession, sex, category, level of education and specialization etc.

Table 4.16, indicates the profession wise distribution of questionnaire to all the respondents in both types of the institutes, where I received from 256 students, 44 researchers and 24 faculties. The above table also shows that in student categories 60.55% are from colleges and 39.45 % are from universities, in researchers there are only 52.27 % from colleges and 47.72 % from universities and faculties are less in colleges than universities, i.e. in all 58.33% from colleges and 41.67% from universities. It is found that there are less percentage of SC/ST in universities then colleges

Table 4.12
District Wise Institution Taken for the Study
[See also Fig. 4.12]

District	*No. of Univ.*	*No. of Auto College*	*Total Insti. Taken*	*Total Distributed*	*Quest Collected SC*	*%*	*Quest Collected SC*	*%*	*Total Collected (%)*
Balascre	1	1	2	50	22	9.91	5	4.90	27 (8.33)
Bhadrak	-	1	1	20	10	4.50	5	4.90	15(4.63)
Cuttack	-	1	1	20	14	6.31	6	5.88	20(6.17)
Dhenkanal	-	1	1	20	14	6.31	0	0.00	14(4.32)
Gajapati	-	1	1	20	3	1.35	9	8.82	12(3.70)
Ganjam	1	1	2	50	25	11.26	6	5.88	31(9.57)
Jajpur	-	1	1	20	16	7.21	4	3.92	20(6.17)
Khurda	3	2	5	130	62	27.93	32	31.37	94(29.01)
Maurabhanja	1	1	2	50	7	3.15	25	24.51	32(9.88)
Puri	1	1	2	50	28	12.61	6	5.88	34(10.49)
Sambalpur	1	1	2	50	21	9.46	4	3.92	25(7.72)
Total	8	12	20	480	222	100	102	100	324

Table 4.13
University Wise Respondents
[See also Fig. 4.13]

Universities of Orissa	*SC*	*%*	*ST*	*%*	*Total*	*%*	*Rank*
1. Berhampur University, Bhanjavihar, Berhampur	13	13.83	4	9.76	17	12.59	3
2. Fakir Mohan University, Byasavihar, Balasore	12	12.77	3	7.32	15	11.11	4
3. North Orissa University, Takatpur, Baripada	5	5.32	12	29.27	17	12.59	3
4. Orissa University of Agri. & Tech., Bhubaneswar	14	14.89	6	14.63	20	14.81	1
5. Sombalpur University, Jyotivihar, Sambalpur	10	10.64	4	9.76	14	10.37	5
6. Sri Jagannath Sanskrit University, Puri	16	17.02	2	4.88	18	13.33	2
7. Utkal University of Culture, Bhubaneswar	13	13.83	1	2.44	14	10.37	5
8. Utkal University, Vanivihar, Bhubaneswar	11	11.70	9	21.95	20	14.81	1
Total	94	100.00	41	100.00	135	100.00	

Table 4.14
Autonomous Colleges Wise Respondents
[See also Fig. 4.14]

	Name of the Auto.Colleges	*SC*	%	*ST*	%	*Total*	%	*Rank*
1	B J.B. College, Bhubaneswar	11	8.59	9	14.75	20	10.58	1
2	Bhadrak Govt. College, Bhadrak	10	7.81	5	8.20	15	7.94	3
3	Dhenkanal College, Dhenkanal	14	10.94	-	#	14	7.41	4
4	F.M. College, Balasore	10	7.81	2	3.28	12	6.35	5
5	G.M. College, Sambalpur	11	8.59	-	#	11	5.82	6
6	Khalikot College, Berhampur	12	9.38	2	3.28	14	7.41	4
7	M.P.C. College, Baripada	2	1.56	13	21.31	15	7.94	3
8	N.C. College,Jajpur	16	12.50	4	6.56	20	10.58	1
9	R.D Womens College, Bhubaneswar	13	10.16	7	11.48	20	10.58	1
10	Raveshaw College, Cuttack	14	10.94	6	9.84	20	10.58	1
11	S.C.S. College, Puri	12	9.38	4	6.56	16	8.47	2
12	S.K.G.C. College, Paralakhemundi	3	2.34	9	14.75	12	6.35	5
	Total	128	100	61	100	189	100	

where are generally SC/ST do not want to go far distance for education.

The above table clearly indicates that the female percentages (75.65%) of SC population is much higher than the male (63.64%), where as male ST percentages (35.36%) are more than ST female (24.35%). This is due to more perception of SC women for higher education. It shows that in our state ST women are less aware for education than SC.

It follows from the above table that from the study population 324 respondents, 67.90% are from SC and 32.10 % from ST, which are half of the SC in both the institutes of Orissa taken for the study.

Table 30, indicates the educational levels of the respondents. It is seen that a majority of the respondents are from sc, where 81.52 % are PG/M.Phil/PhD, 58.29% are from +3/Degree and 87.88% are other levels of respondents. But at the same time it is seen that in +3 levels the ST percent is very closer to SC (41.71%) and very poor percentage in higher level.

The above table shows the specialization wise distribution of respondents and their percentages. Here we come to the conclusion that more STs (61.54%) are preferring arts topic then any other subject and they are nil in medical related subject, it is due to their ignorance of different field and its impotence to the current situation. Mostly, STs prefer other topics, which are easy to them in economically and socially. It also shows that sc respondents are generally preferred art, science and commerce to read. SC respondents are having 5.91% in engineering whereas ST is 4.81%, which are slightly, less than SC. SC prefer other subject like science (20.45%), commerce (12.73%) more and less in medical (1.36%), on the other hand ST's are not interested in medical and lowest in commerce (2.88%).

4.7 Academic and Social Need of the Respondents

This part of the study is divided into two i.e. educational need as well as social needs of the respondents; include physical development, intelligence, perception, language,

Table 4.15: Categorise Respondents: STU, RES & FAC

	Universities of Orissa	*STU*	%	*RES.*	%	*FAC.*	%
1	Berhampur University, Bhanjavihar, Berhanıpur	12	4.69	3	6.82	2	8.33
2	Fakir Mohan University, Byasavihar, Balasore	11	4.30	3	6.82	1	4.17
3	North Orissa University, Takatpur, Baripada	14	5.47	-	#	3	12.50
4	Orissa University of Agri. & Tech., Bhubaneswar	17	6.64	-	#	3	12.50
5	Sombalpur University, Jyotivihar, Sambalpur	10	3.91	2	4.55	2	8.33
6	Sri Jagannath Sanskrit University, Puri	15	5.86	3	6.82	-	#
7	Utkal University of Culture, Bhubaneswar	9	3.52	5	11.36	-	#
8	Utkal University, Vanivihar, Bhubaneswar	13	5.08	5	11.36	2	8.33
9	B.J.B. College, Bhubaneswar	17	6.64	-	#	3	12.50
10	Bhadrak Govt. College, Bhadrak	12	4.69	2	4.55	1	4.17
11	Dhenkanal College, Dhenkanal	14	5.47	-	#	-	#
12	F.M. College, Balasore	9	3.52	3	6.82	-	#
13	G.M. College, Sambalpur	7	2.73	2	4.55	2	8.33
14	Khalikot College, Berhampur	10	3.91	3	6.82	1	4.17
15	M.P.C. College, Baripada	13	5.08	1	2.27	1	4.17
16	N.C. College,Jajpur	18	7.03	2	4.55	-	#
17	Ramadevi Womens College, Bhubaneswa	20	7.81	-	#	-	#
18	Raveshaw College, Cuttack	11	4.30	6	13.64	3	12.50
19	S.C.S. College, Puri	12	4.69	4	9.09	-	#
20	S.K.G.C. College, Paralakhemundi	12	4.69	-	#	-	#
	Total	256	100	44	100	24	100

Table 4.16: Profession Wise Distribution

Institutions	*Student*	*%*	*Res.*	*%*	*Faculties*	*%*	*Total*	*%*
Colleges (12)	155	60.55	23	52.27	11	45.83	189	58.33
Universities (8)	101	39.45	21	47.73	13	54.17	135	41.67
Total	256	100	44	100	24	100	324	100

Table 4.17: Sex Wise Distribution

Category	*Male*	*%*	*Female*	*%*
Scheduled Caste	133	63.636	87	75.652
Scheduled Tribe	76	36.364	28	24.348
Total	209	100	115	100

Table 4.18: Categorise Distribution of Colleges and Universities

	College	*%*	*Universities*	*%*	*Total*	*%*
SC	126	66.67	94	69.63	220	67.90
ST	63	33.33	41	30.37	104	32.10
	189	100%	135	100%	324	100%

Table 4.19: Education Level Wise Distribution

	+3 Level /Degree/Dep.	*Percent*	*PG/MPhil/ PhD*	*Percent*	*Other*	*Percent*
SC	116	58.29	75	81.52	29	87.88
ST	83	41.71	17	18.48	4	12.12
Total	199	100%	92	100%	33	100%

Table 4.20
Specialization of Respondents

Specialisation	*Scheduled Caste*	*Percentage*	*Scheduled Tribe*	*Percentage*	*Total*
Art	102	46.36	64	61.54	166
Science	45	20.45	12	11.54	57
Commerce	28	12.73	3	2.88	31
Engineering	13	5.91	5	4.81	18
Medical	3	1.36	Nil	####	3
Management	22	10.00	4	3.85	26
Other	7	3.18	16	15.38	23
Total	220	100	104	100	324

socio-emotional development, gender role development, moral development, and developmental issues relating to education of the respondents, which are given in the following tables:

Table 4.21
Information Needs on Special Interest

Sl. No.	*Areas of Interest*	*No. of Responses*	*Percentages*	*Rank*
1.	Artistic	53	16.36	4
2.	Scientific	34	10.49	5
3.	Plants & Animals	65	20.06	2
4.	Protective	57	17.59	3
5.	Mechanical	11	3.40	7
6.	Industrial	9	2.78	8
7.	Government	17	5.25	6
8.	Business Detail	5	1.54	9
9.	Selling	2	0.62	11
10.	Accommodating	2	0.62	11
11.	Humanitarian	66	20.37	1
12.	Leading-Influencing	3	0.93	10

Table-4.21, shows the information needs on special interest of SC/ST, both are more concerned with plants, animals(20.06%) and social/humanitarian(20.37%) and less need on selling, accommodation and leading etc. The ranks among the needs are highest in humanitarian (1), plant/ animal (2).

Reading interest among SC/ST respondents is shown in Table 4.22. It is found that SC 's are interested more in textbooks (25.45%), class notes (18.18%) and newspaper (16.82%) and they have less interested in government publications (0.45%), non-fictions (0.91%). ST's are less interested in govt. publications, fictions, indexing/abstracting and non-fictions (0.96%), havinf more interested in text books (32.69%), class notes (26.92%).

Table 4.22
Reading Interest Among Respondents categorywise

Sources	*SC*	*%*	*ST*	*%*
Text Book	56	25.45	34	32.69
Popular Magazine	28	12.73	12	11.54
Newspaper	37	16.82	18	17.31
Class Note	40	18.18	28	26.92
Reference Book	35	15.91	10	9.62
Abstract/Index	8	3.64	Nil	#
Fiction	11	5.00	Nil	#
Non-Fiction	2	0.91	1	0.96
Govt. Publications	1	0.45	Nil	#
Other Sources	2	0.91	1	0.96
	220	100.00	104.00	100.00

Table 4.23
Use of Other Organization/People for Information Needs Other than Library

Sources	*Frequently*	*Percent-ages*	*Occasio-nally*	*Percent-ages*
Govt. Dept./Agencies	57	7.86	267	10.51
Local Council Office	9	1.24	215	8.46
Post Office	13	1.79	211	8.31
Public Library	92	12.69	132	5.20
Academic Libraries	278	38.34	46	1.81
Public Relation Office	34	4.69	290	11.42
Chambers of CommercE	6	0.83	318	12.52
Profes./Trade Asso.	19	2.62	305	12.01
Professional People	45	6.21	279	10.98
Family & Friends	104	14.34	220	8.66
Any Other	67	9.24	257	10.12
	724		2540	

When they were asked about the sources where did they collect information other than their libraries, majority of them replied that frequently they could use family friends, academic libraries government departments, professional peoples, public libraries and any other sources. Maximum respondents stated that they could visit occasionally to the chambers of commerce, professional trade associations, public relation offices and government departments etc.

Table 4.24

Use of Different Media at Home

	Scheduled Castes			*Scheduled Tribes*		
Media of Information	*1st*	*2nd*	*3rd*	*1st*	*2nd*	*3rd*
Newspaper	113	86	20	55	44	6
Television	7	22	35	2	29	35
Radio	76	81	51	35	18	39
Magazine	21	27	55	8	15	22
Telephone	-	-	7	-	-	-
Computer/Internet	1	4	48	-	1	1
Any Other	2	3	4	4	12	1
Total	220	223	220	104	119	104

Table-4.24, shows use of information sources within their environment among SC/ST community. The above table shows that newspaper, radio and magazines are more useful to them than any other sources; they rarely prefer to use TV and computer. Again, although SC population uses little telephone, it is nil in case of ST, ST's are using half of the SCs. Now a days TV and radio play a significant role in their development.

Respondents were asked to indicate what sources of news were important for their family, including television, radio, newspapers, library, friends, family, neighbors, and others, and the relative importance of those information channels.

Table 4.25

Sources of Information of family

Sources of Information	No. of Respondents	Percentages
1. Radio	86	26.54
2. TV	24	7.41
3. Newspaper	49	15.12
4. Library (Any)	5	1.54
6. Friends	72	22.22
7. Neighbors	81	25.00
8. Others	7	2.16

Most respondents mentioned all sources with other family members as the highest ranked source of news, followed by neighbors, television, and newspaper. This finding reflects the respondents view of a news event — those events that are directly related to family life and children's activities at neighbor. The importance placed on family and neighbors reflects a focus on real life concerns with news as a real life interaction channel. Television, radio, and newspapers were ranked less highly, as were friends and neighbors. Few participants had good knowledge of their environment at libraries. Only approximately 25% of SC participants had knowledge of the library services available to them. Only 6 % of ST participants felt that other family and neighbor and radio was important for them

Table 4.26

If Public Access to Computer is widely Available

Where to keep these	Respondents	Percentage
Public Libraries	68	20.99
Post Offices	161	49.69
Shopping Center	11	3.40
Town Halls	9	2.78
STD/ISD/PCO Booths	32	9.88
Other Public Places	43	13.27

When they were asked about if public access to computer is widely available where to keep these majority of them responded to keep in post office (49.69%), public libraries (20.99%) other public places (13.27%), STD/ISD booths (9.88%) again they have given less impotence to town halls (2.78%) and shopping center (3.40%).

4.8 Information Needs and Seeking Behaviour of Respondents

Information need and information seeking behavior, two of the most important research areas of the user studies, are two complementary concepts, which are affected by many factors. Research results in these areas of user studies indicate that the type of information need and information seeking behavior of respondents are dependent on their field of research, and vary from one discipline to another. Understanding such behavior help us to design services and products, which would transmit the required information most effectively. Such different needs in turn may necessitate offering services (e.g. user education) in academic libraries depending on the academic discipline users come from. This study includes information needs of the students, research scholars and faculties in the concerned academic libraries of Orissa.

Table 4.27

Types of Information Provided in the Libraries

	Universities	*Auto. Colleges*	*Total*	*Percentages*
Sociological	213	101	314	21.73
Economical	136	91	227	15.71
Political	137	75	212	14.67
Educational	220	104	324	22.42
Technical	138	87	225	15.57
Any Other	57	88	143	9.90

From the above Table 4.27, it is observed that educational

and sociological information are more used by the SC and ST communities than any other information in the field of academic institutions. Where as 22.42% of information's are related to educational, 21.73% are sociological and 15.71% are economical, among all the six categories of information given in the above table, which shows that they are less interested to technological information.

Table 4.28

Types of Document Provided in the Libraries

	Universities	*Auto. Colleges*	*Total*	*Percentages*
General	161	91	252	22.34
Special	146	75	221	19.59
Commercial	105	55	160	14.18
Entertainment	94	67	161	14.27
R&D	85	39	124	10.99
I &T	98	30	128	11.35
Other	54	28	82	7.27

Table 4.28, shows that libraries in higher education are much oriented with general types of document (22.34%) and other major collections are course wise. It provides less impotence on R&D and other technological documents. Where it shows that special types (19.59%), commercial (14.18%)and entertainment (14.27%) type of documents are in normal collection.

The most important function of the libraries are to provide efficient services to the users. Users awareness about the services provided by the library is essential for effective use of its collection. Respondents were asked on different services offered in their institute to give their importance. Information collected in this regard has been analyses and presented in the following table.

Table 4.29
Service Offered in the Libraries

	Universities	*Percentages*	*Auto. Colleges*	*Percentages*
Text Books	104	77.04	167	88.36
References Books	58	42.96	61	32.28
Journals/Magazines	23	17.04	15	7.94
Trans./Repro.	43	31.85	24	12.70
News Clipping	9	6.67	2	1.06
Bibliographic	3	2.22	-	######
Index/Abstract	2	1.48	-	######
CAS/SDI	8	5.93	-	######
CD-ROM/Online	13	9.63	1	0.53
Internet Surfing	16	11.85	5	2.65
Inter Library Loan	-	######	-	######
	135	100.00	189	100.00

The details furnished in Table 4.29, show that the libraries in academic environment offered text book circulation more than journals and very less services to interlibrary loan (nil), index/abstracting (1.48%), bibliographic (2.22%), CAS/SDI (5.93%-only in higher institute) services. In comparison to colleges, universities provide less services in text books (77.04%) and more in references (42.96%), journals (42.96%), trans/reprographic (31.85%), news clipping (6.67%), CD-ROM/ON-LINE (9.63%), internet surfing services (11.85%). On the other hand colleges are not well equipped to give reader services like inter library loan, CAS/SDI, CD-ROM/ONLINE, indexing/abstracting and bibliographic services in the state.

Table 4.30

Frequency of Visit to the Library

S.l. No.	Frequency of Visit	No. of Response	Percentages
1	Daily	37	11.42
2	Weekly	83	25.62
3	Quarterly	57	17.59
4	Monthly	39	12.04
5	Occasionally	108	33.33

Among the respondents when they were asked about the frequency of their library visits to the institutions' libraries, majority of them stated that they were not daily visiting the libraries (11.42%), weekly (25.62%) and occasionally (33.33%).

The above table shows that 21.14% SC/ST visit the library for studying among the nine proposes given, out of which 22.48% are students, 30.56% research scholars and no faculties are visiting for study, 1.54% to read newspaper, 15.20% for photocopying, 26.01% for issued and return, 10.10% for references, 5.70% for competitive examination, 8.31% for preparing class note and 3.33% for any other purposes. More percentages of faculties are visiting for internet/database searching to the libraries. Thus the visit to library and its use indicates that most of the users consult the library for course materials its issue and return.

Table 4.32

Use of Information Sources in the Library

	Student	Researcher	Faculties	Total	%
Text Book	245	32	16	293	30.78
Popular Magazine	101	23	15	139	14.60
Newspaper	56	18	-	74	7.77
Class Note	189	11	2	202	21.22
Reference Book	129	29	5	163	17.12
Abstract/Index	21	16	-	37	3.89
Fiction	5	-	-	5	0.53
Non-Fiction	17	-	-	17	1.79
Others	15	2	5	22	2.31

On the above table respondents are giving higher priority to the textbook (30.78%) and class note (21.22%) and sometime they like to go through reference books (17.12%), popular magazine (14.60%) etc, they are not likely giving more impotence to fiction (0.53%), non-fiction (1.79%) and other books (2.31%), than their study materials. Here faculties are not interested to go through abstracting fiction non-fiction at all and researchers are also not interested to read fiction and non-fiction but students are likely to refer these little more.

When satisfaction is concerned to their information (Table-4.33) what they gate most of the respondents suggested the information they gate easy to use (23.43%), easy to understand (22.13%) and relevant (20.00%), comprehensive (10.67%), but majority of then stated that it was not up to date (28.54%) and also not comprehensive (18.81%). Except these some respondents were neutral for giving response regarding accurate (31.53%), up to date (15.92%), comprehensive (17.77%) and it was easy to use (12.83%). Thus, this table shows a conflicts satisfaction on information what they gate from their libraries.

Table 4.33
Satisfaction with Information Obtained

Was the Information	*Yes*	%	*No*	%	*Neutral*	%
Easy to Understand	187	22.13	54	11.95	83	12.83
Relevant	169	20.00	78	17.26	77	11.90
Accurate	75	8.88	45	9.96	204	31.53
Up to Date	92	14.89	129	28.54	103	15.92
Comprehensive	124	10.67	85	18.81	115	17.77
Easy to Use	198	23.43	61	13.50	65	10.05

Table 4.31
Purpose of Visits

Purpose for	*Student*	%	*Researcher*	%	*Faculties*	%	*Total*	*Aver. %*
Studying	156	22.48	22	30.56	-	-	178	21.14
Newspaper Reading	12	1.73	1	1.39	-	-	13	1.54
Photocopying	109	15.71	6	8.33	13	27.08	128	15.20
Search Internet/ Databases	3	0.43	18	25.00	19	39.58	40	4.75
Borrow & Return Books/J.	197	28.39	13	18.06	9	18.75	219	26.01
Reference	75	10.81	10	13.89	-	-	85	10.10
Pass Time	33	4.76	-	-	-	-	33	3.92
Prepare Class Notes	63	9.08	-	-	7	14.58	70	8.31
Competitive Examination	46	6.63	2	2.78	-	-	48	5.70
Any Other Purpose	2		11		15		28	3.33

Table 4.34
Information Needs & Users Satisfaction with the Library Service

	Yes	*%*	*No*	*%*	*Neutral*	*%*
Present Services Offered	75	9.59	82	45.81	167	16.99
More Qualified Staff Required	98	12.53	35	19.55	191	19.43
More Fund for Collection Dev.	109	13.94	17	9.50	198	20.14
Up-to-date Collection Needed	167	21.36	17	9.50	140	14.24
More Mechanical Aids Required	205	26.21	9	5.03	110	11.19
Users Education Programme	128	16.37	19	10.61	177	18.01
		100.00		100.00		100.00

When it was asked about to give their suggestion regarding satisfaction with the library services in their institutions they replied that they were satisfied with present service (9.595), staff (12.53%), collection (13.94%) etc. they have responded maximum on mechanical aid required (26.21%), more fund (26.21%) and collection development (21.36%). Some of the respondents are also not satisfied with present service (45.81%) and more staff requirement (5.03%) but maximum of respondents were neutral on all the category of questions asked

4.9 Summaries and Finding of the Praimary Data

Primary data for the present study was collected largely through questionnaire and at times also through personal interviews. In order to find out the information use pattern among the student's faculties and researchers in autonomous colleges and universities of Orissa, 11 districts are taken to our study, the survey method has been followed for the collection of data required. Among the districts, Khurda district (state capital) has three universities and two autonomous colleges to its credit. All total 20 numbers of institutions are taken for the study, out of which equal numbers of questionnaire were distributed among SC/ST students/ researchers and faculties of eight universities and twelve autonomous colleges. Out of which a total numbers of 324 respondents are found fit for analysis as primary findings.

It is observed that a highest majority of the respondents are from Khurda district (29.01%), followed by Puri district (10.49%), it is only due to more institute taken from Khurda (5) which is mostly based on urban based with state capital of the state and at the same time a poor number of respondents are received from Gajapati district (3.70%), which is a backward district in the state. Again, comparatively a large number of SC are from Khurda 62 (27.93%) and ST are from Baripada 32 (31.37%), the least (SC) are from Gajapati (1.35%) & ST from Denkanal. Similarly, Khurda and Mayurabhanja districts are having more ST respondents (31.37% & 24.51%) than any other district in the state. Among all the 8 Universities in Orissa the researcher received only 135 complete questionnaires from SC's and ST's, where SC candidates are more than ST and also come to find that highest number of SC's are from Sri Jagarnath Sanskrit University (17.02%), lowest number in North Orissa University at Takatpur (5.32%), Similarly, highest ST are in North Orissa University at Takatpur (29.27%) and only 1 person from Utkal University of Culture(2.44%), ranking to the same OUAT and Utkal University are coming under rank 1(14.81%) position among the SC/ST respondents among the 8 universities at the same time, Sambalpur University and Utkal university of Culture are having least respondents (rank-5) among all. Among colleges, out of 189 respondents, only 128 SC's and 61 ST's are in the 12 autonomous colleges. Ravenshaw College, B.J.B College, N.C. College and Ramadevi Womens Colleges are having 10% above respondents of SC & ST than the other colleges. The number of SC (128) is more than double of ST (61) in these institutions. ST's are minimum in compared to SC's in MPC College (21.31%), SKGC College (14.75%), Ramadevi Womens College (11.48%), BJB college (14.75%), where as it is maximum in MPC College (21.31%), Baripada.

The very idea of human resources development establishes a permanent link between education and profession. The role of education is to place the right person at the right place. The relevance of education and different level of profession further increase the purpose of the present study among the less advantaged communities. Here, the present study is related to the personal data of the respondents, include—profession, sex, category, level of education and specialization etc., in student categories 60.55% are from colleges and 39.45 % are from universities, in researchers there are only 52.27 % from colleges and 47.72 % from universities and faculties are less in colleges than universities. i.e. in all 58.33% from colleges and 41.67% from universities. It is found that there are less percentage of SC/ST in universities then colleges where are generally SC/ST do not want to go far distance for education. The female percentages (75.65%) of SC population is much higher than the male (63.64%), where as male ST percentages (35.36%) are more than ST female (24.35%). This is due to more perception of SC women for higher education. It shows that in our state ST women are less aware for education than SC. Again, out of total respondents, 67.90% are from SC and 32.10 % from ST, which are half of the SC in both the institutes of Orissa taken for the study. The educational levels of the respondents indicate that 81.52 % are PG/M.Phil/PhD, 58.29% are from +3 /Degree and 87.88% are other levels of respondents. But at the same time it is seen that in +3 levels the ST percent is very closer to SC (41.71%) and very poor percentage in higher level.

Regarding the finding of educational need and social needs of the respondents it shows that information needs on special interest of SC/ST, both are more concerned with plants, animals (20.06%) and social/humanitarian (20.37%) ground than, selling, accommodation and leading etc. On reading interests, SC 's are more interested in textbooks (25.45%), class notes (18.18%) and newspaper (16.82%) and they have less interested in government publications (0.45%), non-fictions (0.91%). ST's are less interested in govt. publications, fictions, indexing/abstracting and non-fictions (0.96%), having more interested in text books (32.69%), class notes (26.92%). When they were asked about the sources where they collect information other than their libraries, majority of them replied that frequently they use family friends, academic libraries, government depts., professional peoples, public libraries and any other sources. When they were asked about if public access to computer network is widely available where to keep these, majority of them responded to keep in post office (49.69%), public libraries (20.99%).

Finding about their information need and seeking behavior shows educational and sociological information are more used by the SC and ST communities than any other information in the field of academic institutions. Where as 22.42% of information's are related to educational, 21.73% are sociological and 15.71% are economical. Which shows that they are less interested to technological information. Libraries in higher education are much oriented with general types of document (22.34%) and other major collections are course wise. It provides less impotence on R&D and other technological documents. The most important function of the libraries are to provide efficient and effective use of its collection. Respondents were asked on different services offered in their institute to give their importance, findings of this shows that the libraries in academic environment offered text book circulation more than journals and very less services to interlibrary loan (Nil), index/abstracting (1.48%), bibliographic(2.22%), CAS/SDI (5.93%) services. In comparison to colleges, universities provide fewer services in text books (77.04%) and more in references (42.96%),

On the other hand colleges are not well equipped to give reader services like inter library loan, CAS/SDI, CD-ROM/ONLINE, indexing/abstracting and bibliographic services in the state. The finding from their library visits reveals that they are not daily visiting the libraries (11.42%), weekly (25.62%) and occasionally (33.33%). When satisfaction is concerned to their information what they gate, most of the respondents suggested in a manageable response towards their libraries, but majority of then said it is not up to date (28.54%), not comprehensive (18.81%) and some others are neutral on it. When it was asked about to give their suggestion regarding library services in their institutions they replied that for maximum mechanical aid (26.21%), more fund (26.21%) and collection development required (21.36%). Some of them are also not satisfied with the present service (45.81%) and responded for more staff requirement (5.03%) but maximum of respondents are neutral on all the category of questions asked.

5

Academic Libraries Network Model

Over the last decades the libraries have witnessed impact of information technology that has been affecting the structure and functions of the entire library system to a great extent. In addition to print resources, libraries are facing the challenges of increased resources in electronic media; customers are preferences to use electronics media, changing document formats and storage complexities. Moreover, the problems of space, standardization, professional development of the staff, challenges posed by new technologies, drastic cuts in the library budgets have aggravated problem of the present day librarianship. However, the solution to the problems of information explosion, ever changing needs of users, increasing amount required for subscription to same number of periodicals, shrinking library budget, and devaluation of rupee and its impact on the library acquisitions can best overcome upon certain level by the following means:

- Use of computer and communication networks for resource sharing;
- Use of national and international databases through communications networks.
- Access to e-resources in the Internet and full text CD ROM based systems.
- For better sharing and speedy delivery of documents.
- Reducing the operational cost of libraries

To cope with the above factors, libraries should accept

cooperative services; cooperation is the key concept of resources sharing. Once, Allen Kant has suggested "the success and survival of libraries will depend on how much and to what extent libraries cooperate with each other in future". Thus, cooperation among libraries in all respects has become essential for their own sake and survival. Initially library cooperation was limited to interlibrary loan, later extended to cooperative cataloguing and centralized cataloguing or even modern concept of shared cataloguing. Now, sharing of resources is an important issue to cope with present crisis. Therefore, networking is a must for every library. It is the electronic transfer of information between two or more points irrespective of distance. It implies automation, data communication and effective services among libraries.

Library networks have grown mostly during the last thirty years in different geographical environment in order to cater to the specific needs of the users. Several models have emerged that provided specific services in different region of the globe. Not all networks conform to the essential functions of library networks. However, the essential functions should include the promotion of resource sharing, creation of resource sharing tools like: Union Catalogues, rationalization of acquisition and maintenance of international standards for creation of records uniformly. Libraries should be able to join different types of networks depending upon the need and select a model, which conforms to its requirements as per Kaul, (1999).

In the developed countries resource-sharing networking was started long back. For instance the growth of networks in the United States can be traced from the mid of 1960. USA is the birthplace of library networking and by now libraries in each state is networked to local, regional and national network Library of Congress (LC) is one of the most important networked library in the world. It is important to note that the US Department of Education has been advocating a vigorous policy of promoting library networking; It offers networking grants, supports inter-library loan projects, automation and retro-conversion projects, resource sharing schemes, etc. besides providing regular federal grants annually to the public and academic libraries. Resource Sharing works in UK is also well established. The best example is Birmingham Library Co-operative Maintenance Project (BLCMP) in Birmingham, has 13 million bibliographic records of books, serials, music etc. in its database and its catalogues get a hit rate of above 90 per cent with more than 60 libraries comprising public libraries, college libraries, university libraries, national and special libraries. BLCMP has introduced EDI clearing house service in about 25 libraries. In Australia the resource sharing tools have grown from catalogue cards to national databases with the contributions of many older and larger libraries. In Australian Bibliographical Network, the national and central bibliographic databases are maintained and coordinated and maintained by a national agency. The Swedish Model for resource sharing is called the Consortium Model. This model is developed only for six major science and technology libraries in Sweden.

The developing countries like India are lagging behind in library co-operation. The reasons for the same are poor funding and the non-existence of the spirit of give and take or exchange is delaying the prospects of resource sharing programmes. The practice of resource sharing in the Republic of China (Taiwan) has been as limited in scale as has been in India. Greater efforts have been made in China for the development of documentary information resources because it was considered that these resources would work as China's knowledge reserve to promote the development of economy, science, technology and culture. The main effort was made on the rational distribution of the resources with the adoption of new technology. In some countries, at present resource sharing has become an important library programme such as in Thailand. The growth of library Networks in India can be traced to the initiatives made by NISSAT in establishing CALIBNET in 1986, DELNET in 1988 and other networks subsequently. University Grants Commission (UGC) established INFLIBNET in 1988. DELNET has emerged as the first operational library network in India with the support of the National Informatics Centre. No efforts have been made to network public libraries since it is becoming essential to provide networked information to the public. The progress of INFLIBNET has not been at the level as it was planned. There has not been much progress made by BONET and CALIBNET as library networks. They have prepared no union catalogues. MALIBNET has also not prepared union catalogue, which is a must for resource sharing. DELNET, on the other hand, has made considerable progress. More than one hundred and sixty six libraries have joined DELNET as institutional members. The database have increased from one in 1995 to 12 in 1997 with an average increase of about 160 percent in the size of data from 1996 to 1997 and 138 per cent from 1995 to 1996, quoted by Seth and Others (1995). There are various other resource sharing networks have been observed at local, regional, national in our country like—NICNET, INDONET, I-NET, SIRNET, ERNET etc. This has revolutionized not only the information needs of the users but also the role of the library professionals. Librarians are working towards maximum utilization of resources available and in this context we are thinking of networking all the academic libraries of Orissa. The purposes are-

- Facilitating users to have better access to library holdings or services.
- Positive effects on library budget in term of cost, or more services at lesser cost.
- Exchanging of resources for more utilization.
- Enable the users to be more aware regarding the resources not available in their own library.
- For speedy delivery of document to the needful users.
- For better cooperation among libraries.
- For computerized union database.
- For maximizing user satisfaction.
- Linking with other library system and services.

5.1. Factors Influencing for Networking Libraries in Orissa

The effectiveness of library services depends on the ability of librarians to provide quick delivery of documents requested by users either from physical stock or through networks.

The electronics resource sharing is often mentioned, as effective way for meeting the users demand. In order to make the most effective use of the library and information resources, the nature, extent interrelationship and location of the resources must be clearly identified by the users. Libraries of the autonomous colleges and universities of Orissa do not exist in an information vacuum, but are part of a growing information network. The major findings from the evaluation of the libraries under the present study envisage that the need for cooperation in view of the inadequate and uneven availability of library resources among these libraries can be possible, according to Seth & Others (1997). Findings of the present study also indicate that there is an interest in library cooperation among the academic libraries of Orissa. It is also felt that the development of a need-based centralized library information network system among the libraries of the autonomous colleges and universities of the state is essential for the overall development of the academic community of Orissa.

IT scenario of Orissa now is most appropriate to make the libraries fully automated for the development of education and different information needs. In this regard government of Orissa has adopted Orissa Information Technology Policies 1998 for development and growth, Public library Act 2001 and Right to Information Act 2002 are showing positive to this. There are also rapid development of information technology and electronic recourses in the country. Due to explosion of e-resources in every sphere of human activities and awareness about right o information the role of libraries and information centers are also growing day by day with multiple users demands. Therefore, more financial support needed to handle this situation. These can possible in the part of special libraries and private organizations/institutions only. The government of Orissa can't effort special budget for academic libraries, which suffers in multi-angels, needs self sufficient in there own sphere, therefore, there is a growing demand for cooperation among the libraries to promote resources sharing through network within the academic libraries of Orissa by collecting storing disseminating various information for the user.

A Conference on Information Technology (IT) was held at Utkal University, Vanivihar from December 21st to 23rd, 1998 for development of IT in Orissa and took an important decisions for formation of a IT society called 'Orissa Information Technology Society' (OITS) to facilitate growth and development of IT activity in the state. Various IT professionals of OSA suggested for helping some institutions to update their information base in IT. However, we consider the IT scenario of Orissa now is most appropriate to make the libraries fully automated for the development of education and different information needs. In this regard government of Orissa has adopted Orissa Information Technology Policies (ITP) in educational sector as stated by Parida (2000). We are also supporting for the following bases:

- One of the nicest things that have happened regarding IT training in Orissa is the establishment of `Orissa Centre for IBM Software' by IBM in collaboration with OSEDC. They offer a number of very structured courses with faculty training, instruction methodology as well as certification being decided by IBM. The original course materials are developed by IBM, IIT Kanpur, Lotus Corporation and Catapult Inc. and they shall update the same when needed. The infrastructure facilities including Library, Software, Internet access or Computer hardware and networking will be the same as any where else, and much better than whatever can be available elsewhere in Bhubaneswar in the field of IT.
- The programme of Government of Orissa to have IIIT by the help of IIIT at Hyderabad is being processed. This will need an investment of about ten times of what was needed for item above, but the attitude of Government of Orissa is very positive regarding the same. Government has planned to open honours in Computer Science in automated colleges at the B.Sc. level from the next session. These are Khallikot, BJB, Rama Devi, Ravenshaw, Rourkela, and GM College. The faculties are getting trained by OCAC. OCAC has been giving training to Computer users or

professionals from time to time as the need arises, depending on its available resources.

- Different Computer courses/trainings are also expanding in Orissa by Private computer farms. However almost all these institutions are trying to do the best they can, because of heavy competition, and are making their own arrangements to get experts as well as get their own people trained. Silicon, SATYAM, and INFOSYS, are high-end company of computer professionals with social awareness programmes, has now a branch at Bhubaneswar with export market mostly outside India. They are often running various programmes on computer learning for the students.
- At present there are different Internet Service Providers in Orissa working successfully like; NIC, OCAC, VSNL and STPI. STPI provides this facility to software entrepreneurs as well as research establishments. Infosys, Institute of Physics and RRL are using Internet connection from them. NIC (National Informatics Centre) at Bhubaneswar is primarily meant for Government organisations. However, it also extends service for Internet to Universities and educational and engineering establishments, as well as semi-Government organisations. It has the advantage of there being about sixteen-antenna spread all over Orissa, so that with local telephone linkage one can subscribe to Internet services at the district level. OCAC provides Internet service (shell account with TCP/IP) under ERNET. It also has some antennae outside Bhubaneswar, and hopes to expand its activities. Now VSNL in Bhubaneswar is going ahead of all in this regard by DOE and DOT of Government of India.

Thus, in order to permit the libraries to join together to share their library and information resources for the growing demands and requirements of the present time, government of Orissa and department of education should come forward.

5.2 Why Networking in Academic Libraries of Orissa

Orissa is a backward state among the other states of the county. It has various limitations for its overall developments. It can't effort special budget for higher academic libraries. The findings of the study suggested that that there are various problems with the educational institutions of Orissa (chapter-III &IV), which needs self sufficient in there own sphere, therefore, there is a growing demand for the followings:

- To create awareness among and draw cooperation from the authorities.
- To reduce or stagnate the budget provisions.
- To increase reliance or demands on information.
- To promote resources sharing among the academic libraries of Orissa by collecting storing disseminating various information for the user.
- To coordinate efforts for suitable collection development and reduce duplicating of document in the academic institutes of Orissa.
- To enable the user to acquire the needful material not available in there own library from other libraries.
- To establish a referral center for maintaining a central on-line union catalogue of the participating libraries.
- To develop a bibliographic databases of libraries collections of all the academic libraries for search and accessing
- To posses and maintain e-library or automated library for easy and fast communication of information.
- To evolve standards and uniform guidelines in techniques, methods, procedures, and services among coordinating libraries
- To establish communication linkages at national and international levels among the various libraries for exchange of information.
- To create a database of projects, specialists, consultants and institutes for providing online information services.

- To ensure effective bibliographic control of the literature in the areas.
- To maximize user satisfaction.
- To take initiative for promotion of academic research, development and innovation of information technology in educational field.

The other factors influencing networking the libraries of Orissa could be: For making the libraries to look at alternative ways of improving and extending library resources, For combating existing barriers on cooperative library & information network., For making the existing library resources readily accessible among the members and other interested parties., For delivery of documents at a cheaper rate and faster speed. For standardizing the activities of libraries among academic institution in Orissa. For reducing duplicating of collection building. For innovation and to modernize traditional library operations. For increasing reliance or demands on information. For more user-friendly ways of accessing information. For assigning new managerial roles to libraries and information centers. For supply of information in bibliographic, textual form and multi-media form etc.

5.3 What are the Requirements

On the basis of the above need dimensions, it is highly necessitated to have a network based academic library system in the state. The below mentioned are essential for networking of academic libraries in Orissa.

- Firstly, to discuss with the government authority about the project in briefly.
- Financial and moral support from State Government, UGC, INFLIBNET and other external agencies with participant willingness of libraries (node) to share their data.
- Participant libraries to have standardized computer hardware and software with telecommunication facilities. Selection of proper networking hardware and software with servicing guarantee/warrantee from

the reputed vender/suppliers within the local areas, keeping in mind with future change/development of the network

- Installation, loading and configuring of the software and hardware may be done with experts from the branded suppliers/engineers. Proper training of own staff members and end user for effective use of electronics media.
- Provision for adequate photocopying, scanners, barcode and other electronics equipments for effective document delivery.
- A computerized database of bibliographical records of library materials is to be created in each of the participating libraries. A computerized union catalogue is also to be developed to provide a broad perspective about information resources available in various libraries in the network.
- A set of bibliographical standards for the participating libraries is required to ensure compatibility. Creation of bibliographical records in network environment requires the adoption of uniform standards by participating libraries.
- Cooperative acquisition and collection development and lending codes and coordination policies to be formulated among libraries. Regular updating of collection and interaction.
- Above all, a commitment from the management to provide such facilities and appropriate budget allocation for installation and operation expenses.

5.4 The Proposed Network

The proposed network model (fig.5.2) is a part of centralized co-coordinative information network among the academic libraries, with decentralized services in the state of Orissa. The objective is to eliminate duplication in acquisitions to the extent it is possible. Further, the member libraries undertake to give services such as information access and document delivery. This model leads to the concept of centralized development of collection and also to decentralized system of giving services. The individual libraries, participating in the programme, determine their level of support to the programme for building the shared resources. The higher their budget, the higher is their support. The geographical area of co-operation could confine to the state of Orissa.

Before proceeding further regarding the network model, it is better to review different types of network models, working in local, national and international basis. A Network in twin city of Orissa was proposed by Parida (2002) to orient the existing library professionals in computer application in different library operations. A proposed network of libraries in Bhubaneswar was proposed by Seth & Others (1997). Some popular types of network models are given below:

Model Type 1. Centralized Collection Development and Services at National, or Regional Level Resources: acquired centrally and stored at a Single site. Funding: Contribution by Participating libraries. Grants are also sought from government and private agencies. E.g. National Lending Library, UK

Model Type 2. Centralized Collection Development and Services By Subject Resources: Subjects specific collection of documentary resources. Acquired centrally and stored at a single site City, region, or country may limit the geographic distribution of libraries. Funding: Marketing of services and grants from the government and private agencies. E.g. National Science Library at INSDOC, New Delhi.

Model Type 3. Centralized Collection Development at Organizational Level Resources: Libraries belonging to a single bigger organization collaborate. The shared collection is acquired centrally at a single site. Funding: Organization backing the Library provides funds. The participating libraries may also contribute towards the central funds CSIR, DRDO, DOE, and ISRO etc.

Model Type 4. Coordinated Collection Development at Institutional Level Resources: Eliminates duplications. Serves at the level of participating libraries. The geographical area of cooperation could confine to a city, region, a state or country. Funding: The individual libraries determine their level of support. The higher there budget the higher their support. User libraries pay for the services they avail of. DELNET, BONET, MALIBNET and INFLIBNET etc.

Among the above types of model, type -4 is most popular and fit for coordinated collection development at academic institutional level. A brief review of this type of the latest trend on the national network needs to be brought in order. Before proceeding for it we need the help of following national networks like: INFLIBNET, UGCNET and ERNET. Therefore, it is essential to clarify their objectives and functions.

ERNET India, an autonomous society under Ministry of Information Technology, is providing Internet access to education and research community in the country for over 10 years. ERNET is a nationwide terrestrial and satellite network with points of presence located in major cities. ERNET backbone is being upgraded to cater for growing bandwidth requirements and the satellite network is being expanded to offer Internet access in remote area. R&D and training are also integral parts of ERNET activities. In fact the recently started UGCNET is the brainchild of the older ERNET India.

UGCNET features an open IP platform deploying technologies like IP based multicast and IP spoofing and internet technologies that provide interactive education on PC or TV enabling online response through open systems internet architecture for variety of applications carrying real time audio, video and data.

INFLIBNET is a major programme of the UGC initiated in 1991 with its Head quarters located at Gujarat Univ. campus, Ahmedabad. The programme is directed towards modernization of libraries and information centers, and establishment of a mechanism for information transfer and access, to support scholarship, learning and academic pursuits. It is also aimed at establishing a national network of libraries and information centers in Universities, institutions of higher learning and R&D institutions in India.

It is basically a cooperative endeavor in resource development, sharing and utilization at national level, Its major activities include library automation, software development, standardization, digitalization, human resource development and nonetheless the development of union databases. Till now, 142 universities have been given grants for the automation purpose. As a part of essential requirement of skilled human resources at each university certain training programmes have been initiated like Computer Applications to Libraries and Information Services (CALIS), Workshop on Automation and Networking of University Libraries under INFLIBNET Programme (WANLIP), Regional training programme in library automation (IRTPL) and Convention for Automation of Libraries in Education and Research Institute (CALIBER).

Thus, as per the above national networks standard, Orissa shall form one of the regions or zones for its linking with them. Accordingly, a High Level Committee (HLC) will be formed by authorities from UGC, INFLIBNET, ERNET, Dept. of IT, NIC Regional Centre, Minister of Education and SC/ST Welfare Dept., Directorate of Higher Education and Network Administrator of the proposed network. All the heads of college and universities libraries of Orissa proposed under this network will represent the core committee to aid and advice, activate, implement and review the network policy of its own. A coordinator may be appointed to serve as the chief administrative and planning officers for inter library cooperative programmes at Bhubaneswar (HQ). The Central Management Committee (CMC) may also consist of all the districts collector, regional directors of education - Baleswar, Bhadrak, Cuttack, Dhenkanal, Gajapati, Ganjam, Jajpur, Khorda, Maurabhanja, Puri and Sambalpur and institute head, chief librarian of concerned institute, Govt. nominee, not below the rank of deputy secretary. Minister of education, Govt. of Orissa or minister of SC/ST may be the chairman of the committee. The CMC may select the coordinator and Local Committee, who should be responsible for the implementation of all its activities. There may be various special committees on special purposes. The network coordinator is to serve as network administrator/coordinator of the CMC and perform the following duties:

- To implement specific programmes under the direction of the CMC.
- To develop and present recommendations to the CMC for additional cooperative programmes and modifications.
- To maintain adequate communications with the members of the network.
- To represent the network to the various professional communities.
- To collect compile and present statistical information and to prepare annual budgets, annual reports.

5.5 Different Angles of the Proposed Network

The execution of any action requires careful planning. Effective sharing require willingness to cooperate by all institution involve in the group. The proposed network should function in such a way that all the universities and colleges of the state would act as local operating centers (nodes) or information gateway. The information gateways may often be accessible as menu driven basis in an online catalog. Catalogs and other electronics links should reflect the diverse needs of libraries and users and should be accessible from remote locations via the INTERNET. The proposed network will be work with the funds and facilities support from UGC New Delhi, and education department government of Orissa, and act as a vital link between the union government and state government with its various institutions in three different stages:

Stage I Inter-linking between National & International Institute/University/Organisation in the field of Education. INFLIBNET will to act as a central (Hub) co-coordinator for all networking activities including ERNET, UGC NET and the proposed OALNET. Central Operating Hub of the proposed OALNET will be remain under Dept. of Education Govt. of Orissa, and supposed to get all information from the INFLIBNET (National Hub).

Stage II The Central Operating Hub (Operating Center)

accumulates all the information of local, regional, national and international level and disseminated to its Local Node at different Districts of Orissa and will act as the gateway of all communications. The different colleges and universities in the district will receive their links from district nodes from directly or indirectly through Central Hub. Then, this links can be extended further up to Village institutions or club or post offices, but the decision will be taken by the CSP. To make this process of information dissemination more effective and useful, the two-way communication should be encouraged.

Stage III After the networking with international, national, regional colleges/university, situated at regional level will disseminate information at the local level institutions, which also includes Non-Govt. Organization (private). The research library resources systems should play a leadership role, on behalf of libraries and diverse scientists and library users, in negotiating and developing agreement for licenses to access databases of OALNET. In this stage the network will be linked with other technical institutions in the state and private colleges existing at other district headquarters, subsequently at the fourth stage, they will be linked with other sub divisional headquarter and Village level educational institutes in the state. However, colleges in the state of Orissa are basically funded by state govt. will be brought under the larger national interest of UGC facilitated ERNET and INFLIBNET. The various information gateways in OALNET will be act under the aid and advice of different committees: High Level Committee (HLC), Central Management Committee (CMC), and Local Committees at Institution (LCI) and Committees for Special Purpose (CSP). The brief objective and functions of different committees are given in Table No-5.1.

Two to three years after the implementation of the proposed network plan, the Central Management Committee shall take appropriate feedback from the member libraries and other allied library systems to review and evaluate the administrative and technological progress made, based upon this plan and to decide upon the appropriate step needed to continue to extend nationwide library technology planning in respect of other allied institutions. Every year there will be at least two meetings of the CMC one at January and other on July.

In order to create a viable framework for the activities of the network, it is proposed that a written agreement or by laws should be drafted and signed by the participating libraries. A written agreement simply may list the activities while bylaws may contain more detail, stating the purpose of the network and enumerating the roles and functions of the officers and rules for membership. Various working committees on cooperative services should be established and made responsible for planning and presenting proposals for cooperative action in the specific functional areas. It is expected that the proposed organizational structure will be an efficient and effective model for the academic libraries of the state as well as nation.

5.5.1 Objectives

A Network in the first instance is envisaged as a physical structure of links among the libraries established by means of computer and telecommunication links. The primary purpose of OALNET is to foster more effective inter-institutional cooperation in the state, through sharing of resources and information, providing a forum for the exchange of ideas on issues related to libraries/information centers and facilitating and supporting leadership in our profession.

Resources sharing are based on the concept that the collective strength and effectiveness of group of libraries is greater than that of its member taken individually and then added up. The major objectives of the proposed network are as follows:

- To promote the sharing of the resources of the membership through traditional and non-traditional library activities as well as other activities deemed appropriate by the CMC.
- To encourage the development of library and information services and research at member institutions.

Table 5.1

Different Committees with there Functions

Levels	*Different Committees and its Organisations*	*Objectives*	*Function*
National	High Level Committee	The overall development in connection with resource sharing through networking	➢ Co-ordinate
	1. Chairman/VC-UGC		➢ Development
	2. Chairman/VC- INFLIBNET		➢ Fund Rising
	3. CMD/MD-INFLIBNET		➢ Supervise
	4. Director, Depts. IT, Govt. of India		➢ Administrate
	5. CMD/MD-ERNET		
	6. Minister of Education		
	7. Director of Higher Education		
	8. CMD-OALNET		
	9. Network Administrator		
State	Central Management Committee	To carryout the effective development and function of the OALNET	➢ Planning/Co-ordinate ➢ Budgeting/Fund rising
	1. Minister of Education		➢ Developing
	2. Director of Higher Education		➢ Supervise
	3. CMD-OALNET		➢ Administrate/Maintain
	4. Network Administrator		➢ Police Making
	5. SCST Development Department		➢ Database Making

	6. Director-SCSTR&TI 7. Concerned District Collectors 8. Institution Head/Authority 9. Chief Librarian of Concerned Lib.		
Institu-tional	Local Committee at Institution 1. Institution Head/Authority 2. All the Department Heads 3. Chief Librarian 4. Network Manager/Engr	To fulfill the larger interest of the institution as well as resource sharing.	➢ Cooperating/Sharing ➢ Planning/Co-coordinating ➢ Collection Developing ➢ Man Power Training ➢ Users Education ➢ Electronics Publishing ➢ Administrate/Maintain ➢ Inter Lib. Loan /DD Serve
Miscell aneous	Committees for Specific Purpose 1. CMD-OALNET 2. Network Administrator 3. Concerned District Collectors 4. Concerned Instit. Head/Authority 5. Chief Librarian of Concerned.Ins 6. Network Manager/Engr.	To overcome the specific goal of the network as a whole.	To Discuss on: ➢ Development ➢ Disputes ➢ Investigate ➢ Infrastructure ➢ Service ➢ Marketing Inf. Any Other

- To disseminate current knowledge about library and information sciences resources and other technological advancements.
- To seek solutions to mutual problems.
- To cooperate with other networks and similar organizations, as appropriate.
- To pursue grant, gift, and other funding sources to further support the OALNET services.
- To welcome additional academic library members as appropriate.
- To have motivation and clear aims to provide efficient services to the users of their institutions as well as other users.
- To establish communication linkages according to certain rules or network protocols at local, national and international levels among the libraries. By which the sender, transmitter and recipient are clearly identified with the actual content of the message.
- To ensure effective bibliographic control of the literature in the areas.
- To facilitate and promote document delivery and library lending services.
- To permit and share the library resources with other institutional members reciprocally.
- To maximize the utilization of existing information resources by sharing.
- To maximize user satisfaction.
- To share database services like: bibliographic (catalogue), textual (abstract, index), full text (complete article, books) and conceptual (directory etc).
- To collect, store, organize and retrieve information on all aspects of academic requirements of the user.

5.5.2 *Membership*

There shall be two classes of membership: A. Classes (Full) and B. Classes (Affiliate) members.

1. Full membership shall be limited to the libraries of the all-autonomous colleges and universities of Orissa.

Representatives of these libraries shall be entitled to participate fully in policy-making decisions of the CMC.

2. Affiliate membership shall be open to other academic libraries that share the stated objectives. Representatives of these libraries shall not participate in making decisions of the CMC. Members of affiliate libraries may participate fully in the programs, activities and ad hoc committees of the OALNET.
3. Applications for membership shall be made in a form and on such terms as determined by the CMC.
4. Requests for changes in classes of membership shall be given due consideration by the CMC, when received in writing by the January meeting and shall become effective on July 1.
5. Requests for membership withdrawal shall be given due consideration by the CMC, when received in writing by the January meeting and shall become effective on 1st July.

5.5.3 Important Features

On the basis of the above objectives some most important features of the proposed need based information network model is presented below:

5.5.3.1 New Dimensions to be Undertaken

The concept of library network now became easy to transmit required information to any part of the world almost simultaneously, at a very low cost without any difficulty and that also without parting with the documents physically. It is for these reasons that computerized networking continues to attract the attention of libraries and information center. Now, the conventional method in the libraries cannot be continued in future due to its cost, growth, space, time and labour, because, most of the document are published in electronics form and can be accessible through network. Through electronic means the user also get a vast area of interest in his subject field. Therefore, considering the existing infrastructure facilities, financial recourses, manpower and technical aspects the implementation of the proposed network model can be made by introducing computer culture in the academic libraries and setting up of networking infrastructure in the libraries for the proposed model and users. In order to build the network effective and efficient the following points should be undertaken:

- ❖ Team spirit
- ❖ Design and develop appropriate networking service field
- ❖ To maintain network standard
- ❖ Data processing and database building:
- ❖ Cooperative acquisition of resources
- ❖ Centralized Union Cataloguing Decentralized service
- ❖ Inter-library lone and document delivery services
- ❖ Users need satisfaction
- ❖ Online interaction

5.5.3.2 Cooperative Acquisition & Collection Development

Since, the participating libraries are coming under the network system, the first priority is to make a cooperative acquisition policy statement for various activities of purchasing and building library collections. Which can be serving as guidance for the network. Under the policy of cooperative acquisition, a scheme of combined acquisition should be adopted by participating libraries with the objective in view that all the participating libraries should have access to all the material that is acquired under the scheme. The second priority is to formulate a written collection development policy for the need based library and information system as a tool, which should enable the librarians of participating libraries:

- ❖ To work with greater consistency towards achieving a target collections within a limited funds with more wisely.
- ❖ To communicate the users, authorities and other as to the scope and nature of existing collections and future plans.

- ❖ To define the library's goal, objectives and its various needs with limitations of the existing resources.
- ❖ Knowing the users and their needs of present and future.
- ❖ Careful analysis of the existing collection and determining its strength and weakness.

5.5.3.3 Database of Union Catalogue

The exchange of bibliographic data or information can occur in a number of ways, one of which is participation in a union catalogue. So, the union catalogs should be most comprehensive and standardize. This catalogues form one of the main building block for the resource sharing among the libraries to study the resources available, which can make convenient for interlibrary loan, cooperative cataloguing, cooperative preservation and collection development activities. All the participating libraries should maintain a uniform code of conduct or standard and provide access to their other bibliographic records for users from both inside and outside the library.

The inclusion of all records and holding of the library in the union catalogs is necessary to maximize the benefits of resource sharing for library users and among the participating libraries. Libraries that are just getting started with retrospective conversion should develop plans to complete this process in a timely fashion. Cataloguing of library materials is a very time-consuming and arduous process for any library, therefore centralized cataloguing is very important for each library. It eliminate duplicating new documents and puts the document on the shelve sooner. It is proposed that at its mature stage of the implementation of the model each member library should first compile their own list of holdings under the leadership of their respective local operating center. The local operating center should take the advantage of this union catalogue and also cooperate in updating the union catalogue.

5.5.3.4 Inter Library Loan (ILL) and Document Delivery (DD)

The activity of inter library loan include borrowing and

lending books and other materials between libraries and permitting faculties and students to use the library of other. The finding of the survey reveals that in higher academic libraries there is no inter library loan system, even through this activity was recognized as a device of conventional resource sharing. This is due to lack of clear guidelines or state library act or lack of any cooperative agreement for inters library loan system. But, this can be more effectively possible by the proposed network. The effective ness of ILL depends on:

- ❖ Commitment to share
- ❖ Linking with other automated libraries or networks
- ❖ Computerized union databases of the library
- ❖ Electronics publishing
- ❖ A clear-cut ILL code

To provide efficient ILL service and reduce the processing cost, the libraries should regularly examine ILL policies and delivery mechanisms in light of expanded availability of electronics information. The network system should be informed about the ILL protocol, to understand the benefit it can provide and should have ILL protocol compliant software for its feasibility and feedback. The protocol should be internationally approved for Internet browsing. Generally the protocol is based on client/server technology, in which the architecture is the requesting machine and the server is the supplying machine. The client and server are connected with one another via a Local Area Network (LAN) or Wide Area Network (WAN). The client contains the user interface and may perform some or all of the application processing while the server stores information and responds to queries from the client.

There should be ILL code agreed by the participant libraries. Each library will assume responsibility for borrowed material subscribing to borrowing privileges established by the inter library loan code. The inter library loan code is very important because it would be made possible to know, the types of materials to be included and excluded for the same. For any types of irregularity or violation of the clientele to be served, the core committee will take decisions.

The following pre-requisites are necessary for formulation of an ILL Code.

- ❖ A uniform code applicable for all the member libraries should be adapted faithfully.
- ❖ In each university and autonomous colleges there should be a Local Lending Centre (LLC), where all the Govt./Private colleges within 50 KM can have the facilities
- ❖ The LLC should also be responsible for compilation of union databases.
- ❖ All the SC/ST student, researchers and faculties within the area can gate high preference for the same.
- ❖ The LLC should have sufficient trained professionals, sufficient infrastructure in all respects.
- ❖ It should have photocopying machine
- ❖ A standard request forms should be followed in all libraries and LLC.

5.5.3.5 Manpower Training

The achievement of the objective of the network, every library becomes a center of technology, information for its community of users is important to the overall success of the proposed network. However, sophisticated networks and electronic resources are no value unless people know how to use them. Training is required in order to use, and benefit fully from, services provided by electronic doorway libraries. For many years library personnel and users could peruse the card catalog and find books and information. But with the introduction of technology and the Internet, access to library information is undergoing dramatic changes. These changes, while improving and expanding access to information, alter the procedures that library personnel and users traditionally have followed to find resources. Libraries need to provide the training required for people to work in and use electronically sophisticated libraries. Training will vary based upon the needs of the individual library. Factors that will influence needs are the library's mission, diversity of its users, and size of staff and collection. Although there is no definitive training program that will met the needs of all libraries. Certain elements should be part of every library-training plan. At a minimum, these include:

- ❖ Decide training objectives
- ❖ Identification of trainees
- ❖ Descriptions of training and its cost.

Libraries and library systems should regularly assess library personnel and user training needs. Assessments of training needs should take into account library personnel and users who are from diverse cultures, use different learning styles, and or are visually or physically challenged. There are various training programs on computer application to library: computer hardware or software, tele-communication library, library automation, networking, Internet browsing, training on different library software etc., but the local committee will decide for this. Once the Library personnel have been trained, the electronics libraries should also provide training for its user regarding the various services, its operation, limitations etc. As is the case of training of library personnel, training of users should focus on how to obtain needed information and resources including use of the Internet.

5.5.3.6 Educating/Publicizing the Information Access

The success and the aim of any resource-sharing project via network depend upon its proper impimentation and wide publicization among the users. It should be the duty of any library professionals to publicize its different services available and benefit obtained from it. The trained manpower in the library should educate its other subordinate and also to the users on various angles of the electronics machinery and its different applications, limitations etc. Whenever users contact the library personally or through remote access they may interact with any or all the formats in the library while seeking information. They may also encounter library staff to satisfy their information needs and way to find from the electronics means. Therefore, the user must know which source (print or electronics) to access and how to access. It should be clearly publicized in a simple and convenient step-by-step process. The information access process assumes an interaction cycle consisting of query specification, receipt and examination of retrieved result, and then either stopping or reformulating the query until a desired result is abstained. The library staff, also highlight that the user's information need is static and the information seeking process refines until the query retrieves the documents relevant to the original information need. Further, they should describe a sample and popular interaction model for the entire information access process.

5.5.3.7 Online Network

The success of any cooperative network system depends on effective communication system. Mail, Telephone, telegraphs, teleprompt, telex, and facsimile transmission, satellite and computer technology are various means for transmission. Generally, it is pointed out that mail service is too slow, telegraph is too expensive, telephone message can be misinterpreted and must be supplemented by written records, and teletype/telex information transmits information rapidly and eliminates possible errors. Facsimile transmissions the rapid transmission of printed pages from one points to another using electronic devices. Computer communication via modern connections has the greatest impact on inter lending system. However, recent developments in communication technology and computer technology have made the libraries easier to extend cooperation among them. Now, every library can provide access via the internet both to its own information resources in a local online catalog and/or union or virtual catalog and to the cast array of information resources available elsewhere on the Internet. Internet is an international network of networks connected by TCP/IP protocols. The Internet may be used for remote login, electronic mail, news, file transfer, and other services, Use of the internet has increased dramatically in recent years due to the widespread availability of graphical user interfaces (CUIs) and the World Wide Web (WWW).

In view of the rapidly changing face of the Indian telecommunication industry in respect of the existing telephone, telegraphs and telex services as well as the introduction of digital technology in switching and transmission systems among these libraries should undertake to evolve a computerized networking system that would be connected through satellite links, microwave links etc., on the similar lines of DELNET, CALIBNET, MALIBNET, BONET HYLIBNET and other existing proposed library and information networks in the country etc. The UGS through its INFLIBENT and ERNET of Ministry of Information Technology should play a leadership role to help for coordinate digitization among libraries and other institutions in order to: broad access, digitized records, avoid duplications and much better information services.

5.6 Barriers to Resource Sharing Network

Hybrid media is going to be fashion of libraries of future, yet there is uncertainty with this every time. For a long times print media has been tested and verified for its access and stability in the world and replaced by electronics media, but numbers of books published in the world is not going to down these days also. Thus, both have their positive and negative aspects of use. However, most of the developed countries are using electronics information through networking themselves, in India these trends are also continuing in the metropolitan cities since last two decade. It is common assumption that larger libraries can be net lender and smaller libraries can be net borrower. Among the obstacles that have been inhibiting smooth networking are: infrastructure cost, feeling of self-sufficiency, skilled manpower, loss of autonomy, traditional/institutional barriers, lack of institutional support, lack of determination and dedication among librarians and proper cooperation among different libraries are major problems on the way to resource sharing. These problems can be overcome, if we can judge its benefit aspects.

5.7 Concluding Observations

The researcher is an user of information technology in the profession of library and information field, since last 15 years, but always find pleasure in what other more competent and responsible people in IT achieve. I strongly feel that IT development in Orissa can be fast; for this purpose we should do what we can individually, and get together for a few things when we feel it necessary, and not a waste of our own or other people's time. I feel here Govt. of Orissa and different authority of the concerned institute libraries may have a very positive role to play. The other non -government institute may join with this cooperative network immediately if they so desire. They may watch and wait for its implementation and effectiveness. A Conference on Information Technology was held at Utkal University, Vanivihar from December 21st to December 23rd, 1998 for development of IT in Orissa and took an important decisions for formation of a IT society called 'Orissa Information Technology Society' (OITS) to facilitate growth and development of IT activity in Orissa. IT professionals of OSA also given words for helping some institutions to update their information base in IT.

It can be concluded that in a backsword state like Orissa, steps are being taken to disseminate knowledge in various ways. Like passing of Orissa Public Library Act-2001, application of IT in the field of education, introducing computers in the academic libraries and formation of Orissa Information Technology Society, availability of different library software and hardware in the open market etc. The capacity is being built up with the help of Government of Orissa, UGC and international funding agencies for this purpose. With the explosion of knowledge and constraints on the financial resources in the state, the resource sharing networking has emerged as an important alternative for the department of education government of Orissa. The information technology has facilitated the resource sharing among the institutions located in different districts of the state. It enables the participating libraries to obtain material from each others may be the list of books, indexes and abstracts of required articles, facsimile copies of required pages or documents, charts, figures, graphs, drawings by using computer terminals attached to a large or very large network system and data bases coupled with visual display units (VDUs) and attached with printing facility. Information can be scanned first on the screen, and if required, relevant information can be obtained in the print form.

Access to information infrastructure, the ability to produce and consume are the determinants of individual 's economic success and social mobility, he may be any kinds of user or may the poorest of the poor in the remote village. There is no limit to gain any types of information any where of the globe by pressing a networked computer key. It is also very interesting, acceptable, easy to use and also convenient among the student, researcher and faculties in the educational institutions of Orissa. Therefore, the proposed network system is the right path in a right time for the state government, the department of education and SC/ST development department to implement conveniently for reducing the illiteracy among SC/ST communities and more helpful to the higher level educational system in Orissa.

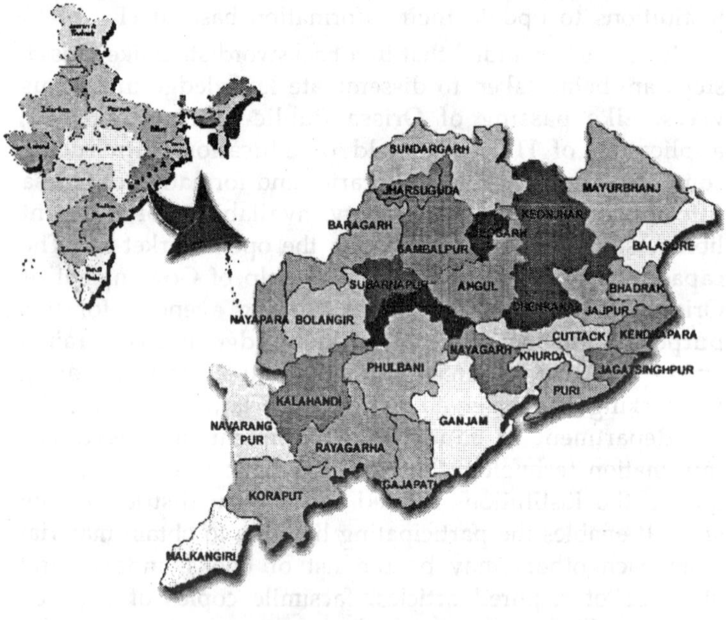

Fig: 5.2: Proposed OALNET Model

Network Activities

Cooperative Acquisition & Processing, Collection Development, Centralized Control, Decentralized Monitoring and Disseminations, Union Catalogue, Inter Library Loan/ Document Delivery, Standardization, Education & Training, Library Automation and HRD and Online Information and Feedback.

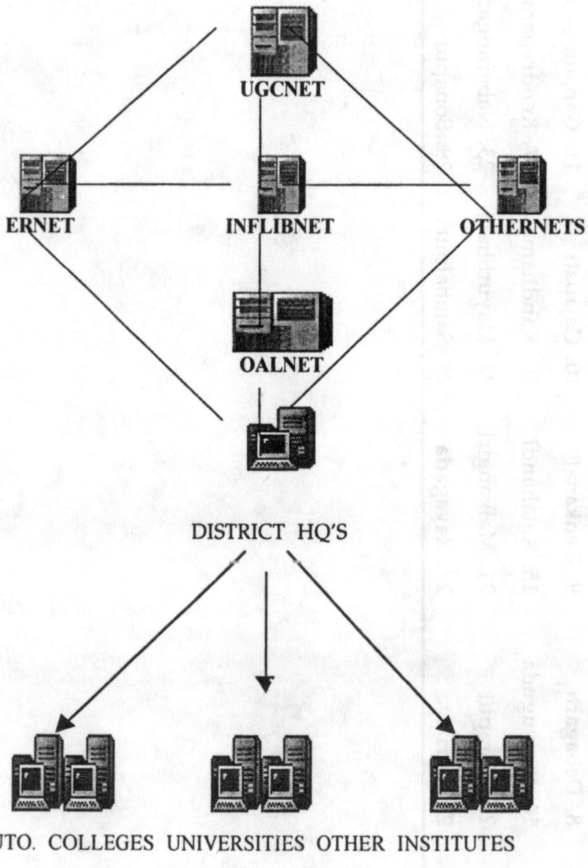

District Wise Latest Map of Orissa in India

1. Anugul	2. Balangir	3. Baleswar	4. Baragarh	5. Baudha	6. Bhadrak
7. Cuttack	8. Debagarh	9. Denkanal	10. Gajapati	11. Ganjam	12. Jagatsinghapur
13. Jajapur	14. Jharsuguda	15. Kalahandi	16. Kandhamal	17. Kendrapara	18. Kendujhar
19. Khorda	20. Koraput	21. Malkangiri	22. Mayurbhanj	23. Nabarangapur	24. Nayagarh
25. Nuapada	26. Puri	27. Rayagada	28. Sambalpur	29. Sonapur	30. Sundergarh

6

Conclusions and Suggestions

Findings from different studies reveals that Indian higher education has not been exempt from the force and urgency with which educational reform is politically advocated to respond to the economic imperatives. The expansion of enrolment and increase in the number of institutions has entailed increased expenditure on higher education, which is faced with the formidable problem of the development of mass higher education. The challenge of mass higher education has still not been met adequately, particularly from the disadvantaged communities in our country. This is time to re-examine the role of higher education. Private interest in education contributed a lot to higher education in India in the earlier period. But today they are driven by profit motive and not quality education; thus, they are neglecting the poor SC/ST communities. However, the rapid spread of higher education has also resulted in the deterioration of the standard of education in every sphere- ill equipped laboratories, poorly stocked libraries with conventional thinking make it ineffective, totally inadequate space in buildings and play grounds, neglected and remote campus setups, uninterested and ill qualified teachers, inexperienced administrators and managers, non involvement of parents and guardians in the affairs of institutions of higher education, lack of vision of the academic and executive bodies of the universities, all these factors have contributed to the all round decay of higher education.

The laws under which the universities had been

constituted did not adequately respect autonomy and independence, which constituted the soul of the University. No university can grow to its full potential in the absence of freedom and autonomy. Introducing autonomous colleges should change the affiliation system of the universities. The basic objectives in the establishment of autonomous colleges have been reducing the workload of autonomous colleges in the university system, decentralization of academic administration, promotion of creativity innovations and higher standard. An autonomous college is expected to have the freedom to prescribe rules of admission, determine the course of study and methods of teaching and evaluation and conduct of examinations. However, this process will not materialize into tangible results unless there is unreserved participation on the part of the entire academic community. Upward revision of pay scales of the teachers in colleges and universities was to go side by side with the teachers taking up certain increased responsibilities like increased workloads. Teacher training in the university system is rather weak. Teacher who are recruited into the university and college system are not given adequate training. Quality in higher education depends primarily upon the commitment from government, the education department and the academic community to the maintenance and improvement of standards

This is shown that after independence, India's education expenditure has never touched the four percent mark of the GDP. Three decades ago, Kothari Commission had recommended that it should not be less than six per cent and the recommendation had been accepted in principle but not implemented so far in spite of repeated promise by successive governments. Thus, a large number of newly started universities and colleges due to paucity of funds and facilities remain academic slums. Moreover, the considerable share of the benefits of higher education of the last 50 years was cornered away by elite sections of the country.

Although, the present study is based on information needs of scheduled caste and scheduled tribe student, research scholars and faculties in the higher academic environment in Orissa, it is essential to specify the different angles of education and library system in our country as well as in Orissa in general and SC/ST communities in particular. The literature review reveals that the Indian higher educational system is growing in quantities without quality, in the process of evolution the higher academic libraries are also thrown up various problems that call for analysis, examination, and solution. On one hand there is knowledge explosion and heavy inflow of information, on the other there is heavy demand for pinpointed information without the loss of time. Manual methods for the retrieval and dissemination of information are becoming inadequate, and these are being replaced with the information technology by the developed countries in the world. Thus, libraries are not operating in isolation now, but are becoming partners of various networks for mutual benefit and providing access to information is the principle goal in the western countries now. Today academic libraries are in transition from manual to electronics system basically in developing countries like India, where it still face several challenges of information technologies for library automation like manpower, infrastructure for IT, communication facilities, limited budget, library software, training and awareness among library personnel. The computer technology has greatly affected libraries and promises to increase that effort etc. With all this, the organization and the operation of the university and college libraries in India is becoming more complex due to inadequacy in finance, housing, and professional manpower. It is also observed that active library services are not been provided because of the reasons like- under-utilization of information sources, duplication of information sources, growth rate of libraries and complexities of users' demands.

Regarding disadvantaged communities as a whole, various studies show that India have adopted the policy of special privileges and introduced various programmes and schemes for the deprived sections i.e. Scheduled Castes and Scheduled Tribes communities for equality and justice. These policies have gained lot of importance and have been introduced in the constitutional commitments for development of these communities in the society. But, without proper education among them all these peogramme are fruitless, so, education is considered as an important mechanism for their all-round development that is directly linked to better jobs and higher income. But, these sections of our society were traditionally and historically deprived of their basic rights and education was far away from their reach. After completing 55 years of independence and having experimented with special welfare programmes for them, it is high time to assess their achievements now. Considering the key role of education as an agent of change, it is worth seeing educational achievements among these deprived sections. But, it is not possible for these communities to access, sustain and perform better in education due to their poor social and stigmatized background without governmental support and will of the upper caste. Although, they have been provided with various material and non-material facilities including reservation of seats in admissions at all levels of education.

However, during last five decades of the experimentation of the policy; the literature review revealed that the educational condition of SCs and STs has not improved as much as it should have—despite the existence of several constitutional guarantees and welfare schemes and different educational facilities to them—the study examines the causes for this failure. Several options for accelerating improvement in the socio-economic conditions of these people's lives have been put forward in the study. An Overview of the problems faced by SCs and STs.noted by different studies that despite abolishing unsociability, prejudice against SCs and STs persists in some form or the other—be it overt, covert or subtle in expression. "Whatever has been done in this regard has been done hesitatingly half-heartedly and as a measure of concession forgetting that this relates to their constitutional rights and not concession to them. Atrocities against SCs and STs continue to occur frequently. More and more SCs/STs are becoming illiterate, landless and are joining the ranks of agricultural labourers. Since the 1980s there has been a steady decline in the allocation of government funds for SC and ST development and welfare projects.

The studies reviewed that, there has in general been an inherent lack of interest and seriousness on the part of the planning and implementing machinery to achieve the objectives of the Constitutional benefits secured by the SCs and STs do not appear commensurate with the funds spent so far. The representations of the SCs&STs in academics, either as students or employees in Schools, Colleges, Universities, other Autonomous Institutions or Centers of Higher Learning are still very poor. Thousands of qualified job seekers are deliberately refused employment in the schools colleges' universities etc. Hundreds and hundreds of SC&ST students aspiring for higher studies are turned out every year denied admissions, or even after admissions are thrown out or forced to get out under some pretext or the other from the Colleges, Universities, Autonomous Institutions and other Centers of Higher Education. The upper caste people are unwilling and are actually incapable of teaching the SC&ST students in the academic environment.

It is also reviewed that the likelihood of talented children achieving their potential depends on their socio-economic background. Talented children from well to do families have much better chances of doing well in life than those from poor families. The talents of children from weaker sections of society waste or wither away due to lack of opportunity.

The numbers of SC&ST professionals in the colleges, autonomous colleges, universities, deemed universities, research centers and other institutions of higher learning in the country are extremely poor. There are various examples of this all over the country. Yet, the authorities: Government and the Dept. of Higher Education have managing successfully. The UGC is not even allowing or facilitating the SC&ST students to acquire the requisite higher qualifications of M Phil and Ph D essential for teaching in the universities and colleges Social study circle, (http//www.dalitindia.com). They do not provide them any scholarships and fellowships to pursue these long and costly studies. The Government and the Ministry of Social Justice and Empowerment is not helping the poor SC&ST students wanting to go for such essential higher studies. The upper caste professors and universities are also doing their best and contributing their shares in denying the SCs&STs admissions to these courses, and also in rating them deliberately lower so that they do not become eligible for teaching, even if the SC&ST students manage to do these essential higher Courses. Such is the situation in the country today.

Despite providing reservation quotas in educational institutions and jobs, the representation of SCs and STs in private educational institutions and the higher levels of all public services remain very poor. The amendments to departmental orders concerning recruitment and promotion of SCs and STs have adversely affected their interests. The paper believes that the private sector in India is likely to grow more rapidly in the future as a result of the government's economic reform policies. Due to the withdrawal of the government from several areas of economic activity (because of privatisation of government owned industrial, mining, service and infrastructure facilities) there is a growing worry that employment opportunities for SCs and STs would also reduce drastically. Unlike the State, the private sector has no constitutional obligation to implement job quotas for the weaker sections of society. Nor has it responded in an understanding manner to create employment opportunities for these sections of society.

Recently, the process of globalization and privatization has posed a serious threat to the Affirmative Action Policy and thereby to the basic constitutional commitment of social equality and justice. Globalization demands merit and excellence that will suit to the economic interests of the corporate sector. The merit and excellence would come from good quality education that has been the monopoly of few upper castes/class people. Majority masses will further get marginalized due to their continued backwardness and disabilities because the policy is not applicable in the private sector of education and employment. A fresh empirical probe in the era of new challenges of globalization is proposed considering its implications on the Affirmative Action Programmes.

The Opportunities for studies abroad available to Indian students are by and large still kept as a secret from the

SCs&STs, even though hundreds of Indian students are to be found in many foreign countries with various scholarships and other schemes that help them to pursue their studies abroad, without taxing their families. Even Dr. Ambedkar's Dream of educating select SC&ST students abroad, accepted by the then British Indian Govt., has been badly twisted beyond recognition by the Welfare Ministry over the years. A similar scheme of Dr. Ambedkar Overseas Fellowships for students to study abroad, through Dr. Ambedkar Foundation has been in the cold storage for quite sometime, and many students already selected for the award of the fellowships have not been permitted to avail of the Fellowships. A silent effort is said to be in the offing, to turn it as a facility only for SC&ST University and College Teachers those are already in job. Thus, the scheme meant for the students is being distorted, and at the same time, the UGC and other authorities would be washing off their responsibilities in providing opportunities to train abroad, the SC&ST lecturers and professors working in the Colleges and Universities. Thus by one change, two opportunities available to SC&ST students and teachers are now being cleverly and silently closed.

In fact this has been the history of India, where the teachers instead of teaching the poor are denying them education, instead of equipping them with knowledge are condemning them, turning them as unfits and deliberately rating them low. The provision of facilities, are inadequate and proves meaningless as they do not reach on time and has stigma of caste and of being inferior attached to it. It is empirically established that most of the SC/STs are first generation learners and therefore find it difficult to cope with over all educational standards, quality and surrounding environment. Being first generation, the over all environment at home front is not conducive neither motivating.

The issue of equality and justice gained high relevance in contemporary societies. However, the goal of equality cannot be achieved without special planning and programmes; especially for those communities that have been traditionally-historically deprived on various grounds of race, ethnicity, caste or gender. Social deprivation is universal but methods of combating it are different in different societies. Most of the democratic countries have adopted the special measures to do away with deprivation and introduced policies and programmes to achieve equality in social and economic spheres. The social and economic development is directly linked to higher education and the employment. However, growth of higher education in India has taken place more in response to political pressures and demands from the upper sections of the society than to cater to the development need of the nation as a whole stated by Aikara, (1994).

Thus, the issues and problems emerged during last five decades behind a developed India are manifold: the political; social, economic and educational needs proper evaluation. Among all importance and relevance of formal education continues to occupy major space in the process of social development and change. In India, where one-fourth portions of population are illiterate, belongs to SC/ST Communities. Studies have revealed that the policy has certainly contributed to the educational progress of the SC/ST, but the progress is steady and minimal at higher level of education. It is because of the following drawbacks within the system itself needs evaluation and proper rectification.

- The socio-economic background that has direct links with educational access, retention and performance got thoroughly ignored. Consequently, a few urban-based families/castes within the SC/ST communities have benefited. Again, within them SCs are more advanced than STs, which led to regional and caste-to-caste imbalances.
- With reference to implementation of the provisions, it has been very poor due to bureaucratic attitude of upper castes, lack of will power and politicization of the issue; on one hand, and on the other, these communities in general, lack awareness. The people in general carry prejudice against them, due to inherent feelings of superiority resulting into anti-reservation protests and litigations.
- It is also argued by some sections of people that the caste criteria should be replaced by economic criteria

with certain time limit for such provisions. And very importantly, there has been an argument that the reservation policy lowers down the quality and standards. However, a small section of educated Scheduled Castes elites has emerged that is always being targeted against fall victim to new forms of discrimination and crisis.

- Academic libraries in India are facing several challenges of information technologies for library automation like manpower, infrastructure for IT, communication facilities, limited budget, library software, training and awareness among library personnel. Therefore, the active library services are never provided, under-utilization of information sources, duplication of information sources, growth rate of libraries, users are not satisfied by the service.
- Under the active leadership of the present Central Government's liberalization policy, the govt. is being championed as a means to facilitate the progress of the national economy into the global arena in the 21st century, but simultaneously the central government is giving enormous latitude and power to the state governments to attract various industries and plan their expansion. In the wake of this massive industrialization and discriminations the states: Maharashtra, Gujurat, Haryana, Punjab and even West Bengal have increased their stake with sheer dynamism and vision in all spears. The states that are lagging way behind include Bihar, UP, MP, Assam, Rajasthan and Orissa.

However, the main objective of the study is based on information needs of scheduled caste and scheduled tribe student, research scholars and faculties in the higher academic environment in Orissa, the finding of the present study shows that, there are major regional and internal imbalances among the Non- SC/ST and SC/ST in the state. It is seen that the basic problems, which be devil the Indian education system, continue in large measure in Orissa as well, which the National Policy on Education 1986 as modified in 1992 (Chapter-I) has not been able to effectively resolve. The reasons are absence of accountability and lack of incentives among decision makers, poor quality of education system are major obstacles to the implementation of the policies. Although, there is growth of educational institution increasing, yet the quality of education is decreasing.

According to the Sixth All India Educational Survey (1993), about 11,655 habitations in Orissa do not have primary schools within a distance of one kilometer and 16,317 without upper primary schools within a distance of three kilometers. According to the National Norms the state should have 26,500 upper primary schools as against which 11,510 such schools are in existence and there should be one upper primary school for every two primary schools, the gross enrolment ratio (GER) in respect of primary school (class 1-V) in Orissa is 71.8%(rural-70.9, urban-76.7. Enrolment in upper primary level is 38%, dropout rate at the primary (43.5%) and upper primary stages (57.0%) are very high., and dropout rate at elementary level (girls) is 72.1% in the state compared to all India ratio of 68.1%. There are also wide variations in levels of learner achievement among boys and girls, urban and rural, SC/ST and non-SC/ST communities in the state. The resulting short fall acts as a deterrent, particularly for girls, for enrolment in upper primary schools. The average teacher-student ratio for the state as a whole is 1:39 (Kothari Commission Report-1966, said for 1: 40) at the primary level, it is highest in Balaswar & Puri (1:48), where as Phulabani is the lowest (1:11). The poor levels of educational attainments are a cause for serious concern. In the nineties, however, with increasing government support and funds made available for education, community participation in education has almost been reduced to a trickle leading to greater dependence on government. According to the Census of India Report 2001, the overall literacy rate in the state is 63.6% among males 75.95% and females 50.97%. Khurda district has the highest literacy (80.2%) in Orissa and the lowest is Malkangiri (31.3%). For the above problems Govt. of Orissa and Central Government are initiating various programmes and at present Orissa is developing in its education sphire.

The task force on education, set up by the government of Orissa to prepare its Vision-2020 document, notes in its report that for three years, 27 high schools in the state have shown 'Nil' results. All 27 schools are located in tribal-dominated areas. An ongoing nation-wide enrolment drive—Sarva Siksha Abhiyan—whose slogan is 'School-Chale-Hum' (Let's Go To School), may be having the desired impact, but there are schools in Orissa where, for several years, not a single student has managed to pass the high school certificate (Class X) examination. For example Gopalpur Girls High School in Kalahandi district is one such school, where not a single student has passed the HSC (Higher Secondary Certificate) examination between 1996 and 2000. Again, out of 27 schools in the backward areas, eight schools in Koraput, eight in Rayagada, two each in Malkangiri and Nawarangapur districts, four in Kalahandi district and one each in Phulbani, Gajapati and Sundargarh. Officials at the school and mass education department and the SC and ST development department blame each other for the dismal state of education in Orissa's tribal areas. A task force member said: "A kind of double administration by the welfare officers of the SC and ST department and the inspectorate of schools has ruined these special schools. No one is bothered about teacher absenteeism, lack of mid-day meals and the absence of facilities." Officials at both departments agree that the objective of promoting primary and secondary education in tribal areas has not been achieved.

According to an umbrella body of tribal legislators, Adibasi Bidhayak Parishad, the issue of education for tribal children has not been seriously dealt with. Even in the government of Orissa one of the MLAs claim that not a single school has an adequate number of teachers. The government still has to provide books to the tribal students, they say. In Orissa, 10,000 out of the 40,000 schools have no school buildings, and 40% of classrooms do not possess a blackboard. Three thousand schools are single-room schools with just one teacher. Fifty-five per cent of schools do not have drinking water facilities.

The first and foremost indicator of educational progress of the state or the disadvantaged community in the field of higher education is the number of standard institutions, its faculties and student enrolment. The secondary data provides on Orissa educational scenario. Shows there has been a spurt in the enrolment of SC/ST students in higher education in autonomous college level. The SC students are better placed as compared to ST's. The majority of disadvantaged students are in the Arts stream and as such the goal of economic empowerment of this population in the state seems to be illusive. The state is for behind as compared to the national average literacy as per the census of India during entire census since independence, again the literacy levels, particularly female literacy are extremely low for landless wage earners, marginal landholders SC/ST. The gender disparities are also wide especially among this category. Higher dis-continuation rates as well as enrolment rates further investigation to find out the casual factors. However, the performance of the state regarding SC women's higher education seems to be satisfactory in terms of number and percentages, but it is only in urban areas. It could be said that in spite of constitutional obligations, legal provisions, central and state level policies and programmes affirmative actions the benefits of higher education are availed by a small number of SC/ST communities only.

The type of higher institution shows during 1998/99 that the educational institutions, student enrolment, numbers of scholars and teachers available in Orissa are very poor. The numbers of general colleges are 1367 with 555000 students and having 23003 teachers in all and there are only 171476 students in 591 institutions having 8934 teachers in all. The teacher student ratio is 1:19 in our higher education system, which is much less than the national average. The distribution of student enrolment as per their level of education in higher academic system during 1996/97 to 1999/00 gives the percentages of SC/ST students in higher-level education have been increasing every year during last five years. But in PG level, there are little differences during 1998/99((20.69%) and 1999/00(20.05%), in professional level more student enrolled during 1999/2000 (32.5%) than others. In the mentioned four level of education non-SC/ST percentages of enrolment is lesser and lesser during 1996/97 to 2000.01 perhaps this is for more awareness and attention of education department government of Orissa and middle class people, but it reveals SC/ST enrolment is not so increased as non-SC/ST in all the five years except 2000/01. During the year when a comparison has made it shows that in Ph.D. SC/ST-(79) 0.41% and non-SC/ST-(451) 0.27%, in professional level SC/ST-(1087) 5.58% where as non- SC/ST (4193) is only 2.46%. The year wise distribution of only SC/ST shows that in all level of education the percentages are increasing better except professional levels (23.85%) during 1999/00. Thus, credit goes to the governmental actions for their overall development and different educational facilities provided time to time during the year. All this reveals that in higher level there are some developments. This may be due to government's role played for the same or people are more aware about higher educational benefits or student may not having employment during there educational period hoping for it.

To conclude the progress of scheduled caste and scheduled tribe in higher education is unsatisfactory due to the defective education system in it, followed by the unfavorable socio-economic conditions, biased attitudes of the upper castes. At the level of educational institutions, the teachers, fellow students, administrators carry their biases and prejudices and treat the disadvantaged students badly. As a result these students fall victim to all sorts of discrimination, humiliations and negligence. Again, it is very difficult to get admission in good colleges for all including the reserved quota candidates. Minority and Private institutions are excluded from adopting reservation policy so the admissions become more difficult for reserved category students. The students are admitted on merit basis or financial basis and the difference between open and reserved quota candidates' percentage of marks is very little and they can't able to effort big amount of donations in the institutions. In some places the academic performance is judged with caste biases. This is especially true of professional/technical education where they have internal assessments and practical e.g. medical, engineering etc. Consequently, these students suffer from alienation and isolation, all sorts of complexes and mental-emotional blocks resulting into poor performance, stagnation or dropout in Orissa.

Findings from the Orissa academic library system reveals that this comprises in three levels i.e. school and college and the university libraries. Excepting very highbrow private schools, most schools in Orissa do not have a library as per the present situation. This area of librarianship is very neglected and needs immediate and continuous attention. As regards to college libraries, most colleges have libraries but other than very well known colleges in city areas, the ordinary colleges do not run libraries of any consequence. There is some library development in costal area institutions. But on the other hand universities are having their own libraries within their campus. For all these higher academic libraries the budgetary provision available from state government, UGC and ICSSR through grants, aid etc, sometimes-special grant, and donation are also received for library infrastructure. Thus there is no separate budget for the libraries. What to speak of providing modern equipment and scientific technology to the existing libraries and upgrading the existing libraries with better infrastructure, even the existing books in the libraries are not properly catalogued and they are not maintained properly due to lack of funds, manpower, training, expertise, space and technology. Therefore, Orissa faces the challenges of actually preparing a perspective plan from scratch i.e., from collection development to networking through IT solutions, and will need a complete blueprint to develop higher academic libraries during the coming centuries.

Summary of the above Limitations

To summarise above obstacles we come to conclude that the poor socio-economic background and struggle for daily survival in the SC/ST communities in Orissa create greater dependence on upper castes and being rural based, most of them are deprived of education and information at primary and elementary level only. This deprivation is supported by their lack of awareness, discrimination, lack of library system, lack of access due to distance, lack of affordability and lack of motivation resulting out of social background. At school front, the poor quality of educational contents, teaching methods, teachers' and fellow students' discriminative attitude as well as unattractive atmosphere result in poor enrolment, poor performance and high dropout rate among the children. This leads to creation of imbalances among and between regions, castes and gender.

But, this does not mean that they are not developing and their facilities provides by the government (see Chapter-III & IV) do not help them improving their plight. Their access to higher education is made easy by these programmes but could be made more effective and result oriented by implementing them properly. Although education has served as a positive contributor to the process of planned change, one finds that this change have been restricted to the urban areas, to particular regions, and to particular castes and individuals among the SC/STs. There have been regional, rural urban, male-female and caste-to-caste variations across the country. For example, states like Kerala, Maharashtra, Punjab, West Bengal, Andhra Pradesh among others have showed a better response in educational development of Scheduled Castes and Scheduled Tribes communities. But, Orissa is lacking behind since our independence, even though it is one of the richest states in India for its mineral resources, wide forest range, marine base and cultural heritage. This is because of the bureaucracies controlled by the politician perpetuate to a corrupt system of governments planning. However, there are some common obstacles on its progress as follows:

- Orissa is overburdened with debt every year. It has deficit budgets in its developmental programs. Its annual state revenue is going by paying the salaries of the government employees.
- The majority of the educated public craves to be

government employees. Once employed, they think it is their birthright to hold the position notwithstanding their performance. During their tenure in office, bureaucrats and politicians are guided by the personal goal to amass wealth at the expense of the public funds that would carry them through not only their own lifetime but also that of their next two generations.

- There is no strategic long-range planning or coordination for future project developments in Orissa. The different avenues that can help Orissa put forward a futuristic outlook to envision Orissa into a developed one, if it can look after in its socio-economic and political will.
- The well-being of a community in general whether we think of improving day to day life of women or children is innately connected with the level of education or training they get in uplifting their own individual life.
- Even our cultural heritage and religious belief has encouraged strong family values and bondage over centuries, the inherent conservatism in them also has propagated the belief in caste system and the acceptability of a dowry system during marriage.
- In the process of "me and mine only" thinking, individuals accumulate wealth for themselves never thinking of others in distress. Hence, a society not believing in "giving" is where the rich gets richer and the poor gets poorer.
- Lack of education among the (40% SC/ST) majority of population has led to lack of birth control leading to massive population explosion.
- Defective educational systems in the state. It is fairly safe to assume that the primary goals of most, if not all the courses (undergraduate and postgraduate) offered by universities and autonomous colleges in the Orissa are theoretical in essence. One course may vary from another in the degree to which an emphasis is placed on theory rather than practice, but this

distinction is between the theory and the practice of information work.

- Educators design different curricula with the intention of providing students with the best preparation for employment opportunities; students enroll on the institutions in order to gain a qualification and get a job in the jab market and employers are expected to respect the validity of that qualification as an indicator of the level of knowledge and skill that the holder is likely to have-not surprisingly, much space in the literature is given over to discussion on questions of curriculum content.
- In higher education SC/ST students are more in arts stream and their percentages in graduation level are more than post graduations, they do not prefer to have the most expensive science and technological (professional) subjects. This may be due to their financial and social weakness. They are not sound on information technology and they have known idea about their right to information.
- In the academic environment the library and information system is badly affected in many angles like financial, collection building, manpower development, space, electronics infrastructure etc.

Various studies and survey reports have endorsed these constraints and highlighted the two most important factors that is education and proper information are the root causes of all the above hindrances in our development programme. In our study also, it is clearly indicated that in the majority of instances, education is undertaken without objectives and without goal or result oriented planning, it is based on social discrimination and prejudices. Most of the part of Orissa is covered with tribal people in the remote areas and there are no communication facilities for spread of education and information. Again, Government facilities can't reach to them easily. There is lack of proper guidance in the backward areas to guide them for education, as often the parents of SC/ST are illiterate or semi-educated. In addition, most of them are forced to work hard labour to earn for themselves as well as for their families. There is lacking of libraries and information centers in backward districts of Orissa like KBK, and the higher academic institutional are not well equipped with all the spears due to government and bureaucratic will in these areas except coastal plains (urban), yet, the urban area libraries suffer with applications of information technologies in the in the twentieth-century. The academic library system also suffers in its conventional method without application of new technologies in the information age. Mostly they come to a lost distance for their higher study eager to fulfill their information needs, but they don't have awareness about different collections in the libraries. They generally are not so broad-minded and financially sound to have any informative document for them. Most of them are not aware of the Governments provisions and programmes for them and major groups of these communities don't know what help they can acquire for upgrading their knowledge and skill in their subjects from the libraries. The findings in their higher education shows, they are of opinion that the class notes are sufficient to pass their examination. and have a jab any where to feed themselves. Some have interest to study more by visiting library, but do not get the materials of their needs and interests at right time and some don't have idea to find out an information he actually want, others don't worried about any new document in the library.

Suggestions

Therefore, it is suggested that, Orissa, which comes under backward state in India, has a great role to play for implementing right to educating and right to information to the weaker sections comprising mostly SC & ST communities, because they constitute 40% of Orissa's population and are mostly illiterate. Their role is more important in our developmental planning and this can be fulfilled if there is a regular traffic of information and consultation between the citadels of knowledge and the users. These levels being preparatory ground for higher education, is crucial to understand and bear in mind when one talks of higher education for them. All these can be solved on the basis of the following few measures:

Proper implementation of the constitutional provisions and special facilities for them. in the state, without any discriminations. Implement both in letter and spirit compulsory, universal and free education for SC/ST. Make the reservation quota mandatory for all private educational institutions at different levels- from primary to technical and professional. Take total responsibility for making SC/ST communities literate within a specified period of ten years. Our High Court should declare right to education as fundamental right of SCs and STs, like the High Court of Andhra Pradesh as published in -The Hindu (2003).

Established members in faculty positions at different universities and colleges could encourage bright students (not necessarily relatives) from Orissa for further studies. They could initiate regular seminars and symposia on different topics of interest at various universities in Orissa in addition to encouraging basic and fundamental research in liaison with the faculty there.

We feel that it is necessary to identify and groom talent amongst boys and girls belonging to SC, ST and other OBCs and train them in special talent schools. This will enable them to compete with the rest of society in an equal manner.

Within the next decade computers, television, telephone and telecommunication industries are going to merge into a giant playground and by punching few buttons one can gain access into global information technology. This can be implemented in Orissa like other developed state. Fortune 500 companies have taken significant inroad into South India and other states but not into Orissa. We need our computer information scientists to galvanize forming a consortium in this direction.

It is high time that the State Govt. to take some specific steps and positive action for the all round development of SC/ST community in the states. It is only they, who can understand the needs and aspirations of the SCs&STs. As Baba Saheb Dr Ambedkar had long ago rightly said, it is only the servile class who can lead them. Definitely not their antagonists, nor the classroom city products just in the Universities, or those with foreign education or reservation of seats trainings and mandates. The Government at the Center and the State should at least give them total literacy and socio-economic status by establishing-

- National and State Level Administrative and Professional Training Establishments for the SCs&STs, to develop and improve their Administrative and Professional Competence and Capabilities. Planning for, SC&ST Education and Employment, separate educational institutions in there local areas
- Recognition of individuals and institutions, working for the development and integration of the SCs&STs.
- Special social security schemes, insurance for the SCs&STs, especially the educated and unemployed in the state.
- Special concessions in private education and information access, to educate their children, and for sending them for higher studies or studies abroad, and or for specialist and advanced courses and trainings.
- Special Concessions for building their own homes, fee government land for there cultivation to eliminate the slums and the growing problems associated with them that dehumanizes the people.
- Special schemes and concessions to SC&ST entrepreneurs for taking up self-employment, starting their own business, and setting up their own industries.
- Special programmes, to harness and utilise the talents, knowledge and experiences of retired library and defense professionals, for the development and improving their standards of leaving.
- Proper implementation of National Policy on Education 1986 as modified in 1992 for them. Specially opening of public libraries in their area with mobile library facilites.
- The government should also regularly Constitute an High Power Committee, at least every two years, to review the allocation, utilisation, appropriation and diversion of the funds meant and budgeted for the education welfare and development of the SCs&STs both in the States and at the Center.

- There should also be schemes and programmes, evolved and structured to suit specific communities/ castes/ tribes, and also sub-castes, sub-tribes and part of the castes and tribes living/ settled in different areas. This is absolutely necessary, in view of large scale migrations due to education, employment, and search of livelihood and for survival; and also the uprooting/shifting/relocation of whole villages, communities and the people of different regions, particularly the ST's and also the SC's of many small pockets, as a result of development programmes and mega-projects.
- Adequate funds have to be separately earmarked for poverty alleviation, ameliorative, assets creation, welfare, infrastructure development, education including grant of various free ships scholarships fellowships and provision of hostels and messes, entrepreneur development, financial assistance for purchase of land/house building/starting business, and for establishing cottage/mini/small-scale/ medium/big/large industries, and such other identifiable schemes and programmes.
- Funds should be separately budgeted, allocated and released to NGO's run by others for the welfare and development of the SC&ST, to NGOs headed or patronised by SC&ST leaders and individuals, and to NGOs run and personally managed by the SC&ST Communities themselves. Their utilities and effectiveness must be carefully assessed, separately in different areas and regions, and for different schemes and programmes, for taking up timely and appropriate corrective and remedial actions, and for a better utilisation of the funds and maximisation of the results.
- The academic institutions and department of education should also properly implement the provisions and facilities meant for them without the academic environment.
- To conclude the present study the academic libraries well organized by its parent institute may satisfy the intellectual needs and interests of the SC/ST

community more than any others. Because we are living in the information age, right to information is the motto of everybody now. The driving force is technological, pushing forward through advances in the fields of computing and telecommunications; the essence of the information revolution lies in the socio-economic sphere, resulting in change in the typical activity of people not just at work, but in every aspect of their lives.

Thus, library has got a very important role to play in education. Without a good and efficient library in place, education cannot attain its desired objective. In fact, this is the reason each educational institution should have a library with adequate fund, infrastructure, adequate collections and, technology resources, matching with the course requirement and current needs. Besides, efficient personnel to handle the library, hitch equipment including computer with required packages and on top of everything, a set of personnel who should be adequately trained to run the library is of utmost importance to match the education level with the global trend.

But it is a matter of regret that despite mushroom growth of educational institution in the country in recent times, the quality of library in the country is no where near the international standards as it is not coping with the international standards. On the contrary it is losing it's efficacy and effectiveness. Unless it matches with all its the requirements in the information age and the library personnel are not trained adequately for management of the modern library efficiently, there is every possibility that the libraries which are expected to be great help to the students and as well as to the research communities will adversely effect both the teaching and research environment in the country. In order to ensure better quality of teaching, research and efficiency of the students, a better and efficient library with well-equipped technology and training, is the necessity of the day. The libraries and colleges are two faces of a single coin namely, learning satisfying the mental needs of the students and faculties. Library supplements classroom lectures in the promotions of education. The academic institution ideal objectives of speeding the light of education by making students library minded by attracting them with modern electronics information systems.

In Orissa even though we are not having electronics form of information's and information technologies in the academic libraries yet, in some private and govt. organizations, institutions and agencies are going ahead for its applications and implementations in their day-to-day information needs. However, in our neighboring states like: Andrapradesh, West Bengal and Madhya Pradesh etc are more advanced to use electronics media in their higher academic libraries. Government of Orissa recently highlighted to use IT in its governance. It is a good sign for Orissa LIS that the 11th Public Library Act has been passed in 2001 and published in Orissa Gazette on 11th March. There are also many other reasons responsible for application of IT in academic libraries of Orissa given in our previous chapter (V). Thus, it is not bad to say for networking Orissa's academic libraries. In the state of Orissa, computer literacy program has been implemented at the school level. Students passing out from these schools will definitely expect a well equipped library with facilities of IT for accessing information when they enter in the collegiate level. Therefore, it has become operative on the part of the Government and college authorities to think for introduction of IT in their college libraries. This will facilitate the students to access information from their library in order to prepare themselves for the challenges that they will face in the forthcoming 21st century. Accordingly, it is also realized that unless the library staff is well acquainted with the technicalities of IT they will be proved the computer specialist will invade misfit the profession and the digital age of the knowledge society. But, in the absence of a study on effective utilization of these facilities by the college libraries, it would be difficult to know the past and present status on IT at college level.

We are living in a society, which is characterized as information society and where the development is very much dependent upon availability of the right information at a right time for taking effective decisions in every sphere of life. But the availability of the right information cannot be ensured unless the scattered information at different sources are collected, processed and disseminated in a systematic manner. The processing and retrieval of information can be done both manually and also using the computer. Though the manual processing of information is in existence from the time immemorial and done by the library professional, it has become outdated and very much slow. Realising this, libraries have started thinking and introducing information technology (IT) for the last three decades. Thus, libraries are at the heart of the information society. According to UNESCO/IFLA (2003) "Libraries and librarians and should have a key role in helping to deliver an equitable global information society" This was the core message of the delegates from over 70 countries attending the Pre-Conference to the World Summit on the Information Society that was organized by the International Federation of Library Associations and Institutions (IFLA) in Geneva 2003.

For the above reason as well as various reasons mentioned in the previous chapter (V) of the present study, it is suggested that the different problems and limitations mentioned in the academic environment of Orissa can be better solved by implementing the proposed "Orissa Academic Libraries Network" (OALNET) for the benefit of Orissa in general and SC/ST communities in particular. If this can be successfully implemented the aim and objective of the higher education can be achieved under the following heads-

- Today computers are available which can compute at very high speed and also have large disc storage space with multimedia facilities at a very low cost investment.
- A networked library shifts the "library System" to the user just like: "home delivery", "fast food"—a fashion in our daily life now. Thus, there is no need of user to come regularly to the library for a particular piece of information.
- The various information needs of the students, researchers and faculties in the higher academic institute can be encouraged for better use of the

networked libraries, round the clock within their institutional campus.

- It offers economies in government educational fund and spread government decisions without delay for the total literacy programme. It also informative for the common people, decision makers, specialist, researcher, scientist to gate right information in right time in front of a networked PC.
- It is mostly beneficial to the academic libraries and its librarians in many aspects like: quicker access to the information, saving of processing time for reference work, increased or higher demands for library services, getting more cost-effectiveness and efficiency in library operation.
- It maintains better cooperation among different institution/librarians, students, researchers and faculties within the region to share their resource within themselves.
- It reduces extra budget, time, space, manpower, and unnecessary paper works, pressure on the librarian and information professionals in the network region.
- It offers better learning to the academic environment with a single key command on the networked computer system in the library.
- Helping students, researchers and faculties to find resources in digitally chaotic worlds with a greater obtains.
- It enable self-learning among the users community with sensitivity to different learning styles and continuous assessment of educational progress.
- In general it provides a greater and wider control over the learning process within state, anywhere and any time in the networked area.
- It can facilitate to use other information, which is not related to a subject, even a private educational institution connected to it in the remote area can access any information.

Thus, in this information age our academic institutions should be self-sufficient. But, self-sufficiency cannot be maintained without proper education or knowledge, and there is no knowledge without information. Therefore, information is the right of every citizen in the world, where there is no right to information, there is illiteracy, which creates all shorts of problem in the society and all these problems make us dependant to others. We certainly need to move from dependant to independent, independence to inter-dependence by changing our self from conventional to electronics. In order to achieve these, in a greater spirit the academic libraries of Orissa should undertake the following measures for proper implementation of the proposed network.

Considering the existing infrastructure facilities, financial resources, manpower and technological aspects in the libraries the implementation of the model (OALNET) can be made in three different steps:

1.1 Purchasing different network infrastructures like- computers hardware and library network software with different network components- physical interface (network card), different connectors for the interface to a communications medium (cables), hubs to distribute electronics data from one input port to several out ports (repeaters) and router (to manage the transport of data pockets over the borders of internal networks and communications media).

1.2 Introduction of computer culture in the academic libraries, institutions all over Orissa. Setting of network management, security management and deciding different department in the institutions to give network connection for larger benefits of the users etc.

1.3 Providing computer and network training to the existing library professionals in the state and automating the entire libraries by crating machine readable databases as per the standard based on national and international.

1.4 Creating various machine-readable databases as per the standard.

2.1 Setting of different workstations in different departments within the institution campus.

2.2 Connecting with the local hub/district hub/central hub for resource sharing among the libraries and information centers.

2.3 Motivating and educating different student, research scholars and faculties about how to use a networked computer and how to search for specific information. It should be clearly published within the workstation.

3.1 Bringing all other nearby libraries within its membership. The private academic/training institutes in the state can accept its membership.

3.2 Different schools, junior colleges in a district can be connected by the recommendation of CMC.

3.3 This system can go to the village Pathasala/Post Office/primary School level in the back word/hill areas by the positive steps taken by the Government of Orissa.

Contributions of the Study

The contribution of this study to the field of library and information science in India lies in several directions. By examining a complex phenomenon, from the perspectives of the key players, the study has been able to identify the problem areas of this process of introducing IT in libraries. It has highlighted the strengths and weaknesses of the detail educational library system in India as well as Orissa. Suggestions for implementation of computer network have been made on the basis of the ground realities. Special emphasis has given for networking the educational institutions in the backward region of Orissa.

Additionally, the use of the phenomenological methodology has been of benefit to the US and UK field. In all probability, this methodology was used for the first time in India in this study. The application of this method to research problem and the validation of its findings through triangulation open up the possibility of using this approach in the field of LIS. The findings were based on different primary and secondary data collected all over India, especially from Orissa. The present study had based on the information needs of scheduled caste and scheduled tribe communities in the higher academic institutions of Orissa and suggested to be self-reliance by implementing the proposed resource-sharing network in the academic libraries.

Scope for Further Research

This study has suggested the department of education and government of Orissa for application of resources sharing network in the academic libraries of Orissa, but before doing so, there is a need to understand the macro levels of it, to explore the effect of external variables such as government policies, economic situations, business environment and IT industry etc. Thus, co-relationship and causality between macro and microenvironment and implantation of networking system in the various types of libraries is a worthwhile area of study. Since, the different types of libraries functioning within varying macro environments, it would be useful to examine the problem of implementation of this, in specific types of libraries starting from school. The introduction and level of networking in libraries are inextricably interwoven with the type and culture of the organization. Another interesting line of investigation could be to examine the effect of organizational structure and librarian's status in the organization and implantation of this model. A study of immediate value may also understand the role and dynamics of resource sharing network vis-à-vis role of librarian in Orissa. It may even be possible to work out some basic do's and don'ts for the resources sharing to yield fruitful results and not become a platform for ego clashes.

The users behavior towards the networked information sources; their search criteria and the librarians' knowledge of networking, attitude towards computer system can be some other areas of study. Individual aspects of implementation-such as finance, staff development etc. can be the focus of future in depth studies. Longitudinal studies of a few libraries over a period of time would provide valuable insights into how different managerial issues over time and how their resolution also varies.

Bibliography

Abell, Angela (1998). Skills for the 21st Century editorial, *Journal of Librarianship and Information Science,* 30(4), p. 211-214.

Agarwal, S.P and Lal M (1997). Information needs of social scientists. *International Library Review,* 19(2), pp. 287-299.

Ahmad, Karuna (1983). 'Towards equality: consequences of protective discrimination', *Economic and Political Weekly,* 13(.2), pp. 69-72.

Ahmed, Karuna (1986). Sponsored social change and positive discrimination: The Case of the Scheduled Caste and Scheduled Tribe, *Social Change,* 16(2), p. 27.

Aijaj, Roohi and Monga, M (1988). Educational development of SCs and STs in Maharastra, Tamil Nadu and Orissa. *Social Changc,* 18(1), p. 70.

Aikara, J. (1994). 'Social context of education in India', *Journal of Education and Social Change,* 34 (20), p. 223.

Aikara, J. (1996). 'Inequality of educational opportunities: The case of Scheduled Castes in India', *Journal of Educational Planning and Administration,* Vol. 10(1), p. 1-14.

Akeroyd, John (1990). Information seeking in online catalogues. *Journal of Documentation,* 46, (1) Mar.

Allen, B. (1990). 'The effects of academic background on statements of information need,' *Library Quarterly,* 60(2), pp. 120-138.

Allen, B., Qin, J. & Lancaster, F. W. (1994). Persuasive communities: a longitudinal analysis of references in the philosophical transactions of the Royal Society, 1665-1990, *Social Studies of Science,* 24, pp. 279-310.

Alvin Toffler (1970). Information society the striking changes. *JASIS,* 34(2), pp. 12-17.

Ambedkar Research Institute (1991). Future trends of SC/ST population and socio-economic, education and political potentialities in India. Published by Directorate of social welfare, Government of Karnataka.

Annual Report (2002/03). Department of Education, Government of India, New Delhi.

Appleton, M. (1994). Investigating library services for postgraduate off-campus students. In Research in distance education 3: revised papers from the third Research in Distance Education conference, Deakin University, Eds. Terry.

Association of Indian Universities. Internet Search: http://www.aiuweb.org/index.htm

Auster, E and Choo, C. W.(1991). Environmental scanning: a conceptual framework for studying the information seeking behaviour of executives. In: ASIS 91. Systems understanding people. Proceedings of the 54th Annual Meeting of the American Society for Information Science, Volume 28, Washington, D.C., 27-31 October 1991. Edited by Jose-Marie Griffiths, Medford, Learned Information, Inc., for Am. Society for Information Science, pp. 3-8.

Babu, A.D., (1994). *Information Generation and Library Use by University Teachers.* Gyan Publishing House, New Delhi.

Badapanda, Sudipta Kumar. (1999). What all-primary education in tribal areas. *Exchanges.* No. 25/26; 1999; pp. 43-47.

Bal, B.K., and Swain, C.R. (1999). Academic excellence and teaching skills: there impact in teaching at college level: an experiment in Mayurbhanja, Vision. 18(3-4). Jan-June, pp. 1-7.

Bates, M.J., (1997). Learning about the information seeking of interdisciplinary scholars and students. *Library and Information Science Research,* 19 (3), pp. 217-48.

Behera, G. B(1995). A journey of twenty five years: chemistry Dept. Sambalpur University. Univ. News. 33(4), pp. 14-15.

Belkin, N. J (1987). Information concepts in information science. *Journal of Documentation.* 34, (1), pp. 55-85.

Belkin, N.J., Cool, C., Stein, A. and Thiel, U. (1995). Cases, scripts, and information-seeking strategies: on the design of interactive information retrieval systems. *Expert Systems with Applications,* 9, pp. 379-395.

Bernal, J. D. (1948). The social function of science. Cambridge Publication, M.A: MIT Press, UK.

Bhat, V.N (1999). Higher Education for 21st Century India: a critical reflection, *University News,* 37(31), pp. 6-10.

Bhattacharyya, A (1978). Information sciences: Unenvied view through a system approach., *IASLIC J.* 23(2), pp. 34-45.

Bhattacharyya, G.(1975). Project on Study Of Subjects. Library Science with a Slant to Documentation. No. 12; Paper G).

Brittain J.M (1982). Pitfalls of user research and some neglected areas. *Social Science Information Studies,* 68 (2), pp. 139-148.

Brookes, B.C. (1980). Foundation of information science. *Journal of Information Science,* 23(2), pp. 3-4.

Brown, M. E. (1991). A general model of information-seeking behaviour. In: ASIS 91. Systems understanding people. Proceedings of the 54th Annual Meeting of the American Society for Information Science, Volume 28, Washington, D.C., 27-31 October 1991 9-14, Edited by Jose-Marie Griffiths, Medford, Learned Information, Inc., for American Society for Information Science, 1991. Meadows A.J. *Communication in Science.* Butterworths, London 1974, pp 248.

Brown, R. H. (1998). Toward a democratic science: Scientific narration and civic communication. New Haven, CT: Yale University Press.

Buchanan, D. and Huczynski, A. (1997). *Organizational Behavior: An Introductory Text.* 3rd edition. London: Prentice-Hall. pp. 276-280.

Case, D.O. (2002). Looking for information: a survey of research on information seeking, needs, and behaviour. San Diego, CA: Academic Press. New Delhi.

Census of India (1991). Government of India, New Delhi

Census of India (1991). ORISSA Primary Census Abstract: scheduled caste and scheduled tribe, Part II-B (iii)

Census of India (2001). Government of India, New Delhi.

Chakrabarti, B. and Basu (1999). A Information needs of the totos: a sub-Himalayan tribal community. *IASLIC Bulletin* 44(4), pp. 177-184.

Chakraborty, G and Ghosh, P.K. (1997). Education among SCs and STs in rural Orissa. Evidence form a recent survey. *Vision*. 17(1-2); Jul-Dec., pp. 35-54.

Chamis, Y., Saracevic, T. and Trivison, D. (1986). Research on information seeking and retrieving: a progress report. National Online Meeting., edited by Martha A. Williams and Thomas H. Hogan, Medford, New Jersey, Learned Information, Inc., 1986 National Online Meeting. Proceedings of the 7th National Online Meeting, New York, 6-8 May 86, 67-72. Presented at the 7th National Online Meeting organised by Online Review, held in New York, 6-8 May.

Chanana, K. (1997). Accessing Higher Education: The Dilemma of Schooling: Women Minorities Scheduled Castes and Scheduled Tribes in contemporary India, in *Higher Education Reform in India,* Edited by Suma.

Chatman, E. (1991). Life in a small world: applicability of gratification theory to information-seeking behaviour. *Journal of the American Society for Information Science,* 42 (6), pp. 438-449.

Chatman, E. (1996). The impoverished life world of outsiders. *Journal of the American Society for Information Science,* 47(3), pp. 193-206.

Chatman, E. (1999). A theory of life in the round. *Journal of the American Society for Information Science* 50(3), 207-217.

Chen, C.C., (1982). *Information Seeking: Assessing and Anticipating User Needs.* New York, Neal Schuman Publishers, Inc., USA.

Chen, C.C. & Hernon, P. (1982). *Information Seeking: Assessing and Anticipating User Needs.* New York: Neal Schuman. USA.

Chottopadhya, M. (2003). Role of Govt. in the Development of Social Aspects of level of living in India, *Man & Development,* June, pp. 49-90.

Christie, Bruce (1981). *Face to File Communication: A Psychological Approach to Information System.* John Wiley Publications; Chichester, England.

Cronin, Blaise.(1981). Assessing user needs. *ASLIB Proceedings,* 32(2), pp. 37-47.

Das, Sunita and Hazary, N. (1986). Educational administration under stress: a study of college Principles in Orissa. *Indian J. Pub. Administration.* 32(4), pp. 89-55.

Debi, Sailabala (1985). Private Profitability or profession education in Orissa, *Utkal Econ. Papers.* Oct. pp. 79-84.

Debi, Sailabala (1987). Private return to higher education in Orissa. *Indian Econ. Rev.* 22(3), pp. 63-77.

Dept. of Education (2003). State of Education Orissa: an overview, Govt. of Orissa, pp. 1-18.

Derr, R.L. (1984). Information seeking expressions of users. *Journal of the American Society for Information Science,* 35 (2), pp. 124-128.

Dervin, B. (1983). Information as a user construct: The relevance of perceived information needs to synthesis and interpretation. In: S.A. Ward & L.J. Reed (Eds.), Knowledge structure and use: Implications for synthesis and interpretation. (pp. 155-183). Philadelphia: Temple University Press.

Dervin, B. (1992). From the mind's eye of the user: the sense-making qualitative-quantitative methodology. In: J. D. Glazier & R. R. Powell, (Eds.), *Qualitative Research in Information Management.* (pp. 61-84). Englewood, Co: Libraries Unlimited.

Dervin, B. and Nilan, M. (1986). Information needs and uses, *Annual Review of Information Science and Technology,* No. 21, pp. 3-33.

Dervin, B. et.al. (1982). Measuring aspects of Information

seeking: *A text of a quantitative/qualitative Methodology. Communication Year Book.* No. 6, Sage Publication, Thousand Oak.

Devdason, F.J., (1989). Identifying information needs: Discussion Paper at the Regional Consultation on Provision of Information Services to End Users, UN/ESCAP Fertiliser Advisory, Development and Information Network for Asia and the Pacific - Network of Fertiliser Information Systems (FADINAP/NFIS). Bangkok, 20-24 Nov. 1989.

Devi, Sailabala (1984). Cost structure of higher education– A case study of Orissa, *J. Higher Education* 10(1-2); p. 57.

Devrajan, G. (1989). *User's Approach to Information in Libraries.* Ess Ess Publication, New Delhi.

Dhanyi, K., (1986). Psychological needs and source linkages in undergraduate information-seeking behaviour. *College & Research Libraries* 47 (5), pp. 475-481.

Dhawan, S.M. and Sachdeva, D.C. (1987). User's Approach to information in Social Science: An Overview. *ILA Bulletin.* 22(3-4), pp. 103-110.

Dixit, R.P. (1992). Assessment of health literature/information needs of medical scientists. *Library Herald* 31, (1-2), pp. 76-92.

Donohew, Lewisn (1978). Tipton Leonard and Haney Roger Analysis of Information seeking strategies. *Journalism Quarterly* 55, Spring, pp. 25-31.

Dreze, Jean and Amartya Sen(1995). Basic Education as a political Issue, *Journal of Education Planning and Administration,* 9(1), pp. 1-26.

Drucker Peter F. (1993). *Managing for the Future: The 1990s and Beyond,* 1993, Tata McGraw Hill, New Delhi.

East India Human Development Report (2004). National Council of Economic Research, Oxford University Press, New Delhi, pp. 175-236.

Economic Survey (2002-2003). Government of Orissa. 2003, p. 14/12-20/12.

Educational Statististics (1997-2002). Directorate of Higher Education and Department of Education, Government of Orissa.

Ellis David (1993). Modeling the information seeking patterns of academic researchers; a guided theory approach. *Library Quarterly,* 63(4), pp. 469-486.

Ellis, D. (1989). A behavioral approach to information retrieval system design, *Journal of Documentation,* 45(3), pp. 171-212.

Ellis, D. (1992). The physical and cognitive paradigms in information retrieval research. *Journal of Documentation* 48(1), pp./45-64.

Ellis, D., Cox, D. & Hall, K. (1993). A comparison of the information seeking patterns of researchers in the physical and social sciences. *Journal of Documentation* 49(4), pp. 356-369.

F.J. Devadason and P. Pratap Lingam (1996). A Methodology for the Identification of Information Needs of Users,Presented in 62nd IFLA General Conference-Conference Proceedings-August 25-31.

For a collection of relevant articles, see Gerard B. McCabe and Ruth J., (1995). Person. *Academic Libraries: Their Rationale and Role in American Higher Education.* Westport, Conn. Greenwood Press, (Contributions in Librarianship and Information Science; No. 84).

Ford, Geoffrey (1973). Researcher in user behaviour in university libraries. *Journal of Doc.* 29(1), pp. 85-106.

Galanter, Marc (1984). *Competing Equalities,* Oxford Universlty Press, New Delhi.

Gandhe, S.K. (1999). Access and Equity—Need of the Disadvantaged, *University News,* 37(3). pp. 23-27.

Giorija Kumar (1989). *Library Development in India.* Vikas Pub. House; New Delhi.

Gould, C. C. & Handler, M. (1989). Information needs in the social sciences: An assessment. *Mountain View,* CA: Research Libraries Group.

Government of India. *Economic Survey–2002/2003,* Education, pp. 222-226.

Govinda, R. (1998). *Issues and Concerns in School Education,* NIEPA, New Delhi.http://www.un.org.in/JANSHALA/octber98/issues.htm

Guha, B. (1983). *Documentation and Information: Services, Techniques and System,* World Press, Calcutta.

Gupta, Aruna K. and Dhar, Neelam (1999). Youth anxiety in and through higher education system. *University News,* 37(31), pp. 1-5.

Gupta, S.P. (1992). College education in Orissa. *University News,* 30(10) 9th March. pp. 13-77.

Hanna, Nagy (1991). Information technology revolution and economic development: World Bank Discussion. Chicago. USA.

Hanson, R J (1996). *Library, User's Guide, 1990-1996,* by Visual Numeric, Inc. Subtitled: Fortran 90 Subroutines and Functions for Scientific Applications, Texas.

Herner, S. and Herner, H. (1967). Information Needs and Uses in Science and Technology In : Cuadra, CA (ed). *Annual Review of Information Science and Technology.* 2, pp. 1-34.

Hewins, E.T. (1990). Information Need and Use Studies. *Annual Review of Information Science and Technology.* 25, pp. 145 172).

Hindustan Times (2003). Vision 2020 seeks private initiative in education, 21 Oct. Calcutta Edn.

Hjorland, B. (1993). Subject representation and information seeking: contributions to a theory based on the theory of knowledge. *Svensk Biblioteks Forskning,* (2-3), pp. 80-6.

Höglund, L. et al. (1995). Tusen studenter om biblioteket - vanor, attityder och krav. Stockholm: BIBSAM. (Delstudie 2)

Höglund, L., Thorstéinsdóttir, G. (1996). Students and the university library. Attitudes to and use of university libraries among students and faculty. *Svensk biblioteksforskning* 4: pp. 29-42.

Hollend, W.E (1972). Information potentials: a concept of the importance of information sources in a research and development environment. *Journal of Communication.* 22, pp. 159-173.

Hyldegaard, J. (1997). Visual information seeking: browsing and navigation through a desktop VR user interface.

Proceedings of the 2nd British-Nordic Conference on Library and Information Studies, Edinburgh, 1997. Organized by the British Association for Information and Library Education (BAILER). Edited by Michelin Beaulieu, Elisabeth Davenport and Niels Ole Pors. London: Taylor Graham, pp. 79-89.

Indian Library Association (1999). Library Vision 2010: Indian Libraries and Librarianship in retrospect and prospect: 45th ILA Conference, Hisar, ILA, New Delhi.

Indian Library Association (1999). National Seminar on Challenges before the University Libraries in India in the 21st century, Vadodara, ILA, Delhi.

Indiresan, P.V. and N.C. Nigam (1993). 'The Indian Institutes of Technology: Excellence in Peril' in Chitnis, Suma and Altbach, Philip (1999). *Higher Education Reform in India: Experience and Perspectives,* Sage Publications, New Delhi.

INFLIBNET, Ahmedabad. http://www.inflibnet.ac.in

Ingwersen, P. (1989). Psychological aspects of information retrieval. *Social Science Information Studies,* 4 (2/3), pp. 83-89.

Ingwersen, P. (1995). Information and Information Science". In: A. Kent, ed. *Encyclopedia of Information and Information Science.* Volume 56, Supplement 19.p. 137-174, New York, NY: Marcel Dekker. ISIC Proceedings

Internet Search - http://orissagov.nic.in/index.htm

Internet Search http://shikshanic.nic.in/cd50years/12/8I/6W/8I6W0301.htm

Internet Search - www.ignou.ac.in/divisions/library/edu.htm

Internet Search. http://www.ntu.edu.sg/sci/is/resgrps-14.htm#Anc_ISP7

Internet Search. Social study circle, http//www.dalitindia.com

Internet Search: http://www.education.nic.in/htmlweb/iamr1.htm

Internet Search. http://www.ambedkar.org/ssc/resvn.htm

Itoga, M. (1992). Seeking understanding beneath the unspecifiable: an alternative framework for mapping information needs in communication. *Libri,* 42 (4), pp. 330-44.

Jain, M.K. (1998). *50 Years of Library and Information Services in India;* Shipra Publications, New Delhi.

Jain, Jasbir (1999). *Excellence and Creativity in Higher Education: Restrospect and Prospect,* Edited by M.I. Sisodia et.al. University Book House (P) Ltd. Jaipur.

Jha, S. (1988). A study on the Secondary School climate in selected tribal district in Orissa. *Progress in Education.* 62(7); pp. 158-62.

Julien, H. & Duggan, L. J. (2000). A longitudinal analysis of the information needs and uses literature. *Library and Information Science Research* 22(3), pp. 291-309.

Julien, H. (1999). Barriers to adolescents' information seeking for career decision-making. *Journal of the American Society for Information Science* 50(1), pp. 38-48.

Kalervo Järvelin and T.D. Wilson (2003). On conceptual models for information seeking and retrieval research, *Information Research,* 9(1), October 2003

Karisiddappa, C. R. (2002). Role and importance of national and state level associations in library development in India. *IFLA Council and General Conference.* Vol. 68 .

Katz, D. and Kahn. R.L. (1978). *The Social Psychology of Organisations.* Ed 2. New York, John Wiley.

Kaul, H.K. (1999). *Library Resource Sharing and Networks.* New Delhi, Virgo Publications.

Kaur, Amritpal (1997). Use of computer and CD-Rom in the libraries of Agricultural Universities and Research Institutes in the states of Panjab, Haryana and Himachal Prodesh, *ILA Bulletin,* 32 (3-4), pp. 1-5

Kejriwal, A. (2003) "More stories of Parivartan", *India Together,* April 2003: http://indiatogether.org/2003/apr/gov-rtidelhi.htm as on 1 October 2003.

King, D.W., Casto, J. & Jones, H. (1994). Communication by engineers: A literature review of engineers' information needs, seeking processes and use. Washington: Council on Library Resources.

Krashen, S. D. (1993). *The Power of Reading: Insights from the Research.* Englewood, CO: Libraries Unlimited.

Krikelas, James (1983). Information seeking behaviour: Pattern and Concept. *Drexel Lib. Quarterly,* 19(2), pp. 5-20.

Krishna Kumar (1992). *Research Libraries in Developing Countries.* Delhi, Vikas Pub. House. India.

Krishnamurty, M. (2002). Digital library gateway for library and information science; a study, *SRELS J. of Inf. Management,* 39 (3), pp. 245-254.

Kuhlthau, C. C. (1991)Inside the search process: Information seeking from the user's perspective. *Journal of the American Society for Information Science,* 42 (5), June pp. 361-371.

Kuhlthau, C. C. (1993). A principle of uncertainty for information seeking. *Journal of Documentation,* 49 (4) Dec, pp. 339-55.

Kuhlthau, C.C. (1993). Inside the search process: Information seeking from the user's perspective. *Journal of the American Society for Information Science,* 42 (5) June, pp. 361-371.

Kuhlthau, C. C. (1993). Seeking meaning: A process approach to library and information services. Norwood, NJ: Ablex. US.

Kuhlthau, C. C.(1993). A principle of uncertainty for information seeking. *Journal of Documentation.* 49(4); pp. 339-355.

Kuhlthau, C.C. (1991). Inside the search process: information seeking from the user's perspective. *Journal of the American Society for Information Science,* 42, pp. 361-371.

Kuhlthau, C.C. (1997). The influence of uncertainty on the information seeking behaviour of a securities analyst," in: Information seeking in context: proceedings of an international conference on research in information needs, seekingand use in different contexts, 14-16 August 1996, Tampere, Finland, edited by P. Vakkari, R. Savolainen, B. Dervin. London: Taylor Graham. pp. 268-274.

Kuhn, T.S. (1962). The structure of scientific revolutions. Chicago, IL: University of Chicago Press. USA.

Kumar K (1983). Educational Experience of Scheduled Castes and Tribes, *Economic and Political Weekly,* 18(36), pp. 1566-1572.

Kumar, K. (1987). Reference Service: 3rd rev. ed. Delhi; Vikas. India.

Kunz, Werner; Rittel, Horst W.J. and Schwuchow, Werner (1977). Methods of Analysis and Evaluation of Information Needs: A Critical Review. Munchen, Verlag Dokumentation. p. 16.

Lahiri, A. (1992). Problem of document Supply: a Book at Indian sources and NLA-ASTINFO Facility. *NISSAT Newsletter* No. 1, pp. 18-22.

Lahiri, R. (1990). A study on the user of a University Library *IASLIC Bulletin,* 33(2-3), pp. 331- 337.

Lalitha, M. (1995), Information seeking behaviour of medical and engineering personnel: a comparative study with reference to their library use. *Library Science with a Slant to Documentation and Information Studies,* 32 (2) Jun, pp. 65-74.

Latham, S., Slade, A.L. & Budnick, C. (1991). Library services for off-campus and distance education: an annotated bibliography. Ottawa, Ontario: Canadian Library Association.

Lewis, D. (2003) "The Need and Value of Access to Information from Non-State Agencies", CHRI unpublished, p. 9.

Liddy, E. D. and Jorgensen, C. (1993). Modeling information seeking behaviours in index use. Proceedings of the 56th Annual Meeting of the American Society for Information Science, Columbus, Ohio, 24-28 October 1993. Edited by Susan Bonzi, Medford, New Jersey, Learned Information, Inc., For American Society for Information Science, pp. 185-90.

Limberg, L. (1995). Information seeking and learning. University of Boras, Department of Library and Information Science, PO Box 874, S-501 15 Boras, Sweden.

Lok Sabha Secretariat (1999). Report on the Reservation for Employment of SC/ST in Central Medical Institutions/ Colleges Including Reservation for SC/STs in Admissions Therein, Standing Committee on Welfare of SC/ST – Sixty-Fifth Report (1995-96), New Delhi.

Lok Sabha Secretariat (1999): Report on the Reservation for Employment of SC/ST in IITs Including Reservation for SC/STs in Admissions There in, Standing Committee on Welfare of SC/ST – Fifth Report (1998-99), NewDelhi.

Lonnquist, H. (1990). Scholars seek information: information-seeking behaviour and information needs of humanities scholars. *International Journal of Information and Library Research*, 2 (3), pp. 195-203.

Louis, Prokash (2002). Literacy education and the weaker sections in Bihar: issues and perspectives, *Social Change*, 32 (3&4), pp. 73-96.

Louis Prakash (2003). Scheduled Castes and Tribes: the reservation debate, *Economic and Political Weekly*, June 21, pp. 2475-2478.

Mahajan, S.L. (1999). Alienation of students in higher education. *University News*, 37(24), pp. 8-11.

Mahapatra, D. (1983). A study of school climate in the Secondary School of selected tribal districts of Orissa. *Vision*. 3(1-2), pp. 75-84.

Maheswarappa, B.S. and Trivedi, S.K. (1986). Information needs of Indian Food Scientists. A Case Study of C.F.T.R.I., Mysore. *Ann of Lib Sc. and Doc*. 33 (1-2), pp. 67-75.

Maheswarappa, B.S. and Hiremath, C.M.(1995). Information Use Pattern of Social Scientists in a University Environment in India" In RAJU (AAN) Ed. *New Vistas in Library and Information Science*, Vikas Publ, New Delhi.

Malmsjo. A., (1997). Information seeking in context. Proceedings of the international conference on research in information needs, seeking and use in different contexts, 14-16 August 1996, Tampered, Finland. Edited by Pertti Vakkari, Reijo Savolainen and Brenda Devin. London: Taylor Graham, pp. 222-35.

Manjunath, K. and Shivalingaiah, D. (2003). Information acess in libraries, *Annals of Library and Information Studies*, 50(2), pp. 85-90.

Marchionini, G. Information seeking in electronic environments. *Journal of Education for Library and Information Science*, 37 (1) Winter 96, pp. 81-83.

Marchionini, G. (1989). Information-seeking strategies of novices using a full-text electronic encyclopedia. *Journal of the American Society for Information Science*, 40 (1) pp. 54-66.

Marchionini, G. and Sandra Dwiggins(1990). Efforts of search and subject expertise on information seeking in a hypertext environment. In: ASIS'90. Information in the year 2000: from research to applications. Proceedings of the 53rd Annual Meeting of the American Society for Information Science, Toronto, Canada, 4-8 November 1990. Volume 27 Edited by Diane Henderson, Medford, New Jersey, Learned Information, Inc., for American Society for Information Science, pp. 129-142.

Marchionini, G. Interfaces for end-user information seeking. *Journal of the American Society for Information Science,* 43 (2), pp. 156-163.

Marchionini, G., Lin, X., Katz, A. and Dwiggins, S(1993). Information seeking in full-text end-user-oriented search systems: the roles of domain and search expertise. *Library and Information Science Research,* 15 (1) winter 93, pp. 35-69.

Menzel, H. (1964). The information needs of current scientific research, *Library Research,* 34(1), pp. 4-14.

MHRD Annual Report (1999-2000), Ministry of HRD, Government of India, New Delhi.

Mick, Colin K. (1980). Towards usable user studies. *JASIS,* 31(5), pp. 347-350.

Ministry of Human Resource Development (2003). Education becoming a fundamental right, and stress on vocationalisation and quality upgradation of Higher Education thrust areas in 2002-03, Press Releases, 23 March.

Ministry of Human Resources Development (1997). Selected Educational Statistics–1996-97, Government of India, New Delhi.

Ministry of Human Resources Development (MHRD-1997)). Selected Educational Statistics–1996-97, Government of India, New Delhi.

Mintzberg, H (1977). The Nature of Managerial Work. New York, Harper. 1973. Quoted in Wilson, T.D., and Streatfield, D.R. Information Needs in Local Authority Social Service Departments: an interim Report on Project Iniss. *(Journal of Documentation.* 33 (4), p. 290).

Mizzaro, S. (1998) "How many relevances in information retrieval?" *Interacting With Computers,* 10 (3), pp. 305-322.

Mohanty, B. and Senapati, C. (1983). Socio-economic profile of technical graduates or in OUAT. *J. Higher Education* 8(3); Sept., pp. 363-373.

Mohanty, M. S. (2000). A projection of the finances of the Utkal University for the year 1999-2000, *Southern Econ.* 15(1-2); Oct., pp. 12-14.

Mohanty, S.B. (1984). Innovation in student – teaching through NSS in ORISSA. *State. Educ. Rev.* 90(2); Feb., pp. 21-24.

Mohanty, S.B. (1992). Improving the functioning of autonomous college in Orissa. University News, 30(18), pp. 13-16.

Mohapatra, P.C.(1989). Problems of tribal education in Koraput district of Orissa. *Tribal Res. Bull.* 5(2); March 1989, 28-33.

Nanda, P.(2000). Ensuring quality higher education in ORISSA is the priority. *Organiser* 52(2), p. 14.

National Board of Employment, Education and Training (1990). Library provision in higher education institutions. Commissioned report No. 7 (Ross report), Australian Government Publishing Service.

National Council of Applied Economic Research (2004). *East India Human Development Report*, Oxford University Press, New Delhi.

Nayak, D.K., (2002). Gender caste and discrimination: a geographical perspective on the pattern of literacy among the scheduled caste women in Orissa, *Ambedkar J. of Social Development,* 10(9), pp. 167-182.

Nazan Ozenc Ucak and S. Serap Kurbanoglu (1998). Information need and information seeking behavior of scholars at a Turkish university, Presented in 64th IFLA General Conference August 16-August 21.

NCERT (2001). Educational problems of tribal children: a project sponsored by UNICEF and funded by World Bank, NewDelhi.

Neelameghan, A. (1992). Information for Small Enterprises. Bangalore, Sarada Ranganathan Endowment For Library Science. p. 50.

Neelameghan, A. (1975). Modern Business Environment and Environmental Scanning. *Library Science with a Slant to Documentation.* 12(1), p. 5-15.

Nicholas, D(1997). The changing information environment: assessing the impact of the Internet on information seeking behaviour. City University, Department of Information Science, Northampton Square, London EC1V 0HB, UK.

NPE 1986 updated 1992, MHRD, Publication No. 1723, MHRD, Department of Education, New Delhi.

Ocholla, D. N. (1996), Information-seeking behaviour by academics: a preliminary study. *International Information and Library Review,* 28 (4) Dec, pp. 345-58.

Odongo, R.I. (2001). A study of the information needs and uses of the informal sector in uganda: preliminary findings, *LIBRES: Library and Information Science Research,* 11(1), pp. 1-13

Oliver, R. and Oliver, H. (1997). Using context to promote learning from information-seeking tasks. *Journal of the American Society for Information Science,* 48 (6) Jun, pp. 519-26.

Osiobe, S.A. (1988). Information seeking behaviour. *International Library Review,* 20 (3) July, pp. 337-346.

Pais Richard (1999). Scheduled castes, employment and social mobility, in S.M. Michel (Ed.), *Dalit in modern India: Vision and Values,* Vistar Publications, New Delhi, p327.

Pandey, Soroja (1993). Education of SC and ST girls in Orissa. *Soc. Change.* 23(4); Dec. pp. 71-77.

Paper, 120, World Bank Report, Washington.USA.

Parida, Baman (1992). Status and job satisfection of librarians in colleges and universities of Orissa: an evaluation in Indian context, Ph.D. thesis, Utkal University, Bhubaneswar.

Parida, Baman (1999). Status of library professionals in academic institutions of Orissa: an evaluation, *Asian Libraries;* 8 (8), pp. 265-274.

Parida, Baman (2000). National IT action plan and ORISSAinformation technology policy in educational sector. *In Information Services in a Networked Environment in India*/ed by Vengan, Mohan and Raghaban; CALIBER-2000 Seminar papers.-Ahamedabad: INFLIBNET, pp. 4.46-4.52.

Parida, Baman (2002). Library networks in twin cities of Orissa: Cuttack and Bhubaneswar, Souvenir: XIX IATLIS, National Seminar, December 1-3, pp. 31-34.

Pathy, J. (1982). Politics of Tribal Welfare Some Reflections, *The Eastern Antropologist*, Vol. 45 (4), pp. 285-300.

Pattnaik, N. (1991). A study on self-concept and academic achievements of scheduled caste and scheduled tribe high school students. *Asian J. Psychological Edn.* 24(5-6); pp. 47-51.

Pattnaik, Nihar Ranjan (1992). Growth of Education among the Kandha tribe in the 19th century. *Adivasi*. 32(3); pp. 5-13.

Pors, N.O. (1995). Studerende og biblioteker. En undersøgelse af studerendes bibliotesbenyttelse. Statens Bibliotekstjeneste: København. (Skrifter fra Statens Bibliotekstjeneste, 9).

Power, K.B. (1997). Higher Education in India Since Independent: Restrospect and Future options, AIU Occasional Papers, 1- 21-pp + appendix 20.

Pradhani M.A. and Goutam (1997). Library services in the universities in North East. *IASLIC Bulletin*, 42(4), pp. 165-174.

Prasad, H.N. (1992). *Information Needs and Users*. Indian Bibliographic Center, Varanasi. India.

Prasher, R.G. (1991). Information and its Communication. Medalicom Press, New Delhi., India.

Pratap Lingam, P. (1985). Some Selected Extra Curricular Components in Information Science. *Library Science With a Slant to Documentation*. 22(4), p. 196.

Pratap Lingam, P. (1986). Towards a methodology for developing a mechanism for business environmental scanning. *IASLIC Bulletin*. 31(3), p. 84, 92 96.

Pratap Lingam, P. (1987). Manpower Planning for Sectoral Information and Documentation System in India with an Illustrative case study of Textile Industry. *IASLIC Bulletin*. 32(1), pp. 24 26.

Presentation by Secretary Mass Education (2002). Draft paper on: ORISSA2020–an education vision, held at Bhubaneswar.

Prasad, H.H and Tripathy, H., (1998). Information seeking behaviour physical scientist and social scientist: a report, *Annals of Library Science and Documentation*, 45(2), pp. 41-48.

Provisional Census Report (2001). Govt of India., New Delhi. India.

Ramesh, D.B., Seth, M.K. and Sahu, J.R., (1996). Use of Digital Information A Study on CD-ROM and ON-LINE Databases., *Lucknow Librarian*, 28(1-4); pp. 1-3.

Ranganathan, S.R., (1957). The five laws of library science, Blunt and Sons Ltd, Publications, UK.

Ranganathan, S.R., (1963). *The Five Laws of Library Science*. Bombay: Asia Publishing House. 2nd ed. (Ranganathan Series in Library Science; No. 12)

Ranganathan, S.R. (1964). *Colon Classification*. 6th ed., with amendments. Bombay, India: Asia Publishing House.

Rath, R. (1975). The study of scheduled caste and scheduled tribe college students in Orissa, Department of Psychology, Utkal University, Bhubaneswar.

Reddy, S.H. and Karisiddappa, C.R. (1997). Information seeking behaviour of the professionals in the field of disabilities with special reference to mental handicap in India, *Annals of Library Science and Documentation*, 44(2), pp. 54-64.

Reneker, M.H. (1993). A qualitative study of information seeking among members of an academic community: methodological issues and problems. *Library Quarterly*, 63 (4) Oct 93, pp. 487-507.

Report of the activities of SC&ST Development and Minorities, Backward Classes Welfare Department (2002/03). Govt of Orissa.Bhubaneswar.

Rhode, N.F. (1986). Information Needs. Advances in Librarianship. 14, pp. 49 50. New York, Academic Press.

Rissanen, K. (1994). Opiskelijat terveydenhuoltoalan tietoa etsimässä. Case-tutkimus Tamperen terveydenhuolto-oppilaitoksessa. Tampere. Ammattikasvatushallinon koulutuskeskus. (Ammatti-kasvatushallinnon koulutuskeskuksen julkaisuja 1/1994).

Rout, R. K. (1988). Teaching literature in Ten Plus Two stages with special reference to Drama: A content method analysis. *Vision*, 8(1-2), Jul-Dec., pp. 81-92.

Roberts, A. (2003) "Challenges to the right to information", CHRI unpublished, p.1. Ontario Court (General Division), Jane Doe v. Board of Commissioners of Police for the Municipality of Metropolitan Toronto et al., Court File No. 87-CQ-21670, *Judgment* July 3, 1998 cited in

Rudd, E. (1984). Research into postgraduate education. *Higher Education Research and Development*, 3, pp. 109-120.

Sahoo, F.M. and Padhi, S. (2001). Work and job involvement in university teachers: An empirical examination of need salience theory. *Sankalpa*. 9(1), Jan-June, pp. 12-26.

Sahoo, P.K. and Patri, Kalpataru (1997). Development of higher education in Orissa. *J. Edn Planning & Admn*. 11(2), p. 203.

Sahoo, S.K., (1998). Innovative and experimental education in remote tribal pockets in Orissa. *J. Edn. Soc. Change*. 12(2-3), p. 7-17.

Salman, Lamia (1981). The information needs of the developing countries: an analytical; case–studies. *UJISLAA*, 3(4), pp. 241-247.

Sandstrom, P. E. (1994). An optimal foraging approach to information seeking and use. *Library Quarterly* 64, 414-449.

Sangameswaran, V. and Gopinath, M.A (1987). User studies in NICFOS: a review. *ILA Bull*. 22(2-3), pp. 142-151.

Sasikela, C (1994). Information seeking behaviour of managers in industry. *IASLIC Bulletin*, 39 (1) Mar 94, pp. 27-31. Paper presented at the 19th All India Conference of the Indian Association of Special Libraries and Information Centres (IASLIC), Mesra, Ranchi, 26-9 Dec.

Satija, Mohinder Partap and S.P. Agriwal. (1990). *Book Numbers* (Some Indian Methods). (New Delhi, India: Ashok Kumar Mittal, 1990.)

Satish, N.G (1994). *Attitude Towards Information: A Study of Social Scientists,* Concept Pub. Company, New Delhi.

Savolainen, R. (1995). Everyday life information seeking: Approaching information seeking in the context of "Way of Life". *Library and Information Science Research* 17(3), pp. 259-294.

Savolainen, R.(1993). The sense-making theory: reviewing the interests of a user-centred approach to information seeking and use. *Information Processing & Management,* 29 (1), pp. 13-28.

Schilling, K., Roth, L. H., Mickelson, P. and Ginn, D. S.(1995). Integration of information-seeking skills and activities into a problem-based curriculum. *Bulletin of the Medical Library Association,* 83 (2), pp. 176-83.

Seth, M K (1992). Trends in information technology industry-38th All India Library Conf. held on 21-24 Nov 1992, at Utkal University, Vanivihar, Bhubaneswar-4, Orissa. pp. 233-237.

Seth, M. K. and Dalai, B. K. (1995). Library automation in India., *DESIDOC Bulletin of Information Technology,* 15(3); pp. 29-34.

Seth, M. K., Ramesh, D. B. and Sahu, J. R. (1997). BHULIBNET a proposed network of libraries in Bhubaneswar-16th Annual Convention & Conference of Society for Information Science, Access to Electronic Information at Utkal University Dept. of Library & Information Science, Bhubaneswar 29-31 Jan. pp. 288-294.

Seth, M. K., Ramesh, D. B. and Sahu, J R (1998). Information indiscipline–A challenge to the library and information professionals-18th Natioonal Seminar of IASLIC, held at Kerala Agricultural University, Thrissur December, pp. 73-77.

Shannon, C. (1940). Information, communication theory, the Exploratory Publications, San Francisco, CA.

Sharma, M. C. (2000). Affirmative Action Policies in Higher Education: The Indian Experience' in Edgar Beckham

F. (ed), *Diversity, Democracy and Higher Education: A View from Three Nations,* Association of American Colleges and Universities, Washington D.C.

Shokeen, A. and Kaushik (2003). Information Seeking Behaviour of Perceived by sociologist: a case study, *ILA Bulletin,* 39 (3), pp. 11-15.

Sing, S.P. (1984). Impediments to education of tribals of ORISSA, *Vanyajati* 32(4) Oct., pp. 7-13.

Singh, J.P (2002). The State of Universal Education in India: a sociological appraisal, *Ambedkar J. Social Development,* 10(1), pp. 183-195.

Singh, Jaglar. (1999-2000). End-User Training," *ILA Bulletin* 35(4), Oct.-Mar., pp. 23-27.

Singhal, S. and Das, Rasmita (1998). Power of gender as caste on academic self-concept and academic performance of college student, *J. Edun. Planning and Admn.* 12(2); Apr, pp. 173-85.

Sisodia, M L (1999). Collegiate Education of Disadvantaged Population: education for equity, *University News,* 37(44),. pp. 1-5.

Sitter, S. and Stein, A (1992). Modeling the illocutionary aspects of information seeking dialogues. *Information Processing & Management,* 28 (2), pp. 165-180.

Skelton, B. (1973) 'Scientists and Social Scientists as Information Users: A Comparison of Results of Science User Studies With The Investigation into Information Requirements of the Social Sciences', *Journal of Librarianship,* 5(2), pp. 138-156.

Spink, A. (1996). Interactive information seeking and retrieving: a third feedback framework. Proceedings of the 59th Annual Meeting of the American Society for Information Science, Baltimore, Maryland, 21-24 Oct 1996. Edited by Steve Hardin. Medford, New Jersey: Information Today, Inc., for American Society for Information Science, pp. 10-15.

Sridhar, M. S.(1990). User Research – A review of Information Behaviour Studies in Science And Technology. Bangalore, Biblio Infon Service,,

Sridhar, M.S. (1989). Information seeking behaviour of the Indian space technologists. *Library Science with Slant to Documentation*, 26(2), pp. 127-166.

Stam, D. C. Tracking art historians: on information needs and information-seeking behaviour. *Art Libraries Journal*, 14 (3), pp. 13-16.

Standing Committee on Welfare of SC/ST (2000). Report on the Reservation for Employment of SC/ST in IITs Including Reservation for SC/STs in Admissions Therein, Standing Committee on Welfare of SC/ST – Fifth Report (1998-99), New Delhi.

Summers E.G, Matheson Joyce and Conery Robert (1983). The effects of personal, professional and psychological attributes and information seeking behaviour on the use of information sources by educators. *JASIS*, 34(1), pp. 75-85.

Sumsion, J. (1994) Survey of Resources and Uses in Higher Education Libraries: UK, 1993. Loughborough: Loughborough University of Technology, Library and Information Statistics Unit.

Swain, Dillip (1996). Information- seeking behaviour and Reading habits of creative writers in Oriya. An analytical study, M. Phil. (Unpublished Dissertation). Sambalpur University.

Sypher H.E. and Applegate J.(1984). Organising Communication behaviour the role of schema and construct. In Bosteom Robert W. Ed. *Communication Year Book* No. 8, 1984, Sage publication, Beavery.

Talero Eduardo and Gaddette Philip (1996). Harnessing information for development: A proposal for a World Bank Group Strategy: World Bank discussion paper. World Bank; Washington.

Talja, S., (1995). Information seeking in everyday life: methodological strategies. Tampere University, Department of Information Studies, PO Box 607, FIN-33101, Tampere, FINLAND.

Tapas R. Dash. J., (1991). Inequality in educational development of tribes in Orissa. *Edn. Planning & Admn.* 5(1); p 75.

Taylor Alvin (1991), *Future Shock.*Bentham Books; New York.

Taylor Graham, (2002.). New Review of Information Behaviour Research, *Information Research,* 8(4), review no. R103 Available at: http://informationr.net/ir/reviews/revs103.htm.

Taylor, H.A. (1984). *Archival Services and the Concept of The User: A Ramp Study.* Paris, Unesco. p. 21.

Taylor, M. (1986). *Bacon's Personal Life,* Edited by Michael Century Hutchinson Ltd, 1986, UK.

The Economic Times (2002). The Crisis in higher education, 23 Oct.

The Economic Times (2003). Literacy graph surges above population swell, 6 Dec.

The Hindu (2002). Law soon to implement right to education, Saturday, Nov 30, 2002

The Hindustan Times (2003). Education in Orissa's tribal areas is in a shambles, November 27.

The New Indian Express (2003). Public expenditure on education, 10th December, Bhubaneswar.

The Statesman (2004). Editorial–Reservation race-I : failed education, 9th Feb.

The Statesman (2003). Economics of Education, 30th December 2003.

The Statesman (2003). Task force on education presents vision 2020, 21 Oct.

The Statesman (2003). Economics of Education, 30 Dec.

The Statesman (2003). Education standards: emphasis must be on quality, not numbers article by Atma Ram, 25 March.

The Times of India (2003). Common School System: end apartheid in education article by A.K. Shiva Kumar, 11 Nov.

Toffler, Alvin (1970), *Future Shock.* Bentham Books; New York. USA.

Trivison, D., Chamis, A.Y., Saracevic, T., Kantor, P.B. and Kantor, P. (1987). Effectiveness and efficiency of searchers in online searching: preliminary results from a study of information seeking and retrieval. ASIS 86. Proceedings of the 49th ASIS Annual Meeting. Volume 23. Chicago,

Illinois, September 28-October 2, 1986 Edited by Julie M. Hurd and Charles H. Davis, Medford, New Jersey, Learned Information Inc. for the American Society for Information Science, 1987, 341-349.

UNESCO (1981). Guidelines on Studies of Information Users. Paris, UNESCO.

UNESCO Report (1998). Higher education under WTO region, Egypt.

UNESCO/IFLA (2003). Special report on libraries and librarians, World Summit on the Information Society, in 6th Nov, Geneva.

UN General Assembly, (1946) Resolution 59(1), 65th Plenary Meeting, December 14.

Vakkari, P. and Savolainen, R. (1997). Information seeking in context. Information seeking in context. Proceedings of the international conference on research in information needs, seeking and use in different contexts, 14-16 August 1996, Tampere, Finland. Edited by Pertti Vakkari, Reijo Savolainen and Brenda Dervin. London: Taylor Graham, p. 467.

Vakkari, P. (1998). The growth of information seeking theories. Tampere University, Department of Information Studies, Po. Box. 607, FIN-33101, Tampere, Finland.

Vakkari, P. and Kuokkanen, M. (1997). Theory growth in information science: applications of the theory of science to a theory of information seeking. *Journal of Documentation,* 53 (5) Dec, pp. 497-519.

Vasanthi, C.M (2001). The changing environment of academic libraries: end-user education and planning strategies for libraries in India, *Library Philosophy and Practice,* Vol. 4, No. 1, pp. 24-31.

Wankhede, G.G. (2003). Affirmative Actions and the Scheduled Castes: Access to Higher Education in India, presented in UCLA 21st Century Project Conference On Achieving Diversity in Tertiary Education: Challenges and Prospects 17-21 March, 2003,Bellagio Study and Conference Centre, Italy.

Weedman, J. (1992). Informal and formal channels in boundary-spanning communication. *JASIS* 43(3), pp. 257-267.

Wellisch, H. (1997). From Information Science to informatics: A terminological investigation. *Journal of Librarianship*. 4(3), pp. 158-187.

Wiberley, S. E. and Jones, W. G (1989). Patterns of information seeking in the humanities. *College & Research Libraries*, 50 (6), pp. 638-645.

Wiberly, S. E. & Jones, W. G. (1989). Patterns of information seeking in the humanities. *College and Research Libraries* 50(6), pp. 638-645.

Wilson, T. D. & Allen, D. K. (1999). Exploring the contexts of information behaviour. Proceedings of the second information seeking in context conference, August 1998, Sheffield, UK. London: Taylor Graham.

Wilson, T. D. & Streatfield, D. R. (1977). Information needs in local authority social services departments: An interim reports on Project INISS. *Journal of Documentation* 33(4), pp. 277-293.

Wilson, T. D. (1984). The cognitive approach to information-seeking behaviour and information use. *Social Science Information Studies* 4(2-3), pp. 197-204.

Wilson, T. D., (1999). Models of information behaviour research. *Journal of Documentation* 55(3), pp. 249-270.

Wilson, T.D., and Streatfield, D.R. (1991), 'Structured Observation in the Investigation of Information Needs' *Social Science Information Studies* 1, pp. 173-184.

Wilson, T.D. (2000) 'On User Studies and Information Needs' *Journal of Documentation*. 37(3), pp. 3-15.

Winter, A. & Cameron, M. (1983). External students and their libraries: an investigation into student needs for reference material, the sources they use, and the effects of the external system within which they study. Geelong, Vic.: Deakin University.

Wood, D.N., & Bower, C.A. (1969). The use of social science periodical literature. *Journal of Documentation*, 25, pp. 115-117.

Wood, N.V (1986). College reading and study skills. Orlando, FL: Holt, Rinehart & Winston.

World Bank (1990). Paper, 120, World Bank, Washington.

World Education Forum (2003). Dakar Framework for Action, ICSSR occasional series, No. 4, New Delhi.

World Information Report 1997/98 (1998). Paris: UNESCO Publications, Paris.

Yoon, K. (1997). Exploring the use of certainty in information seeking interaction. Doctoral Thesis. Syracuse University, School of Information Studies, CST 4-211, Syracuse, NY 13244, USA.